Olympiad ACE

A Comprehensive Practice Book
for School Olympiads & Talent Search Exams

BIOLOGY
Class 11

Olympiad **ACE**

A Comprehensive Practice Book
for School Olympiads & Talent Search Exams

BIOLOGY
Class 11

by
Juhi Bhatia, Nisha Jaryal

Bloom Cap Edu Ventures Pvt. Ltd.

꣼ Administrative & Production Office

'Ramchhaya' 4577/15, Agarwal Road, Darya Ganj, New Delhi -110002
Tele: 011- 47630600, 43518550

꣼ PRICE: ₹175.00

꣼ PO No : TXT-XX-XXXXXXX-X-XX

Published by Arihant Publications (I) Ltd.

For further information about the books log on to
www.bloomcap.org

Follow us on

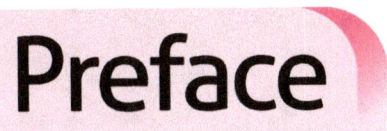

Preface

"Future belongs to those Who prepares for it today"

School Olympiads are National & International level competitions conducted by different Government, Non-Government & Educational Organisations with the purpose of making the children ready to face competitive exams.

The challenging Questions asked in Olympiads motivate them to learn more & more and bring out the best result with improved academic performance. The Awards & Scholarship offered by Olympiads motivate children to aspire & strive for doing better and emerge out to be the best.

Science Olympiads

Being a Scientist or Engineer or Doctor has always been a dream of each school going child. A good command over Science is a must for any of these. Questions of Science Olympiads are structured to help students to develop scientific temperament & motivate them to understand the concepts of science. They also focuses on improving existing knowledge of a student by adding more information.

'Bloom Science Olympiad Study Book Class 11' is a perfect resource to Study & Practice for Olympiad Exams and other National & State Level Talent Search Exams & Other Competitions.

Some Special Features of Bloom Science Olympiad Study Books are;

- Chapterwise Exercises having different types of Objective Questions; Analytical, Applications, Remembering etc, at par with the Olympiad Level.
- Detailed Explanation for each question.
- Olympiad Pattern Practice Sets at the end.

This book is prepared by Expert Panel with the utmost care, still if you have any suggestions regarding its improvement then feel free to contact us at support@bloomcap.org. We will try to inculcate your suggestions in the further editions.

Contents

Chapter 01

Biological Classification, Plant and Animal Kingdom

MCQs 1 Mark Questions

1. Identify the correct statement.
   (a) Biological names are generally in Latin and written in Italics
   (b) The first word in a biological name represents the specific epithet while the second component denotes the specific genus
   (c) Both the words in a biological name, when handwritten, are not underlined, or printed in Italics
   (d) The first word denoting the genus starts with a small letter while the specific epithet starts with a capital letter

2. Classification of an organism is essential because it
   (a) permits systematic arrangement of taxa
   (b) allows new species to maintain their uniqueness
   (c) considers only physiological characters
   (d) considers single-trait for identification of organisms

3. *Aspergillus niger*, represents correct way of writing scientific names.
   (a) Yes
   (b) No
   (c) Cannot say
   (d) No, for genus, Yes, for species name

4. In taxonomic hierarchy, the taxon Phylum/Division is placed between
   (a) kingdom and order
   (b) class and order
   (c) kingdom and class
   (d) class and family

5. Linnaeus system of classification does not distinguish between
   (a) eukaryotes and prokaryotes
   (b) multicellular and unicellular
   (c) photosynthetic and non-photosynthetic
   (d) All of the abvoe

6. Which of the following criteria was not used by Whittaker for classification?
   (a) Cell structure
   (b) Mode of nutrition
   (c) Biochemical dissimilarities
   (d) Body organisation

7. 'Five kingdom system of classification did not differentiate between fungi and green plants'. This statement is
   (a) false
   (b) true
   (c) cannot say
   (d) the information is incomplete

8. Which group holds maximum nutritional diversity?
   (a) Plantae   (b) Monera
   (c) Fungi   (d) Animalia

9. Which of the following shape is not shown by bacteria?
   (a) Bacillus   (b) Pyramidal
   (c) Cocci   (d) Vibrio

10. Halophiles, thermoacidophiles, and methanogens belongs to which domain?
    (a) Monera   (b) Eubacteria
    (c) Archaebacteria (d) Protista

11. 'X' are small prokaryotes lacking cell wall are Gram-negative in nature. Which other features can be used to describe such organisms?
    (a) They are usually motile with certain exceptions
    (b) They are chemo-organotrophic in nature and require proteins for growth
    (c) These are facultative anaerobes, but some may be obligate anaerobes
    (d) These are able to survive at extreme conditions of temperature and pH

12. Identify the smallest living cells known which can survive without oxygen.
    (a) Euglenoids   (b) Dinoflagellates
    (c) Slime moulds   (d) Mycoplasma

13. Aarti placed a drop of marine water under a microscope. She observed a single-celled organism with distinct nucleus and a wall. This organism should be placed in which kingdom of Whittaker's classification?
    (a) Plantae   (b) Protista
    (c) Monera   (d) Animalia

14. Organism 'P' is found in freshwater as well as in marine environments. These float passively in water currents and are the main producers in oceans. Their walls are embedded with silica. These are also referred to as
    (a) herbivores   (b) mycoplasma
    (c) diatoms   (d) sporozoans

15. X represents a category of second major source of marine primary producers. They are an important part of the food web in oceans as they release a large amount of energy into planktonic food webs, along with toxins that kill other marine organisms. Identify the organism 'X'.
    (a) *Euglena*   (b) *Gonyaulax*
    (c) *Trypanosoma*   (d) *Paramecium*

16. Identify the organism shown in the image given below.

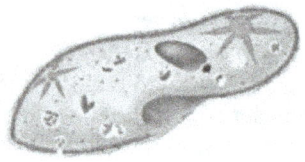

    (a) Dinoflagellates (b) *Paramecium*
    (c) *Euglena*   (d) Slime moulds

17. In a refrigerator, a piece of stale bread with stinking smell is present, which has also become dry and rough in texture. There were colonies of certain microorganisms found growing on it. Which of the following statement is correct with respect to your observation?

    (a) The piece of bread turned black due to bacterial contamination
    (b) The infection occurred due to certain toxins released by *Rhizopus* bacterium
    (c) Colonies of *Volvox* could be seen growing on the bread piece
    (d) The infection caused is due to the fungus *Rhizopus stolonifer* commonly called bread mold

18. Venn diagram given below shows a relation between two fungal species, represented by *P*. What relation do both the species share?

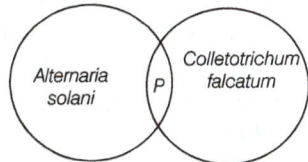

(a) Zygomycotina   (b) Basidiomycotina
(c) Deuteromycotina   (d) Ascomycotina

19. In the organisms associated with kingdom 'S', holozoic mode of nutrition is present. Thus, 'S' could be identified as
(a) Animalia   (b) Plantae
(c) Monera   (d) Protista

20. An organism will be classified as a virus when
(a) DNA is enclosed within a protein coat
(b) outside a living host, the cell remains alive
(c) nucleus is absent
(d) it contains a cell wall

21. Below given information states the names of the viruses that are commonly known to us. How many of these viruses possess single-stranded or *ss*RNA?

Herpes simplex virus, Hepatitis-B virus, Human coronavirus, Polyomavirus, Rabies virus, *Ebolavirus, Adenoviridae*, Bacteriophage, Yellow fever virus, HIV.

(a) 6   (b) 3   (c) 7   (d) 5

22. Which of the following option is incorrect about virus given below?

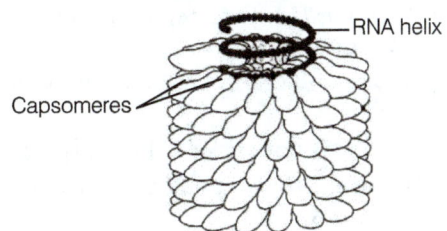

(a) It is a positive sense single-stranded virus
(b) It mainly infects animals
(c) The virus has a very narrow range of survival and infects only certain plants
(d) The virus is negative sense single-stranded RNA virus

23. Read the following statements carefully and identify the correct statement(s) about lichens.
(a) Lichens are permanent symbiotic association of an alga and roots of leguminous plants
(b) They mainly inhabit aquatic areas
(c) They seldom grow near smoky industrial areas and are considered very good pollution indicators
(d) All the statements are correct

24. Cytotaxonomy is based on which of the following?
(a) Uses the chemical constituents of the plant
(b) Number and codes are assigned to all the characters and the data is then processed using computers
(c) Analysing relationships between the various organisms
(d) based on cytological information like chromosome number, structure, behaviour

25. Fusion of two gametes dissimilar in size is referred as?
(a) Isogamy   (b) Anisogamy
(c) Oogamy   (d) None of these

26. Which of the following statements are correct regarding green algae?
   I. Sexual reproduction is by flagellated zoospores produced in zoosporangia.
   II. Green algae usually have a rigid cell wall made of an inner layer of cellulose and an outer layer of pectose.
   III. Green algae usually have a rigid cell wall made of an outer layer of

cellulose and an inner layer of pectose.

IV. The chloroplasts may be discoid, plate-like, reticulate, cup-shaped, spiral or ribbon-shaped in different species.

(a) I and II   (b) II, III, and IV
(c) II and IV   (d) I, II, III, IV

27. Vegetative reproduction in member of brown algae, 'X', is fragmentation. It is also a source of an acid 'Y' which yields a compound of commercial importance. Identify 'X' and 'Y' correctly by choosing the correct answer from the options given below.

	X	Y
(a)	*Chara*	Chlorellin
(b)	*Laminaria*	Agar-agar
(c)	*Sargassum*	Alginic acid
(d)	*Polysiphonia*	Funori

28. A pigment X is responsible for imparting brown or light brown colouration to *Sargassum*. Identify the pigment.
(a) Chlorophyll
(b) Phycocyanin
(c) Phycoerythrin
(d) Fucoxanthin

29. Major pigments found in Rhodophyceae are
(a) chlorophyll-b (b) chlorophyll-c
(c) phycoerythrin   (d) fucoxanthin

30. Elaters are kind of sterile cells. These are produced by sporangia of sporophytes in some bryophytes and pteridophytes. These are associated with/as
(a) spore dispersal
(b) provision for reserve food to developing spores
(c) protection of immature spores
(d) providing moisture to developing spores

31. Identify the incorrect statement regarding mosses.
   I. Leaves are one cell thick except at the midrib and lack stomata.
  II. First gametophyte stage is protonema that is creeping and green.
 III. Rhizoids are elongated and unicellular.
  IV. The second stage is the leafy stage, which develops from the secondary protonema as lateral bud.
(a) Only I   (b) I and II
(c) Only III   (d) II, III, and IV

32. ......X...... and ......Y...... are two plant groups, the examples of which are ferns and mosses. Which among the following statement will be considered as a difference between the two?
(a) Xylem is exarch in roots
(b) Reserve food material is true starch
(c) Oogamous type of sexual reproduction
(d) Gametophytic phase dominant in life cycle

33. Which of the following pairs incorrectly describes the relationship between the plant groups?
(a) *Marsilea* — Presence of companion cells
             in group
(b) *Marchantia* — Xylem and phloem are absent
(c) *Cycas* — Motile male gametes
(d) *Sphagnum* — Growth in dim light

34. Which of the following statement is correct with respect to gymnosperms?
(a) *Selaginella* is heterosporous, but *Salvinia* is homosporous
(b) *Cycas* and *Cedrus* both have unbranched stem
(c) Ovule is not enclosed by ovary wall
(d) *Salvinia*, *Ginkgo* and *Pinus* are not gymnosperms

35. Which of the following option is incorrect about kingdom-Animalia?

(a) Heterotrophic mode of nutrition

(b) Cell wall is present

(c) Organisms with definite shape, have organ system level of organisation

(d) Able to coordinate their body actions, develop rapid responses due to a nervous system in present most members

36. Protostomes and deuterostomes can be taxonomically best distinguished on the basis of

(a) segmentation pattern

(b) body symmetry

(c) pattern of embryonic development

(d) presence or absence of coelom

37. Metameric segmentation

(a) exists in radially symmetrical animals

(b) makes every segment dispensable

(c) possess elements of the essential organ systems

(d) is determined by modes of respiration and circulation in an organism

38. The figures *A* and *B*, show two types of coelom. Choose the option that represents the correct match with figures.

A   *B*

(a) *A*-Aschelminthes, *B*-Echinoderms

(b) *A*-Arthropods, *B*-Aschelminthes

(c) *A*-Platyhelminthes, *B*-Annelids

(d) *A*-Hemichordates, *B*-Molluscs

39. I-Porifera, II-Annelida, III-Mollusca, IV-Platyhelminthes, V-Ctenophora

How many of the above phylum are true coelomates?

(a) 3   (b) 4   (c) 5   (d) 2

40. In some animals, the actual coelom is reduced but spaces between viscera grows and form a large blood filled cavity called haemocoel. This would be found in which pair of animals?

(a) *Astacus* and *Pila*

(b) *Antedon* and *Peripatus*

(c) *Nereis* and *Astacus*

(d) *Pila* and *Antedon*

41. Mostly marine animals with no nervous system would be found in phylum

(a) Ctenophora

(b) Annelida

(c) Porifera

(d) Arthropoda

42. Among the features listed below, which one cannot be associated with an invertebrate?

(a) Radial symmetry

(b) Warm-blooded

(c) Hollow nervous system

(d) Absence of pharyngeal gill system

43. If a taxon of animals is further classified on the basis of 'canal systems', the taxon is most likely

(a) Phylum–Porifera

(b) Phylum–Echinodermata

(c) Class–Osteichthyes

(d) Class–Insecta

44. An unknown organism *X*, is pathogenic in nature. It causes a disease, which is characterised by swelling in legs, arms and the genitalia. Also, it can lead to swollen lymph nodes.

Identify the organism and the correct phylum to which it belongs.

(a) *X-Ancylostoma*, Aschelminthes

(b) *X-Wuchereria*, Nemathelminthes

(c) *X-Nereis* , Annelida

(d) *X-Planaria*, Platyhelminthes

45. The flat body plan of Platyhelminthes helps them to
(a) facilitate reproductive activity
(b) attain effective locomotion in all directions
(c) minimise the loss of body fluid and maximise surface area
(d) maximise exposure of the body cells/tissues to surrounding medium

46. A farmer is more prone to which of the following infections?
(a) Ascariasis
(b) Fascioliasis
(c) Malaria
(d) Schistosomiasis

47. Which of the following options correctly represents the characteristic features of phylum–Annelida?
(a) Triploblastic, segmented body and bilaterally symmetrical
(b) Triploblastic, unsegmented body and bilaterally symmetrical
(c) Triploblastic, flattened body and acoelomate condition
(d) Diploblastic, mostly marine and radially symmetrical

48. Among the figures of animals with segmented bodies, which one shows metameric segmentation?

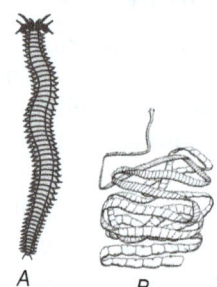

A   B

(a) A
(b) B
(c) Both (a) and (b)
(d) Neither (a) nor (b)

49. Select the correct option with respect to X.

Organism	Level of organisa-tion	Body symmetry	Coelom	Segment ation
X	Organ system	Bilateral	Pseudoco-elomate	No

(a) *Nereis*   (b) *Pila*
(c) *Ophiura*   (d) *Ancylostoma*

50. What is the role of nephridia in phylum–Annelida?
(a) Osmoregulation (b) Digestion
(c) Excretion   (d) Both (a) and (c)

51. An organism A, which inhabits aquatic or terrestrial habitats has a blood anticoagulant that inhibits the activity of thrombin thus, making the conversion of fibrinogen to fibrin possible. Identify the organism along with the phylum (B).

	A	**B**
(a)	*Hirudinaria*	Aschelminthes
(b)	*Nereis*	Annelida
(c)	*Hirudinaria*	Annelida
(d)	*Limulus*	Arthropoda

52. Observe the diagram given below.

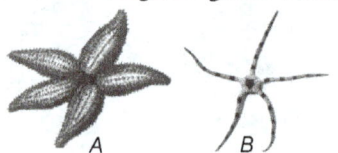

A   B

Choose the feature that is unique to the members of the above phylum.
(a) External fertilisation
(b) Free-swimming larva
(c) Excretory system is absent
(d) Water vascular system is present

53. The body of hemichordates is divided in
(a) proboscis and trunk
(b) proboscis, collar and trunk
(c) proboscis and collar
(d) collar and trunk

54. The schematic representation of a circulatory system is given below.

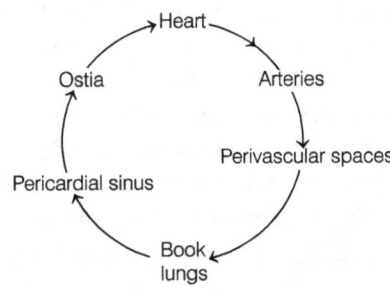

This system is found in

(a) scorpion   (b) earthworm

(c) *Chiton*   (d) crocodile

55. Animals of the same phylum are grouped below.

Mark the group having dissimilar pairs.

(a) *Anopheles, Culex, Aedes*

(b) *Nereis, Limulus, Pheretima*

(c) *Echinus, Antedon, Ophiura*

(d) *Exocoetus, Labeo, Pterophyllum*

56. All vertebrates are chordates but all chordates are not vertebrates, why?

(a) Notochord is replaced by a vertebral column in adult of some chordates

(b) Ventral hollow nerve cord remains throughout life in some chordates

(c) All chordates possess a vertebral column

(d) All chordates possess notochord throughout their life

57. Observe the chart and fill in the missing places from the options given below.

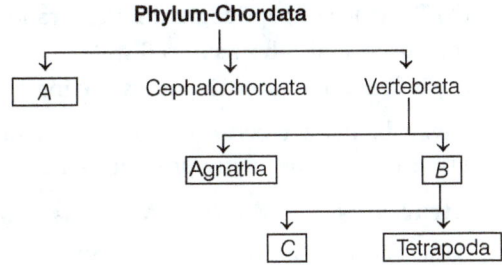

	A	B	C
(a)	Placodermi	Gnathostomata	Pisces
(b)	Urochordata	*Balanoglossus*	Tetrapoda
(c)	Urochordata	Gnathostomata	Pisces
(d)	Placodermi	Gnathostomata	Pisces

58. A jawless vertebrate is

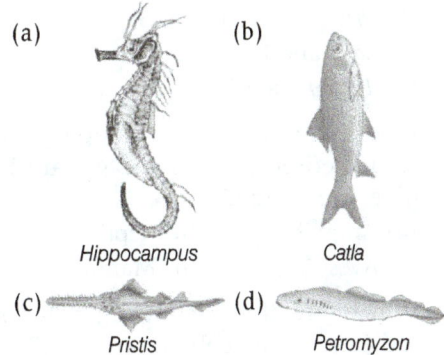

59. Observe the diagrams (*A-B*) given below.

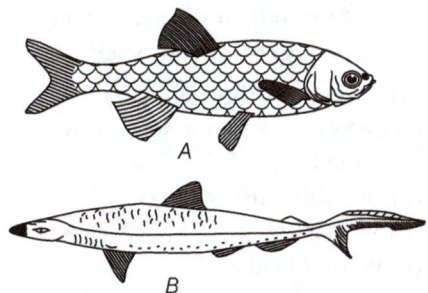

Which of the following option(s) correctly relate to the diagram given above?

(a) *A*-Their body remains covered with minute ctenoid scales

(b) *B*-These fishes breathe by two pairs of gills covered by operculum

(c) *B*-Gill-slits are separate and without operculum

(d) Both (a) and (c)

60. While culturing fishes in a fishery, a person observed an altogether different kind of fish with a streamlined body and terminal mouth, four pairs of gills, skin was covered with cycloid scales.

Based on the above description, which two examples would be the best fit?

(a) *Petromyzon* and *Torpedo*

(b) *Pristis* and *Labeo*

(c) *Catla* and *Exocoetus*

(d) *Trygon* and *Clarias*

61. Identify the vertebrate group of animals characterised by crop and gizzard in its digestive system?

(a) Amphibia   (b) Reptilia

(c) Aves   (d) Mammalia

62. Which one of the following in birds, indicates their reptilian ancestry?

(a) Scales on their hindlimbs

(b) Four-chambered heart

(c) Two special chambers are crop and gizzard in their digestive tract

(d) Eggs with calcareous shells

63. Which one of the following characteristics is not shared by Aves and Mammalia?

(a) Breathing using lungs

(b) Viviparity

(c) Warm blood nature

(d) Ossified endoskeleton

64. Which of the following pairs are correctly matched?

	Animals	Morphological features
(A)	Crocodile	4-chambered heart
(B)	Sea urchin	Parapodia
(C)	Obelia	Metagenesis
(D)	Lemur	Thecodont

(a) Only A and D   (b) Only A and B

(c) B, C and D   (d) A, C and D

MCQs 2 Marks Questions

Direction (Q. Nos. 65-67) Read the passage given below and answer the questions that follows.

While viewing slides in his biology workspace, Anil observed a slide showing the following characteristics.

I. Single-layered thick cell wall.

II. Flagella emerging from cell wall.

In order to experiment further, he placed 3-4 drops of crystal violet stain on the slide and then rinsed it with water after about 30 seconds. A few drops of iodine is added and cells are again washed with 95% alcoholic.

65. What kind of bacteria is present on the slide?

(a) Cannot determine due to incomplete information

(b) Gram-positive

(c) Gram-negative

(d) Gram neutral

66. What will your observation be if the bacteria is Gram-negative?

(a) Crystal violet stain will get washed off

(b) Crystal violet stain will be retained

(c) Bacteria is stained pink

(d) Both (b) and (c)

67. What is the basis for Gram-staining reaction?

(a) Lipid content of bacterial cell wall

(b) Presence of peptidoglycan membrane

(c) Absence of L-lysins in cell wall

(d) Release of endotoxins or exotoxins

68. Given below are certain structures which are a part of the living environment.

Structures	Abbreviations
Virus Particles	VP
Algal Cell	AC
Water Molecule	WM

Structures	Abbreviations
Chloroplast	CL
Phospholipid Molecule	PM

Which of the following graphs would correctly represent these structures in increasing order of their size, i.e. from smallest to longest?

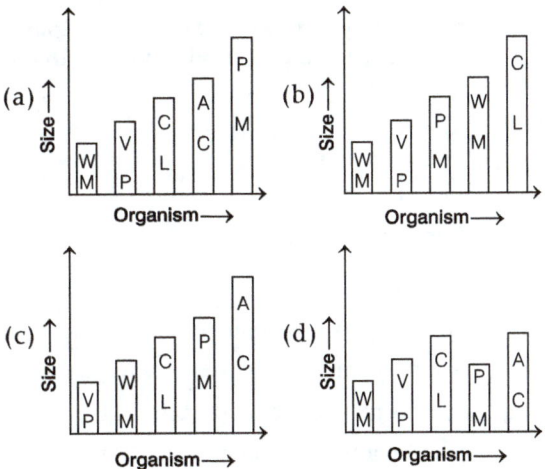

69. **Assertion** (A) Basidiomycetes are the most advanced fungi.

    Reason (R) Motile structures are completely absent in this group of fungi.
    (a) Both A and R are true and R is the correct explanation of A
    (b) Both A and R are true, but R is not the correct explanation of A
    (c) A is true, but R is false
    (d) A is false, but R is true

70. A researcher while experimenting on various freshwater samples, observed a single-celled organism X with a hard cell wall. On conducting more of research work, he found that the organism when given to patients with deficiency of vitamin-B_{12} and C proved to be helpful in combating the deficiency as it contains several vitamins, minerals, antioxidants and omega-3-fats.

    Identify the organism 'X' and select the statement which does not belong to it.

	X	Features
(a)	*Spirulina*	The cells are spherical in shape
(b)	*Chlamydomonas*	It is motile and unicellular
(c)	*Ulva*	This contains two whiplash flagella
(d)	*Chlorella*	The free-floating microscopic species serve as food and oxygen sources

71. Consider the given situation:
    'Vicky while collecting samples for identification of different types of algae, came across some forms growing attached to rocky stones and some growing in deep waters. It was later found that the latter has a pigment P that absorbs the blue-green part of the sunlight's spectrum as it has a short wavelength thus, penetrating deep into the water.'
    Choose the correct statement with respect to the alga referred.
    (a) Cell wall is made up of pectin and cellulose
    (b) Life cycle of many algae exhibits alternation of generation of gametophytic (diploid to haploid generations)
    (c) A number of phycocolloids are extracted from such algae for commercial purposes
    (d) These are rich sources of soda, potash and iodine

72. K, M, N represent three different species of algae having certain characters (as mentioned). [Hint - A tick (✓) represents the presence of the specific feature]. Identify K, M, N from the options given below.

Species	Unicellular forms	Phycobilins	Motile flag-ellated bodies
K	✓	✓	✗
M	✓	✗	✓
N	✓	✗	✓

(a)   *K - Gelidium*
     M - Gracilaria
     N - Chlorella

(b)   *K - Gracilaria*
     M - Laminaria
     N - Sargassum

(c)   *K - Gelidium*
     M - Laminaria
     N - Ulva

(d)   *K - Chlorella*
     M - Sargassum
     N - Laminaria

73. Observe the flowchart given below and identify *A, B* and *C* with respect to the given features.

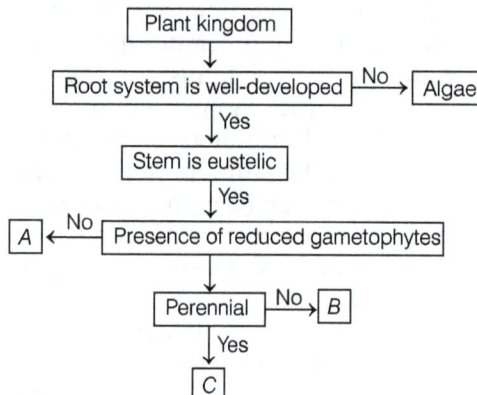

(a) *A*-Algae, *B*-Mango, *C*-Cedrus
(b) *A*-Bryophytes, *B*-Moss, *C*-Equisetum
(c) *A*-Algae, *B*-Mango, *C*-Ginkgo
(d) *A*-Gymnosperm, *B*-Maize, *C*-Ginkgo

74. The table given below depicts certain characteristics possessed by organisms *X, Y* and *Z*.

	Perennial	Vegetative reproduction	Seed production	Spore production
X	✓	✗	✓	✗
Y	✗	✓	✗	✓
Z	✓	✓	✓	✗

Identify *X, Y* and *Z*.

	X	**Y**	**Z**
(a)	Angiosperms	Bryophytes	Pteridophytes
(b)	Gymnosperms	Algae	Angiosperms
(c)	Gymnosperms	Pteridophytes	Algae
(d)	Angiosperms	Pteridophytes	Algae

Darken your choice with HB Pencil

1. ⓐ ⓑ ⓒ ⓓ	14. ⓐ ⓑ ⓒ ⓓ	27. ⓐ ⓑ ⓒ ⓓ	40. ⓐ ⓑ ⓒ ⓓ	53. ⓐ ⓑ ⓒ ⓓ	66. ⓐ ⓑ ⓒ ⓓ
2. ⓐ ⓑ ⓒ ⓓ	15. ⓐ ⓑ ⓒ ⓓ	28. ⓐ ⓑ ⓒ ⓓ	41. ⓐ ⓑ ⓒ ⓓ	54. ⓐ ⓑ ⓒ ⓓ	67. ⓐ ⓑ ⓒ ⓓ
3. ⓐ ⓑ ⓒ ⓓ	16. ⓐ ⓑ ⓒ ⓓ	29. ⓐ ⓑ ⓒ ⓓ	42. ⓐ ⓑ ⓒ ⓓ	55. ⓐ ⓑ ⓒ ⓓ	68. ⓐ ⓑ ⓒ ⓓ
4. ⓐ ⓑ ⓒ ⓓ	17. ⓐ ⓑ ⓒ ⓓ	30. ⓐ ⓑ ⓒ ⓓ	43. ⓐ ⓑ ⓒ ⓓ	56. ⓐ ⓑ ⓒ ⓓ	69. ⓐ ⓑ ⓒ ⓓ
5. ⓐ ⓑ ⓒ ⓓ	18. ⓐ ⓑ ⓒ ⓓ	31. ⓐ ⓑ ⓒ ⓓ	44. ⓐ ⓑ ⓒ ⓓ	57. ⓐ ⓑ ⓒ ⓓ	70. ⓐ ⓑ ⓒ ⓓ
6. ⓐ ⓑ ⓒ ⓓ	19. ⓐ ⓑ ⓒ ⓓ	32. ⓐ ⓑ ⓒ ⓓ	45. ⓐ ⓑ ⓒ ⓓ	58. ⓐ ⓑ ⓒ ⓓ	71. ⓐ ⓑ ⓒ ⓓ
7. ⓐ ⓑ ⓒ ⓓ	20. ⓐ ⓑ ⓒ ⓓ	33. ⓐ ⓑ ⓒ ⓓ	46. ⓐ ⓑ ⓒ ⓓ	59. ⓐ ⓑ ⓒ ⓓ	72. ⓐ ⓑ ⓒ ⓓ
8. ⓐ ⓑ ⓒ ⓓ	21. ⓐ ⓑ ⓒ ⓓ	34. ⓐ ⓑ ⓒ ⓓ	47. ⓐ ⓑ ⓒ ⓓ	60. ⓐ ⓑ ⓒ ⓓ	73. ⓐ ⓑ ⓒ ⓓ
9. ⓐ ⓑ ⓒ ⓓ	22. ⓐ ⓑ ⓒ ⓓ	35. ⓐ ⓑ ⓒ ⓓ	48. ⓐ ⓑ ⓒ ⓓ	61. ⓐ ⓑ ⓒ ⓓ	74. ⓐ ⓑ ⓒ ⓓ
10. ⓐ ⓑ ⓒ ⓓ	23. ⓐ ⓑ ⓒ ⓓ	36. ⓐ ⓑ ⓒ ⓓ	49. ⓐ ⓑ ⓒ ⓓ	62. ⓐ ⓑ ⓒ ⓓ	
11. ⓐ ⓑ ⓒ ⓓ	24. ⓐ ⓑ ⓒ ⓓ	37. ⓐ ⓑ ⓒ ⓓ	50. ⓐ ⓑ ⓒ ⓓ	63. ⓐ ⓑ ⓒ ⓓ	
12. ⓐ ⓑ ⓒ ⓓ	25. ⓐ ⓑ ⓒ ⓓ	38. ⓐ ⓑ ⓒ ⓓ	51. ⓐ ⓑ ⓒ ⓓ	64. ⓐ ⓑ ⓒ ⓓ	
13. ⓐ ⓑ ⓒ ⓓ	26. ⓐ ⓑ ⓒ ⓓ	39. ⓐ ⓑ ⓒ ⓓ	52. ⓐ ⓑ ⓒ ⓓ	65. ⓐ ⓑ ⓒ ⓓ	

Chapter 02

Morphology of Flowering Plants

MCQs 1 Mark Questions

1. Morphological characteristics play a significant role in the identification of plants. Which of the following constitutes the descending part of plant axis?
   (a) Branches   (b) Leaves
   (c) Stem   (d) Root

2. Given below are four features codes *A, B, C* and *D* are given in front of them.
   Presence of nodes-*A*
   Positively hydrotrophic-*B*
   Positively phototropic-*C*
   Negatively geotropic-*D*
   Which of the above features correctly depicts root?
   (a) *B*   (b) *A*
   (c) *D*   (d) *C*

3. Root can be differentiated from stem by the
   (a) presence of root hairs
   (b) presence of root cap
   (c) absence of nodes and internodes
   (d) All of the above

4. The diagram given below shows the regions of root. Select the correct option for parts *A-D*.

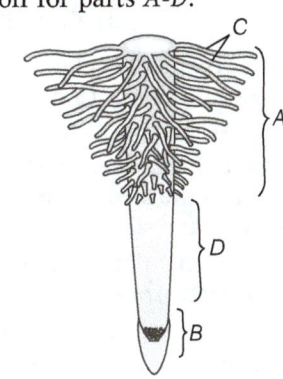

	A	B	C	D
(a)	Root hairs	Region of maturation	Region of elongation	Meristema-tic zone
(b)	Region of maturation	Meristematic zone	Root hairs	Region of elongation
(c)	Region of elongation	Meristematic zone	Region of maturation	Root hairs
(d)	Meristema-tic zone	Region of maturation	Root hairs	Region of elongation

5. Given below is the diagrammatic representation of root parts are labelled as *X, Y* and *Z*.

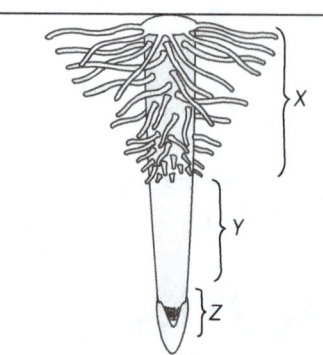

Cells of which of the above labelled zone *X, Y* and *Z*, become elongated and develop a large central vacuole filled with cell sap?

(a) *Z*   (b) *X*

(c) *Y*   (d) *X* and *Y*

6. Roots are organs of a plant that provide anchorage to a plant. Choose the correct statement with respect to root.

(a) Meristematic zone or the zone of cell division is thick walled with no intercellular spaces

(b) Zone of elongation is situated in front of meristematic zone

(c) In tap root system, main root is persistent

(d) Adventitious roots are commonly found in dicots like *Mangifera indica*

7. The roots that originate from the parts of plant other than the radicle are called

(a) adventitious root (b) stilt root

(c) internodal root   (d) nodal root

8. The four zones in the root from root apex to stem base in the correct order will be

Mineral absorption zone-I

Meristematic zone-II

Maturation zone-III

Water absorption zone-IV

(a) II, III, IV, I   (b) IV, III, II, I

(c) II, IV, I, III   (d) I, II, IV, III

9. Consider the following flowchart and identify the correct match for '*X*'.

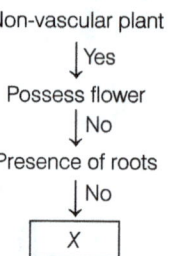

(a) *Equisetum*   (b) Mosses

(c) *Pteridium*   (d) *Pteris*

10. Consider the following parts.

I. Trichomes   II. Nodes

III. Leaves   IV. Flowers

V. Fruits   VI. Branches

How many of the above, can be seen on a stem?

(a) 2   (b) 5

(c) 6   (d) 3

11. Consider the Venn diagram given below.

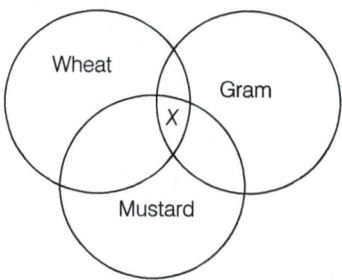

'*X*' is a feature that is similar to all the three plant species given. *X* will be

(a) woody plants

(b) well-developed trunk

(c) short and non-woody

(d) palm-like shape

12. Leaf having purely divided lamina broken up into different segments or leaflets is called

(a) petiole   (b) phyllotaxy

(c) compound leaf (d) simple leaf

13. During an excursion, Sangeeta saw a plant with opposite leaves of two successive nodes, lying in the same plane. The kind of phyllotaxy shown will be
(a) opposite palmate
(b) opposite superimposed
(c) opposite decussate
(d) pinnate palmate

14. In which type of inflorescence main axis continues to grow and the flowers are borne laterally in acropetal succession?
(a) Cymose   (b) Racemose
(c) Either (a) or (b) (d) Both (a) and (b)

15. Spadix is an inflorescence found only in
(a) monocots   (b) dicots
(c) Poaceae   (d) Asteraceae

16. Cyathium inflorescence is of the following type
(a) single male flower is surrounded by female flowers
(b) male and female flowers are borne in different plants
(c) there is only one male and one female flowers
(d) single female flower surrounded by many peripheral male flowers

17. Rajesh, on his way to school, saw an inflorescence. In it, two lateral branches developed on either side of a terminal flower. These lateral branches re-divide to form a branch again.

The inflorescence is
(a) monochasial cyme (b) scorpioid cyme
(c) helicoid cyme   (d) dichasial cyme

18. 'A flower represents the reproductive unit of a plant'. Read the following statements regarding flowers and select the option with correct statements.
   I. A zygomorphic flower is radially symmetrical.
   II. China rose, cotton, *Cucurbita* are examples of unisexual flowers.

III. Poppy is a dimerous flower.
(a) Only III   (b) I and II
(c) I, II and III   (d) II and III

19. A flower was cut horizontally into two halves. Both the halves were symmetrical. The same flower was again cut vertically, and the halves obtained also were symmetrical. Which of the following option matches to the above description?
(a) Zygomorphic   (b) Asymmetrical
(c) Actinomorphic (d) Synandrous

20. Calyx forms the outermost whorl of a flower. They can be polysepalous, e.g. <u>A</u> or gamosepalous, e.g. <u>B</u>.

Choose the examples which best describe *A* and *B*.

	A	*B*
(a)	Rose	Lotus
(b)	Lotus	Mangdia
(c)	*Hibiscus*	Rose
(d)	Mustard	*Hibiscus*

21. The petals of a plant are funnel-shaped, with tube gradually widening upwards and pairing intensively into a limb. What is this corolla shape called as?
(a) Cruciform   (b) Campanulate
(c) Infundibuliform (d) Papilionaceous

22. The figures given below show flower aestivation. Match accordingly.

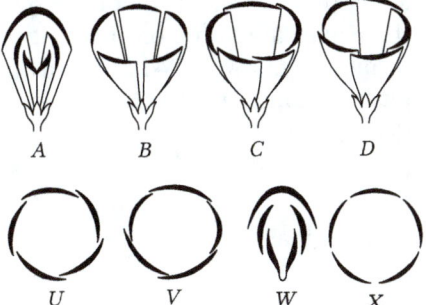

(a) Valvate - *B* - *X*, Twisted - *C* - *U*, Vexillary - *A*-*W*, Qunicuncial - *D* - *V*

(b) Valvate - *A*-*X*, Twisted-*C*-*W*, Vexillary -*B*-*U*, Qunicuncial -*D*-*V*

(c) Valvate -*C*-*W*, Twisted-*A*-*U*, Vexillary-*D*-*X*, Qunicuncial- *B*-*V*

(d) Valvate - *B*-*U*, Twisted-*D*-*W*, Vexillary - *A*-*V*, Qunicuncial-*C*-*X*

23. Study the figures given below and choose the correct option showing how filament is attached to anther?

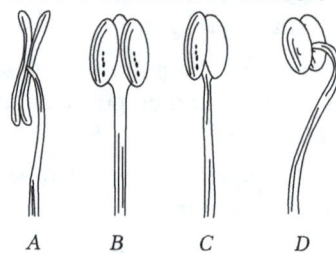

	A	**B**	**C**	**D**
(a)	Adnate	Basifixed	Dorsifixed	Versatile
(b)	Versatile	Basifixed	Adnate	Dorsifixed
(c)	Adnate	Versatile	Basifixed	Dorsifixed
(d)	Versatile	Adnate	Basifixed	Dorsifixed

24. Which of the following matches is incorrect with respect to placentation?

(a) Lemon-Axile

(b) Marigold-Free central

(c) *Pisum*-Marginal

(d) Mustard-Parietal

25. The placenta of a plant forms a ridge along the ventral suture of the ovary and the ovules are borne on this ridge forming two rowes. What is this type of placentation termed as?

(a) Parietal

(b) Basal

(c) Axile

(d) Marginal

26. Which kind of placentation is represented by the given figure?

(a) Marginal   (b) Axile

(c) Parietal   (d) Basal

27. The diagram given below shows different parts of a fruit.

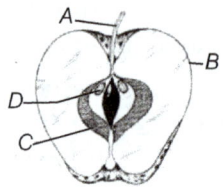

Which part of the following develops from

1. ovary wall   2. funiculus

3. ovule   4. ovary

(a) 1-*B*, 2-*D*, 3-*A*, 4-*C*

(b) 1-*C*, 2-*A*, 3-*D*, 4-*B*

(c) 1-*A*, 2-*B*, 3-*C*, 4-*D*

(d) 1-*C*, 2-*B*, 3-*D*, 4-*A*

28. Study the following diagrams and determine *A* and *B* along with their examples.

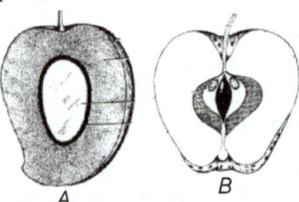

(a) *A*-False fruit; *Ananas* and *Pyrus*, *B*- True fruit, mango and guava

(b) *A*-True fruit; mango and grapes, *B*- False fruit; apple and *Ananas*

(c) *A*-False fruit; guava and grapes, *B*-True fruit; *Morus* and *Pyrus*

(d) *A*-True fruit; *Pyrus* and *Ananas*, *B*- False fruit; mango and guava

29. In *X* type of fruit the endocarp projects inwards forming distinct chambers and epicarp and mesocarp are free to form the separable part. What is *X*?
(a) Pepo   (b) Pome
(c) Hesperidium   (d) Balausta

30. Edible part of mango is
(a) endocarp   (b) epicarp
(c) testa   (d) mesocarp

31. From which part of the coconut, coir is obtained?
(a) Epicarp   (b) Pericarp
(c) Mesocarp   (d) Endocarp

32. The figure shows a gram seed.

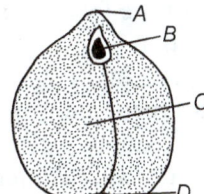

Which of the following part permits water to enter embryo before germination?
(a) *B*   (b) *D*   (c) *A*   (d) *C*

33. The figure shows the longitudinal section of grain. Label the parts *A-D*.

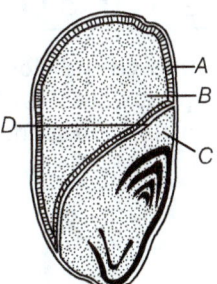

	A	B	C	D
(a)	Aleurone layer	Endosperm	Scutellum	Epithelium
(b)	Scutellum	Epithelium	Endosperm	Aleurone layer
(c)	Epithelium	Scutellum	Endosperm	Aleurone layer
(d)	Aleurone layer	Epithelium	Scutellum	Endosperm

34. A few statements about dispersal of fruits and seeds by wind are given below. Which of the following statement is incorrect?
(a) Fruits develop balloon-like appendages which makes them light
(b) Fruits have persistent and feathery styles
(c) Fruits open with force and scatter the seeds in all directions
(d) Seeds of some plants are sufficiently light and minute in size

35. .... is an elongated scar on the seed coat through which seeds are attached to the fruit?
(a) Testa   (b) Tegmen
(c) Kernel   (d) Hilum

36. At the two ends of the embryonical axis
(a) radicle is present
(b) plumule is present
(c) Both (a) and (b)
(d) None of the above

37. Plant have two cotyledons in its seeds. Such plants are called dicot plants. In majority of dicots, direct elongation of radicle leads to the formation of
(a) primary root which grows inside soil
(b) lateral roots that are referred to as secondary roots
(c) root cap that covers apex of root
(d) root hair that absorb water and minerals from soil

38. ♂ stands for ...*A*... .
⊕ stands for ...*B*... .
% stands for ...*C*.... .
Here, *A* to *C* refers to
(a) *A*–bisexual, *B*–actinomorphic, *C*–zygomorphic
(b) *A*–unisexual, *B*–actinomorphic, *C*–zygomorphic
(c) *A*–unisexual, *B*–zygomorphic, *C*–actinomorphic
(d) *A*–bisexual, *B*–zygomorphic, *C*–actinomorphic

39. Decode the part of floral formula given below.

$$\oplus \male K_{(5)} C_{(5)}$$

(a) Actinomorphic, unisexual flower, polysepalous, polypetalous

(b) Zygomorphic flower, bisexual, gamosepalous, gamopetalous

(c) Actinomorphic, bisexual flower, polysepalous, gamopetalous

(d) Actinomorphic, bisexual flower, gamosepalous, gamopetalous

40. Bicarpellary, syncarpous gynoecium, axile placentation, epipetalous stamens and berry or capsule fruits are characteristic features of which family?

(a) Fabaceae   (b) Liliaceae

(c) Papilionaceae   (d) Solanaceae

41. Which of the following floral formula is correct for the given floral diagram?

(a) % $\male$ $K_5 C_5 A 1+2+2+2+3$

(b) Br or Ebr $\oplus$ $\male$ $K_{(4)} C_4 A_4 \underline{G}_1$

(c) $\oplus$ $\male$ $K_{(5)} \overparen{C_{(5)}} A_5 \underline{G}_{(2)}$

(d) $\oplus$ $\male$ $\overparen{P_{(3+3)}} A_{3+3} G_{(3)}$

42. The diagram of few plants are given below. Which of the following plants belong to Solanaceae family?

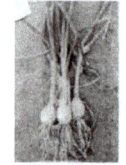    

A   B   C   D   E

(a) C and D   (b) A, C and D

(c) Only C   (d) A and B

43. Which of the following statement is correct with reference to the flowers of family–Solanaceae?

(a) Pentamerous, actinomorphic, unisexual, hypogynous

(b) Pentamerous, zygomorphic, bisexual, epigynous

(c) Pentamerous, bisexual, actinomorphic, hypogynous

(d) Trimerous, actinomorphic, bisexual, hypogynous

44. The partial floral formula of a flower is

$$K_{(5)} C_5 A_\infty \underline{G}_{(5)}$$

Which of the following set of information is conveyed here?

(a) Gamosepalous, polypetalous, syncarpous and superior ovary

(b) Polysepalous, polypetalous, syncarpous and inferior ovary

(c) Gamosepalous, gamopetalous, polycarpous and superior ovary

(d) Gamosepalous, polypetalous, syncarpous and inferior ovary

MCQs 2 Marks Questions

45. The graph given below shows how angiosperms are classified on the basis of their lifespan? What does *A-D* indicate?

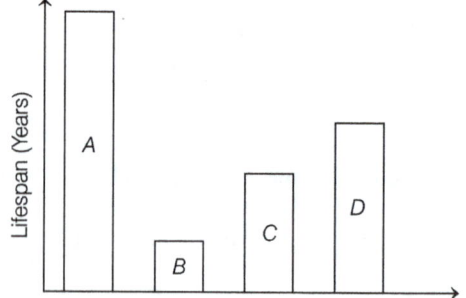

(a) *A*-Ephemerals, *B*-Annuals, *C*-Biennials, *D*-Perennials

(b) *A*-Perennials, *B*-Ephemerals, *C*-Annuals, *D*-Biennials

(c) *A*-Ephemerals, *B*-Perennials, *C*-Biennials, *D*-Annuals

(d) *A*-Perennials, *B*-Biennials, *C*-Annuals, *D*-Ephemerals

46. Consider the following plant species.
Mirabilis, Lemna, Avicennia, Daucus, Pistia
How many of these do not possess any root cap?

(a) 4   (b) 1
(c) 0   (d) 2

47. The main function of stem are

I. it bears, support flowers and fruits.

II. it stores food in aerenchyma cells.

III. it add new cells, tissues and organs.

Choose the correct option.

(a) I and III   (b) Only II
(c) Only III   (d) I and II

48. Complete the following flowchart related to branching of stem.

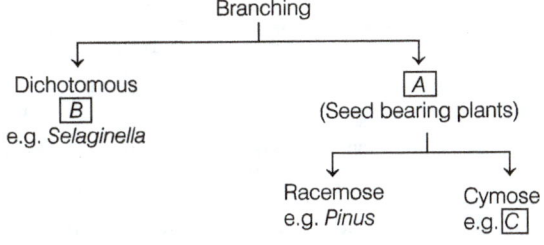

(a) *A*-Lateral, *B*-Spore bearing plants, *C-Datura*

(b) *A*-Monopodial, *B*-Flower bearing plants, *C-Croton*

(c) *A*-Lateral, *B*-Flower bearing plants, *C-Lawsonia*

(d) *A*-Monopodial, *B*-Spore bearing plants, *C-Terminalia*

49. **Assertion** (A) Phyllotaxy, arrangement of leaves is made to allow the leaves get enough light for photosynthesis.

Reason (R) In phyllotaxy arrangement of leaves are on both main stem and branches.

(a) Both A and R are true and R is the correct explanation of A

(b) Both A and R are true, but R is not the correct explanation of A

(c) A is true, but R is false

(d) A is false, but R is true

50. Match the following parts of leaf with their features.

	Leaf		Features
A.	Amplexicaul	1.	Cushion-like
B.	Pulvinus	2.	Lateral outgrowth
C.	Ligules	3.	Leaf base enclosing the stem
D.	Stipules	4.	Splitting sheath forming scaly structures

(a) A-3, B-1, C-4, D-2

(b) A-1, B-2, C-3, D-4

(c) A-3, B-4, C-2, D-1

(d) A-1, B-3, C-2, D-4

51. Among bitter gourd, mustard, pumpkin, brinjal, China rose, lupin, cucumber, sunhemp, gram, guava, bean, chilli, plum, *Petunia*, tomato, rose, *Withania*, potato, onion, *Aloe* and tulip, plants having hypogynous flowers are .... in number.

(a) 6   (b) 10
(c) 15   (d) 18

52. Consider the following table related to a aestivation and match the columns correctly.

Types	Examples	Representation
Valvate	P. *Polyalthea*	I.
Twisted	Q. *Brassica*	II.
Vexillary	R. *Hibiscus rosa sinensis*	III.

(a) Twisted - R - II   (b) Valvate - Q - III
(c) Vexillary - Q - II   (d) Valvate - P - I

53. Match the Column I with Column II and choose the correct answer from the options given below.

	Column I		Column II
A.	Basal placentation	1.	Brinjal
B.	Multicarpellary ovary	2.	*Cucurbita*
C.	Synandrous stamens	3.	Sunflower
D.	Polyadelphous	4.	*Citrus*

Codes

	A	B	C	D
(a)	3	1	2	4
(b)	1	2	3	4
(c)	3	4	2	1
(d)	2	4	3	1

54. Given below are certain terms that represent various morphological terms.

> Basifixed, Synandrous, Valvate, Plumose, Bifid, Extrorse, Axile, Marginal, Discoid, Epipetalous, Diadelphous

How many of the above terms are related to stamens?
(a) 5   (b) 10   (c) 6   (d) 4

55. Consider the following fruits.
  I. *Oryza sativum*
  II. *Triticum aestivum*
  III. *Litchi chinensis*

IV. *Lycopersicum esculentum*
Which of the above fruits bear edible parts as endosperm and embryo?
(a) I and II   (b) I and III
(c) II and III   (d) Only IV

56. **Assertion** (A) Kidney-shaped fruit of cashewnut develops from multicarpellary ovary.

Reason (R) The edible seed with two large cotyledons is enclosed by a hard pericarp in fruit of cashewnut.
(a) Both A and R are true and R is the correct explanation of A
(b) Both A and R are true, but R is not the correct explanation of A
(c) A is true, but R is false
(d) A is false, but R is true

57. Choose the chief edible part in (*A*) groundnut, (*B*) Jack fruit, (*C*) Apple and (*D*) Mango fruit from the options given below.

	A	B	C	D
(a)	Endosperm	Inflorescence	Mesocarp	Endocarp
(b)	Cotyledons	Succulent perianth	Fleshy thalamus	Mesocarp
(c)	Cotyledons	Endosperm	Mesocarp	Fleshy thalamus
(d)	Cotyledons	Fleshy thalamus	Pericarp	Mesocarp

58. Natural breaking of seed dormancy can be done *via*.
  I. leaching of inhibitors and salts.
  II. attainment of maturity during dormant period by immature embryo.
  III. Formation of growth hormones.
  IV. Rupturing seed coats by filling, chopping machine, threshing.
Choose the correct option.
(a) I, II and III   (b) I and III
(c) Only III   (d) Only IV

59. Consider the Venn diagram given below.

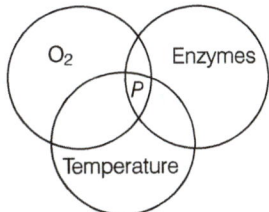

The three factors given in the Venn diagram, are known to affect a process related to seed, denoted by '*P*'.

Identify '*P*'.

(a) Seed dispersal   (b) Seed dormancy
(c) Seed germination (d) Seed viability

60. **Assertion** (A) Seeds of some plants are sufficiently light and minute in size to be easily carried away to great distances by air.

Reason (R) The seeds develop one or more thin membranous wings to ensure their dispersal by wind.

(a) Both A and R are true and R is the correct explanation of A
(b) Both A and R are true, but R is not the correct explanation of A
(c) A is true, but R is false
(d) A is false, but R is true

Darken your choice with HB Pencil

1.	ⓐ ⓑ ⓒ ⓓ	11.	ⓐ ⓑ ⓒ ⓓ	21.	ⓐ ⓑ ⓒ ⓓ	31.	ⓐ ⓑ ⓒ ⓓ	41.	ⓐ ⓑ ⓒ ⓓ	51.	ⓐ ⓑ ⓒ ⓓ
2.	ⓐ ⓑ ⓒ ⓓ	12.	ⓐ ⓑ ⓒ ⓓ	22.	ⓐ ⓑ ⓒ ⓓ	32.	ⓐ ⓑ ⓒ ⓓ	42.	ⓐ ⓑ ⓒ ⓓ	52.	ⓐ ⓑ ⓒ ⓓ
3.	ⓐ ⓑ ⓒ ⓓ	13.	ⓐ ⓑ ⓒ ⓓ	23.	ⓐ ⓑ ⓒ ⓓ	33.	ⓐ ⓑ ⓒ ⓓ	43.	ⓐ ⓑ ⓒ ⓓ	53.	ⓐ ⓑ ⓒ ⓓ
4.	ⓐ ⓑ ⓒ ⓓ	14.	ⓐ ⓑ ⓒ ⓓ	24.	ⓐ ⓑ ⓒ ⓓ	34.	ⓐ ⓑ ⓒ ⓓ	44.	ⓐ ⓑ ⓒ ⓓ	54.	ⓐ ⓑ ⓒ ⓓ
5.	ⓐ ⓑ ⓒ ⓓ	15.	ⓐ ⓑ ⓒ ⓓ	25.	ⓐ ⓑ ⓒ ⓓ	35.	ⓐ ⓑ ⓒ ⓓ	45.	ⓐ ⓑ ⓒ ⓓ	55.	ⓐ ⓑ ⓒ ⓓ
6.	ⓐ ⓑ ⓒ ⓓ	16.	ⓐ ⓑ ⓒ ⓓ	26.	ⓐ ⓑ ⓒ ⓓ	36.	ⓐ ⓑ ⓒ ⓓ	46.	ⓐ ⓑ ⓒ ⓓ	56.	ⓐ ⓑ ⓒ ⓓ
7.	ⓐ ⓑ ⓒ ⓓ	17.	ⓐ ⓑ ⓒ ⓓ	27.	ⓐ ⓑ ⓒ ⓓ	37.	ⓐ ⓑ ⓒ ⓓ	47.	ⓐ ⓑ ⓒ ⓓ	57.	ⓐ ⓑ ⓒ ⓓ
8.	ⓐ ⓑ ⓒ ⓓ	18.	ⓐ ⓑ ⓒ ⓓ	28.	ⓐ ⓑ ⓒ ⓓ	38.	ⓐ ⓑ ⓒ ⓓ	48.	ⓐ ⓑ ⓒ ⓓ	58.	ⓐ ⓑ ⓒ ⓓ
9.	ⓐ ⓑ ⓒ ⓓ	19.	ⓐ ⓑ ⓒ ⓓ	29.	ⓐ ⓑ ⓒ ⓓ	39.	ⓐ ⓑ ⓒ ⓓ	49.	ⓐ ⓑ ⓒ ⓓ	59.	ⓐ ⓑ ⓒ ⓓ
10.	ⓐ ⓑ ⓒ ⓓ	20.	ⓐ ⓑ ⓒ ⓓ	30.	ⓐ ⓑ ⓒ ⓓ	40.	ⓐ ⓑ ⓒ ⓓ	50.	ⓐ ⓑ ⓒ ⓓ	60.	ⓐ ⓑ ⓒ ⓓ

Chapter

03

Anatomy of Flowering Plants

MCQs 1 Mark Questions

1. A few epidermal cells, in the vicinity of the '*A*' become specialised in their shape and size and are known as '*B*'. Identify *A* and *B* from the options given below.

(a) *A*-cuticle, *B*-stomata

(b) *A*-epidermis, *B*-cuticle

(c) *A*-guard cells, *B*- subsidiary cells

(d) *A*-guard cells, *B*- cuticle

2. Choose the incorrect match pair.

(a) Root hair - Unicellular

(b) Stem hair- Multicellular

(c) Trichomes- Cause water loss

(d) Guard cells - Regulate opening and closing of stomata

3. A dicot root at a cellular level is composed of an epidermis, cortex, endodermis, pericycle, xylem and phloem. In the given options which is not a characteristic feature of dicotyledons roots?

(a) Pith little or absent

(b) Secondary growth

(c) Radial vascular bundles

(d) Vascular bundles 20-25

4. Select the incorrectly matched pair.

	X	Y
(a)	Guard cells	enclose stomatal pores
(b)	Stomatal apparatus	guard cells + subsidiary cells
(c)	Trichomes	help in preventing water loss
(d)	Velamen cells	transpiration

5. Which of the following constitute the ground tissue?

1. Cortex, 2. Epidermis, 3. Endodermis, 4. Pericycle, 5. Vascular bundle.

(a) 1, 2 and 5   (b) 1, 3 and 5
(c) 1, 3 and 4   (d) 1, 2 and 4

6. Preeti cut the transverse section of unknown plant stem and observed the conjoint open vascular bundle. On the basis of her observation, choose the correct answer from the options given below.

(a) Tulip   (b) Onion
(c) Garlic   (d) Mint

7. Choose the incorrect pair.
   (a) Cuticle is absent – Roots
   (b) Primary function of epidermis –
                                Protection
   (c) Present on epidermis – Stomata
   (d) Bean-shaped stomatal cells – Subsidiary
                                cells

8. Which of the following statement is incorrect?
   (a) Stomata are minute apertures in the epidermis of leaves and other aerial parts of plants
   (b) Aperture is bounded by two specialised kidney-shaped cells, called guard cells
   (c) The guard cells have evenly thickened wall
   (d) The guard cells contain chloroplast and thus perform the function of photosynthesis

9. From the following figures (a), (b), (c) and (d), the stomatal apparatus that belong to jowar is

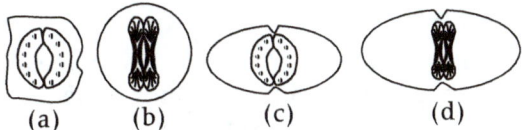

   (a)   (b)   (c)   (d)

10. Ground tissue does not include
   I. epidermis   II. vascular bundle
   III. sclerenchyma   IV. collenchyma
   V. parenchyma
   Select the right combination from the above given options.
   (a) I and II   (b) III and IV
   (c) I and V   (d) I and IV

11. In leaves, the ground tissues consist of thin-walled chloroplast containing cells called as
   (a) epidermal cells
   (b) trichomes
   (c) mesophyll cells
   (d) medullary rays

12. Vascular bundles in monocotyledons are considered closed because
   (a) a bundle sheath surrounds each bundle
   (b) cambium is absent
   (c) there are no vessels with perforations
   (d) xylem is surrounded all around by phloem

13. Identify type of vascular bundle with respect to *A*, *B* and *C* figure.

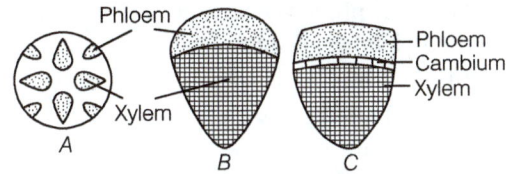

   (a) *A*–Conjoint closed, *B*–Conjoint open, *C*–Radial
   (b) *A*–Radial, *B*–Conjoint open, *C*–Conjoint closed
   (c) *A*–Radial, *B*–Conjoint closed, *C*–Conjoint open
   (d) *A*–Conjoint open, *B*–Conjoint closed, *C*–Radial

14. Water impermeable, waxy material secreted by endodermal cells in the form of Casparian strip is
   (a) lignin   (b) suberin
   (c) conjunctive tissue (d) pectin

15. Which of the following lack stomata in their epidermis?
   (a) Dicot roots   (b) Dicot stems
   (c) Monocot stems   (d) Both (a) and (c)

16. Stomata are structures present in the epidermis of leaves. These regulate the process of transpiration and gaseous exchange. Each stoma is composed of two bean-shaped cells known as guard cells. Specialised epidermal cells surrounding the guard cells are called
   (a) complementary cells
   (b) lenticels
   (c) bulliform cells
   (d) subsidiary cells

17. Which one of the following is incorrectly matched?

(a)	Lenticels	Gaseous exchange
(b)	Quiescent centre	Root tip
(c)	Barley stem	Open in a ring
(d)	Grass leaf	Dumb-bell shaped

18. Which of the following is present between phloem and xylem in dicotyledonous stems?
(a) Conjunctive tissue
(b) Casparian strips
(c) Cambium
(d) Stele

19. Choose the correct option for monocotyledonous root.
(a) Pith is large and well-developed
(b) No secondary growth
(c) Polyarch condition
(d) All of the above

20. Transverse section of a part of a typical monocot root has been shown in the given figure. Identify the different parts (from *A* to *E*) and select the correct option.

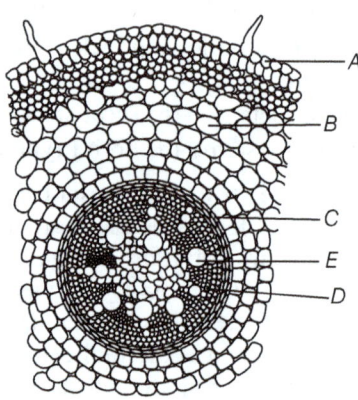

(a) *A*–Epidermis, *B*–Cortex, *C*–Endodermis, *D*–Pericycle, *E*–Metaxylem
(b) *A*–Endodermis, *B*–Cortex, *C*–Epidermis, *D*–Pericycle, *E*–Metaxylem
(c) *A*–Epidermis, *B*–Pith, *C*–Endodermis, *D*–Pericycle, *E*–Protoxylem
(d) *A*–Endodermis, *B*–Pith, *C*–Epidermis, *D*–Phloem, *E*–Protoxylem

21. Choose the incorrect pair for dicot stems.
(a) Hypodermis – Provides mechanical strength to young stems
(b) Starch grains – Present in cells of endodermis
(c) Pericycle – Present above phloem in the form of semilunar patches of sclerenchyma
(d) None of the above

22. The protoxylem in its midrib bundle in a vertical section of dorsiventral leaf
(a) faces the ventral epidermis of the leaf
(b) is surrounded by metaxylem
(c) faces the dorsal epidermis of the leaf
(d) is not distinct

23. The vertical section of a dorsiventral leaf through the lamina shows three main parts namely, epidermis, ...*A*... and vascular system. The epidermis, which covers the upper surface is ...*B*... and lower surface is covered by ...*C*... of the leaf.

Choose the correct option to replace *A*, *B* and *C*.
(a) *A*–mesophyll, *B*–adaxial epidermis, *C*–abaxial epidermis
(b) *A*–endodermis, *B*–adaxial epidermis, *C*–abaxial epidermis
(c) *A*–endodermis, *B*–abaxial epidermis, *C*–adaxial epidermis
(d) *A*–mesophyll, *B*–abaxial epidermis, *C*–adaxial epidermis

24. Vascular system includes...A... bundles, which can be seen in the veins and is ...B.... . The size of vascular bundles are dependent on the size of ...C... . The veins vary in thickness in the reticulate venation of the ...D...leaves.

Choose the correct option to replace A to D.

(a) A–phloem, B–midrib, C–veins, D–dicot

(b) A–xylem, B–midrib, C–veins, D–dicot

(c) A–vascular, B–midrib, C–veins, D–dicot

(d) A–vascular, B–midrib, C–veins, D–monocot

25. Observe the venn diagram that shows the 'X' feature commonly present in monocot leaf. Identify 'X' from the given options.

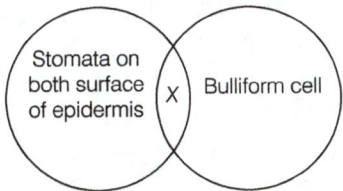

(a) Palisade along both the surfaces

(b) Undifferentiated mesophyll

(c) Palisade towards abaxial surface

(d) Palisade towards adaxial surface

MCQs 2 Marks Questions

26. Read the following statements.

 I. Pericycle give rise to lateral roots only.

 II. Xylem is polyarch type.

 III. Pith is large and well-developed.

 IV. More than six xylem bundles are present.

 V. Do not undergo any secondary growth.

Choose the correct option which correctly depict the given statements.

(a) Monocot roots (b) Dicot roots

(c) Monocot stems (d) Dicot stems

27. Which of the following tissues are present innerside of the endodermis in monocot root of plants?

1. Pericycle 2. Vascular bundles, 3. Cortex 4. Pith 5. Trichomes.

(a) 1, 2 and 5 (b) 1, 3 and 4

(c) 1, 3 and 5 (d) 1, 2 and 4

28. The 'ring' arrangement of vascular bundles is a characteristics of

(a) monocot stem

(b) dicot stem

(c) monocot root

(d) dicot root

29. A are present below the hypodermis and consists of rounded thin-walled B cells with conspicuous intracellular spaces. Identify A and B from the given options.

(a) A- Pericycles B- parenchymatous

(b) A-Corticle layers B- collenchymatous

(c) A-Pericycles B-collenchymatous

(d) A-Corticle layers B-parenchymatous

30. Which of the following is not a function of pericycle?

(a) Initiation of lateral roots

(b) Contribution to the initiation of the vascular cambium

(c) Initiation of the cork cambium

(d) Gives protection to the cortex

31. Below figures represent the transverse sections of A and B, respectively.

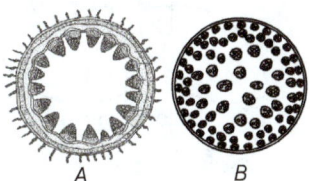

	A	B
(a)	Monocot stem	Dicot stem
(b)	Dicot stem	Monocot stem
(c)	Monocot root	Monocot stem
(d)	Dicot root	Dicot stem

32. Observe the below figures carefully.

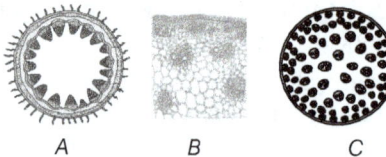

A   B   C

In which of the above figure(s) phloem parenchyma is absent? Select the correct option.

(a) Only A   (b) Only C
(c) Both A and C   (d) Both B and C

33. Given below is the TS of leaf. From A, B, C and D which of the following is responsible for the storage of non-structural carbohydrates and proteins?

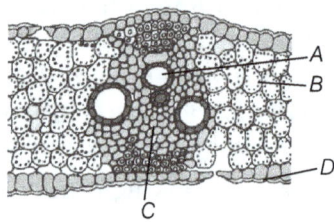

(a) A   (b) B
(c) C   (d) D

34. Observe the below venn diagram carefully and select the correct option from the given options.

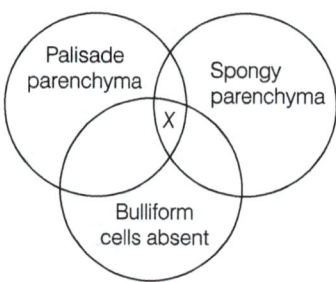

(a) Monocot leaf   (b) Dicot leaf
(c) Isobilateral leaf (d) Both (a) and (c)

35. Which of the following is not the true difference between a stem and a root?
(a) The largest xylem vessel lies towards outside in the stem and inside the root
(b) The xylem and phloem tissues are arranged on the same radii in stem while they alternate in root
(c) Pith is widest tissue in dicot root and cortex is widest in dicot stem
(d) None of the above

36. The diagram given below shows the TS of a dicot leaf. Identify the part that is not correctly labelled.

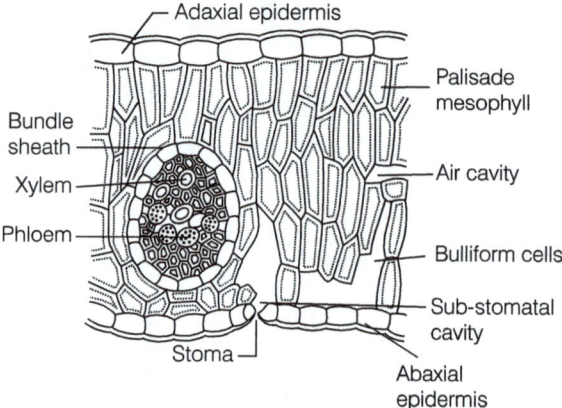

(a) Abaxial epidermis
(b) Palisade mesophyll
(c) Bulliform cells
(d) Adaxial epidermis

37. Which of the following plants contains bulliform cells?
I. *Pistia*
II. *Triticum*
III. Grasses
IV. *Vallisneria*
V. *Isoetes*
(a) I and V   (b) II and IV
(c) III and V   (d) II and III

38. Identify the type of vascular bundle shown in the below figure and select the correct statement regarding it.

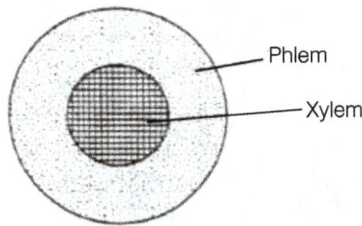

(a) Above figure is ambhicribal, where xylem is surrounded by phloem on all sides

(b) Above figure is amphivasal, where phloem is surrounded by xylem on all sides

(c) Above figure consist leptocentric vascular bundle, where xylem is surrounded by phloem

(d) Above figure consist hadrocentric vascular bundles, where phloem is surrounded by xylem

39. Select the correct statements.

I. Epidermal cells have small amount of cytoplasm and a large vacuole.

II. Waxy layer cuticle is absent in roots.

III. Root hairs are unicellular, while stem hairs/trichomes are multicellular.

IV. Trichomes are branched/unbranched, soft/stiff and secretory or transpiration preventive.

V. Guard cells are dumbbell-shaped in dicots and bean-shaped in monocots.

(a) All except I and II

(b) All except III

(c) All except II and IV

(d) All except V

40. Read the following statements with respect to anatomy of leaf and choose the incorrect statement.

I. In dicot leaf, xylem is towards adaxial epidermis.

II. Stomata are distributed more on the lower surface than on the upper surface on equifacial/bifacial leaf.

III. Stomata are equally distributed on both the surfaces in isobilateral leaf.

IV. Certain adaxial epidermal cells are modified into bulliform cells in grasses in monocot leaf.

V. The vascular bundles are radial and phloem is adaxially placed in monocot leaf.

(a) I and III

(b) II and IV

(c) Only V

(d) I and V

41. Read the following statements and select the incorrect one.

(a) Epidermis is usually double layered, elongated compactly arranged cells

(b) Outside of epidermis covered with a waxy thick layer called the cuticle

(c) Cuticle prevents the loss of water from the plants

(d) The trichomes in the shoot system are usually multicellular

42. Read the following statements and select the incorrect one.

(a) Epidermal cells are sclerenchymatous with a small amount of cytoplasm lining the cell wall and a large vacuole

(b) Guard cells are specialised bean-shaped cells which enclose stomatal pore

(c) Velamen cells are present outside the exodermis and help in the absorption of moisture

(d) All tissues, except epidermis and vascular bundles constitutes the ground tissues

43. Which one is the incorrect statement for the structure labelled as *X*?

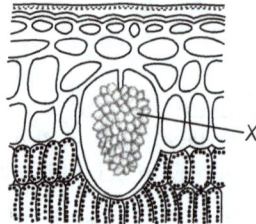

(a) It usually occurs in uniseriate epidermis

(b) Crystals of calcium carbonate get accumulated in these type of specialised cells

(c) These are generally larger than the adjacent epidermal cells

(d) Outer wall of these cells contains cuticle, wax, resin and volatile gums, etc.

44. Assertion (A) Endodermis acts as biological check post between vascular strand and cortex in the roots of angiosperms.

Reason (R) Due to the presence of Casparian strips, the endodermal cells do not allow wall to wall movement of substances between cortex and pericycle.

(a) Both A and R are true and R is the correct explanation of A

(b) Both A and R are true, but R is not the correct explanation of A

(c) A is true, but R is false

(d) A is false, but R is true

45. The diagram given below showing TS of a monocot root labelled as *A-G*. Which part in the given diagram produces lateral roots? Observe the diagram and select the correct option.

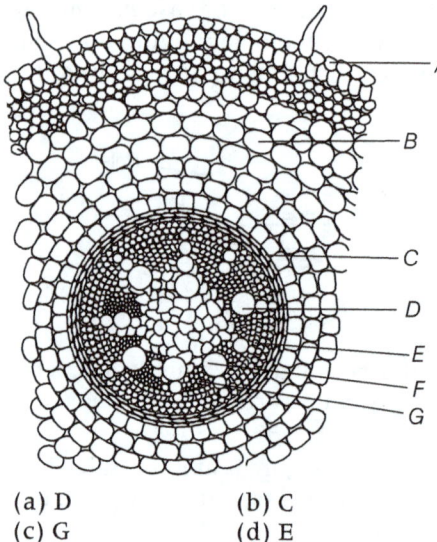

(a) D   (b) C
(c) G   (d) E

46. Assertion (A) Epidermal cells are living and generally do not possess chloroplasts except shade plants, hydrophytes and some ferns.

Reason (R) The outer wall of epidermal cells is thickest, inner is thinnest and radial walls are thick above and thin below.

(a) Both A and R are true and R is the correct explanation of A

(b) Both A and R are true, but R is not the correct explanation of A

(c) A is true, but R is false

(d) A is false, but R is true

47. Assertion (A) Monocotylendons do not form secondary tissues, are referred to as closed.

Reason (R) The vascular bundles have no cambium present in them.

(a) Both A and R are true and R is the correct explanation of A

(b) Both A and R are true, but R is not the correct explanation of A

(c) A is true, but R is false

(d) A is false, but R is true

48. Identify the type of vascular bundle shown in the below figure and select the correct statement regarding it.

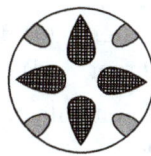

(a) Figure represent the conjoint type of vascular bundle

(b) These vascular bundles are common in stems and leaves

(c) Above figure represent radial arrangement in which vascular bundles occur on different radii

(d) In this type of vascular bundles phloem located only on the outer side of xylem

49. The conductive tissue of dicot root generally form a solid mass in the centre instead bundles being dispersed around a broad pith this contribute to

(a) flexibility without loss of tensile strength

(b) rigidity

(c) positive gravitropism

(d) negative geotropism

50. Refer to the figure given below representing VS of dorsiventral leaf (labellings from 1-4). Which cell numbers are involved in the process of photosynthesis?

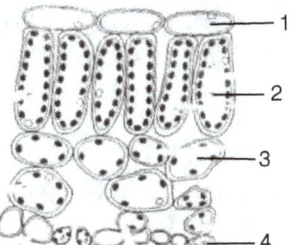

(a) 1, 4   (b) 2, 3   (c) 3, 4   (d) 2, 4

51. Match the Column I with Column II and choose the correct answer from the codes given below.

	Column I		Column II
A.	Bicollateral vascular bundle	1.	*Yucca*
B.	Leptocentric vascular bundle	2.	Fern
C.	Hadrocentric vascular bundle	3.	*Cucurbita*

Codes

	A	B	C		A	B	C
(a)	3	1	2	(b)	1	2	3
(c)	3	2	1	(d)	2	1	3

52. The cross section of some plants stem show the following anatomical features under the microscope.

 I. Sclerenchymatous hypodermis.

 II. Large number of scattered vascular bundles.

 III. Each vascular bundle surrounded by sclerenchymatous bundle shealth.

 IV. Vascular bundles conjoint and closed.

 V. Peripheral vascular bundles are generally smaller than centrally located ones.

Choose the correct option of the following group of plants which shows the above characteristics.

(a) Maize, sunflower and rice

(b) Maize, wheat and rice

(c) Sunflower, pea and rose

(d) Sunflower, wheat and rice

53. Read the different components and codes given to them. Rearrange them in correct order with the reference of their arrangement from inner side to outside in maize root (transverse section). Endodermis → A, Epiblema → B, Pericycle → C, Sclerenchyma cylinder → D, Phloem → E

(a) A → E → D → C → B

(b) A → B → C → D → E

(c) B → A → C → E → D

(d) D → E → C → A → B

54. Match the Column I with Column II and choose the correct answer from the codes given below.

Column I		Column II
A.	Monocotyledonous stem	1. Starch sheath
B.	Monocotyledonous root	2. Conjunctive tissue
C.	Dicotyledonous stem	3. Pericycle forms lateral root only
D.	Dicotyledonous root	4. Endodermis, medullary rays, pericycle and pith are absent

Codes

	A	B	C	D		A	B	C	D
(a)	1	2	4	3	(b)	3	2	1	4
(c)	4	3	1	2	(d)	2	1	4	3

55. A student took the specimen named X , cut it and placed it under the microscope and made the following observation.

I. The epidermis has multicellular hairs.

II. The hypodermis is collenchymatous.

III. The xylem is endarch with two protoxylem being at the centre and metaxylem being at the periphery.

IV. Vascular bundles are open, collateral and conjoint.

The description given above indicates that the X part is

(a) monocot stem   (b) dicot stem

(c) monocot root   (d) dicot root

56. Read the statements and select the correct option.

I. In *Ficus, Nerium, Pepromea* multilayered upper epidermis is present.

II. In *Cynodon dactylon* quard cells are dumb-bell shaped.

III. In submerged hydrophytes, stomata are absent or non-functional.

(a) Only I is true

(b) II and III are true

(c) I, II and III are true

(d) I, II and III are false

Darken your choice with HB Pencil

1.	ⓐ ⓑ ⓒ ⓓ	11.	ⓐ ⓑ ⓒ ⓓ	21.	ⓐ ⓑ ⓒ ⓓ	31.	ⓐ ⓑ ⓒ ⓓ	41.	ⓐ ⓑ ⓒ ⓓ	51.	ⓐ ⓑ ⓒ ⓓ
2.	ⓐ ⓑ ⓒ ⓓ	12.	ⓐ ⓑ ⓒ ⓓ	22.	ⓐ ⓑ ⓒ ⓓ	32.	ⓐ ⓑ ⓒ ⓓ	42.	ⓐ ⓑ ⓒ ⓓ	52.	ⓐ ⓑ ⓒ ⓓ
3.	ⓐ ⓑ ⓒ ⓓ	13.	ⓐ ⓑ ⓒ ⓓ	23.	ⓐ ⓑ ⓒ ⓓ	33.	ⓐ ⓑ ⓒ ⓓ	43.	ⓐ ⓑ ⓒ ⓓ	53.	ⓐ ⓑ ⓒ ⓓ
4.	ⓐ ⓑ ⓒ ⓓ	14.	ⓐ ⓑ ⓒ ⓓ	24.	ⓐ ⓑ ⓒ ⓓ	34.	ⓐ ⓑ ⓒ ⓓ	44.	ⓐ ⓑ ⓒ ⓓ	54.	ⓐ ⓑ ⓒ ⓓ
5.	ⓐ ⓑ ⓒ ⓓ	15.	ⓐ ⓑ ⓒ ⓓ	25.	ⓐ ⓑ ⓒ ⓓ	35.	ⓐ ⓑ ⓒ ⓓ	45.	ⓐ ⓑ ⓒ ⓓ	55.	ⓐ ⓑ ⓒ ⓓ
6.	ⓐ ⓑ ⓒ ⓓ	16.	ⓐ ⓑ ⓒ ⓓ	26.	ⓐ ⓑ ⓒ ⓓ	36.	ⓐ ⓑ ⓒ ⓓ	46.	ⓐ ⓑ ⓒ ⓓ	56.	ⓐ ⓑ ⓒ ⓓ
7.	ⓐ ⓑ ⓒ ⓓ	17.	ⓐ ⓑ ⓒ ⓓ	27.	ⓐ ⓑ ⓒ ⓓ	37.	ⓐ ⓑ ⓒ ⓓ	47.	ⓐ ⓑ ⓒ ⓓ		
8.	ⓐ ⓑ ⓒ ⓓ	18.	ⓐ ⓑ ⓒ ⓓ	28.	ⓐ ⓑ ⓒ ⓓ	38.	ⓐ ⓑ ⓒ ⓓ	48.	ⓐ ⓑ ⓒ ⓓ		
9.	ⓐ ⓑ ⓒ ⓓ	19.	ⓐ ⓑ ⓒ ⓓ	29.	ⓐ ⓑ ⓒ ⓓ	39.	ⓐ ⓑ ⓒ ⓓ	49.	ⓐ ⓑ ⓒ ⓓ		
10.	ⓐ ⓑ ⓒ ⓓ	20.	ⓐ ⓑ ⓒ ⓓ	30.	ⓐ ⓑ ⓒ ⓓ	40.	ⓐ ⓑ ⓒ ⓓ	50.	ⓐ ⓑ ⓒ ⓓ		

Chapter 04

Structural Organisation in Animals

MCQs 1 Mark Questions

1. Identify the correct statement regarding 'frog'.
   (a) It lives both on land and in sea water
   (b) They can survive in freshwater
   (c) *Rana tigrina* is a rare species
   (d) They belong to class Reptilia

2. Which of the following is the most common species of frog found in India?
   (a) *Hyla cinerea*   (b) *Rana henson*
   (c) *Rana tigrina*   (d) *Acris gryllus*

3. Frogs are poikilotherms. Why?
   (a) They can maintain a constant body temperature
   (b) Their body temperature varies with the temperature of the environment
   (c) They do not have a constant body temperature
   (d) Both (b) and (c)

4. The body temperature of a frog is 15°C. The frog is placed in a new environment having temperature of 25°C. What will be the temperature of frog in that new environment?
   (a) 15°C
   (b) 20°C
   (c) 25°C
   (d) Between 15°C-25°C

5. Which of these methods are utilised by frogs for protection?
   (a) Mimicry   (b) Spikes
   (c) Speed   (d) Playing dead

6. Which of the following statement is correct regarding frog?
   (a) They do not hibernate
   (b) They take shelter in narrow burrows to protect themselves from extreme weather conditions
   (c) They take shelter in deep burrows to protect themselves from extreme weather conditions
   (d) They do not aestivate

7. What is the difference between the dorsal side and ventral side of the skin in a frog?
   (a) Dorsal side is pale yellow and ventral side is olive green
   (b) Dorsal side is transparent and ventral side is pale yellow
   (c) Dorsal side is brown and ventral side is dark green
   (d) Dorsal side is olive green and ventral side is pale yellow

8. Frog is divided into how many parts?
   (a) 1   (b) 2
   (c) 3   (d) 4

9. Nictating membrane protects which part of a frog?
   (a) Eyes
   (b) Ears
   (c) Excretory system
   (d) Reproductive system

10. Tympanum receives ....
    (a) food and nutrition   (b) images
    (c) radiations   (d) sound signals

11. Find the incorrect match between Column I and Column II.

	Column I	Column II
(a)	Forelimbs and hindlimbs of a frog	Leaping and burrowing
(b)	Feet of a frog	Jumping
(c)	Digits in forelimbs of a frog	5
(d)	Digits in hindlimbs of a frog	4

12. How are male frogs distinguished from female frogs?
    (a) Tympanum
    (b) Copulatory pad on second digit of fore limbs
    (c) Presence of sound producing vocal sacs
    (d) None of the above

13. Frogs are ....
    (a) herbivores   (b) omnivores
    (c) scavengers   (d) carnivores

14. Identify '3' in the pathway of food ingested by frog.

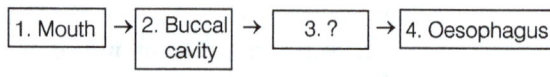

    (a) Pharynx   (b) Larynx
    (c) Crop   (d) Gizzard

15. In the digestive system of a frog, liver secretes .... that is stored in ....
    (a) pancreatic juice; gall bladder
    (b) bile juice; gall bladder
    (c) bile juice; pancreas
    (d) pancreatic juice; pancreas

16. Tongue of a frog is ....
    (a) unilobed   (b) trilobed
    (c) bilobed   (d) dithecous

17. In frogs, chyme is passed to
    (a) duodenum   (b) ileum
    (c) jejunum   (d) cloaca

18. The undigested food in a frog passes out through
    (a) anus   (b) rectum
    (c) intestine   (d) cloaca

19. **A**: The skin of a frog acts as an aquatic respiratory organ which helps in X.
    B: Dissolved oxygen in the water is exchanged through the skin by Y.
    Choose the correct option.

	X	Y
(a)	Cutaneous respiration	Diffusion
(b)	Subcutaneous respiraiton	Diffusion
(c)	Branchial respiration	Osmosis
(d)	Cutaneous respiration	Osmosis

20. What is the location of lungs in frogs?
    (a) Lower part of abdomen
    (b) Upper part of thorax
    (c) Lower part of thorax
    (d) Upper part of abdomen

21. A frog must swallow air to expand the lungs because frog
    (a) has no diaphragm
    (b) has no vagus nerve
    (c) is relatively primitive vertebrate
    (d) normally breathe through its skin

22. Heart, blood vessels and blood are part of which system in a frog?
    (a) Excretory
    (b) Lymphatic
    (c) Reproductive
    (d) Vascular

23. In frog, the ventricle opens into ....
(a) conus arteriosus
(b) sinus venosus
(c) hepatic portal vein
(d) vena cava

24. Which of the following is present in frogs?
(a) 4-chambered heart
(b) Nucleated erythrocytes
(c) Lymph same as blood
(d) Enucleated erythrocytes

25. Which of these statements is true with respect to the anatomy of frog?
(a) The oviduct and ureters are merged in female frog
(b) The urinary and genital ducts are separate in male frogs
(c) The urinary bladder is ventral to the rectum
(d) Frogs are uricotelic

26. Consider the following statements.
I. Kidney of tadpole is pronephros.
II. Excretory product of frog is urea.
Choose the correct option.
(a) Statement I is true, but statement II is false
(b) Statement I is false, but statement II is true
(c) Both statements I and II are false
(d) Both statements I and II are true

27. 'X' is the structure in frog's brain that comprises crura cerebri and optic lobes. Identify X.
(a) Medulla oblongata　(b) Midbrain
(c) Cerebrum　　　　　(d) Cerebellum

28. What lies between the medulla oblongata and spinal cord in frogs?
(a) Foramen ovale
(b) Foramen lacrum
(c) Foramen magnum
(d) Foramen of Monro

29. Which of these is a cellular aggregation in frog?
(a) Tympanum　　(b) Eyes
(c) Nasal epithelium　(d) Internal ears

30. What is the role of mesorchium in male frogs?
(a) Attaches adrenal gland to rectum
(b) Attaches testes to rectum
(c) Attaches vasa efferentia to kidneys
(d) Attaches testes to kidneys

31. How many ova does a female frog lay at a time?
(a) 30 to 40
(b) 10,000 to 20,000
(c) 2500 to 3000
(d) 50,000 to 80,000

32. Following statements are given below
I. They are not the pests for agricultural crop.
II. Legs of frogs cannot be eaten.
III. They play a part in ecological balance.
IV. They are carnivores.
Choose the correct statements with respect to frogs.
(a) I and II　　　(b) II and IV
(c) III and IV　　(d) I, II, III and IV

33. Given below is the diagrammatic representation of internal organs of frog. Identify A to D.

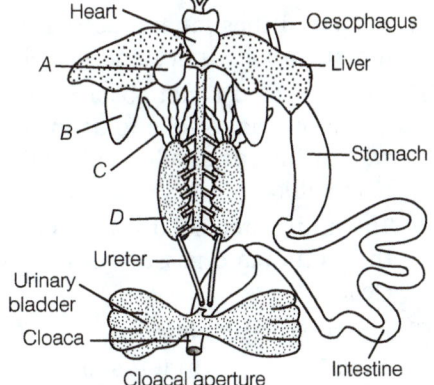

	A	B	C	D
(a)	Gall bladder	Lung	Fat bodies	Kidney
(b)	Gall bladder	Lung	Testes	Kidney
(c)	Gall bladder	Lung	Fat bodies	Testes
(d)	Gall bladder	Lung	Ovary	Testes

MCQs 2 Marks Questions

34. Match the Column I with Column II and choose the correct option with respect to frog.

	Column I		Column II
A.	Alimentary canal	1.	Pancreatic juice
B.	Intestine	2.	Pulmonary respiration
C.	Lungs	3.	Short
D.	Pancreas	4.	Final digestion

Codes

	A	B	C	D			A	B	C	D
(a)	3	2	1	4		(b)	3	4	2	1
(c)	4	1	2	3		(d)	3	4	1	2

35. Choose the correct statement with reference to digestive system in frogs.

  I. Digestion of food takes place by the action of HCl and gastric juices secreted from the walls of the stomach.

  II. Bile emulsifies fat and pancreatic juices digest carbohydrates and proteins.

  III. Digested food is not absorbed by the numerous finger-like folds in the inner wall of intestine called villi and microvilli.

  IV. The undigested solid waste moves into the rectum and passes out through cloaca.

Choose the correct option.

(a) I and III   (b) I, II and III
(c) I, III and IV   (d) I, II and IV

36. Choose the correct statement with respect to respiratory system of frog.

  I. On land, the buccal cavity, skin and lungs act as the respiratory organs.

  II. The lungs are a pair of elongated, pink coloured sac-like structures present in the lower part of the trunk region (thorax).

  III. Air enters through the lungs into the buccal cavity and then to nostrils.

  IV. During aestivation and hibernation gaseous exchange takes place through skin.

Choose the correct option.

(a) Only IV   (b) I and III
(c) I and IV   (d) I, II, III, and IV

37. Match the Column I with Column II and choose the correct option with reference to internal organs of a frog.

	Column I		Column II
A.	Blood	1.	Lymph, lymph channels, lymph nodes
B.	Lymphatic system	2.	Nephrons
C.	Heart	3.	Pumping action
D.	Kidneys	4.	Plasma and cells

Codes

	A	B	C	D
(a)	4	1	3	2
(b)	2	1	3	4
(c)	1	2	3	4
(d)	4	1	2	3

38. Frog's heart, when taken out of the body, continues to beat for sometime. Select the best option from the following statements.

  I. Frog does not have any coronary circulation.

  II. Frog is a poikilothermic.

  III. Heart is autoexcitable.

  IV. Heart is 'myogenic' in nature.

(a) I and III

(b) Only III

(c) I and II

(d) III and IV

39. Which of the following correctly describes the location of some body parts in the frog?

(a) The thin-walled urinary bladder is present ventral to the rectum

(b) Kidneys are situated a little anteriorly in the body cavity on both sides of vertebral column.

(c) Ureters do not emerge from the kidneys in the male frogs

(d) The thin-walled urinary bladder is present dorsal to the rectum

40. Assertion (A) External ear is absent in frogs and only tympanum can be seen externally.

Reason (R) The ear is an organ of hearing as well as balancing (equilibrium).

(a) Both A and R are true and R is the correct explanation of A

(b) Both A and R are true, but R is not the correct explanation of A

(c) A is true, but R is false

(d) A is false, but R is true

41. Match the Column I with Column II and choose the correct option from the codes given below in context to frog.

	Column I		Column II
A.	Vasa efferentia	1.	Small, median chamber
B.	Ovary	2.	Peritoneum and mesorchium
C.	Testes	3.	10-12
D.	Cloaca	4.	No functional connection with kidneys

Codes

	A	B	C	D			A	B	C	D
(a)	1	2	3	4		(b)	3	4	2	1
(c)	4	3	1	2		(d)	3	2	4	1

42. Given below is the diagrammatic representation of the female reproductive system in a frog.

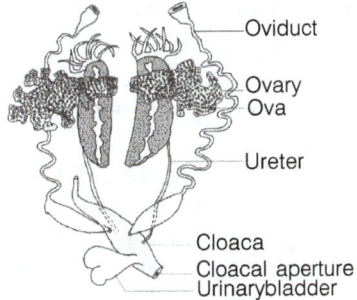

Choose the correct option.

(a) The ovaries are situated near ureters

(b) Cloacal apertures opens into oviduct

(c) Urinary bladder is present in pair

(d) A pair of oviducts arising from the ovaries opens into the cloaca separately

Darken your choice with HB Pencil

1.	ⓐ ⓑ ⓒ ⓓ	8.	ⓐ ⓑ ⓒ ⓓ	15.	ⓐ ⓑ ⓒ ⓓ	22.	ⓐ ⓑ ⓒ ⓓ	29.	ⓐ ⓑ ⓒ ⓓ	36.	ⓐ ⓑ ⓒ ⓓ
2.	ⓐ ⓑ ⓒ ⓓ	9.	ⓐ ⓑ ⓒ ⓓ	16.	ⓐ ⓑ ⓒ ⓓ	23.	ⓐ ⓑ ⓒ ⓓ	30.	ⓐ ⓑ ⓒ ⓓ	37.	ⓐ ⓑ ⓒ ⓓ
3.	ⓐ ⓑ ⓒ ⓓ	10.	ⓐ ⓑ ⓒ ⓓ	17.	ⓐ ⓑ ⓒ ⓓ	24.	ⓐ ⓑ ⓒ ⓓ	31.	ⓐ ⓑ ⓒ ⓓ	38.	ⓐ ⓑ ⓒ ⓓ
4.	ⓐ ⓑ ⓒ ⓓ	11.	ⓐ ⓑ ⓒ ⓓ	18.	ⓐ ⓑ ⓒ ⓓ	25.	ⓐ ⓑ ⓒ ⓓ	32.	ⓐ ⓑ ⓒ ⓓ	39.	ⓐ ⓑ ⓒ ⓓ
5.	ⓐ ⓑ ⓒ ⓓ	12.	ⓐ ⓑ ⓒ ⓓ	19.	ⓐ ⓑ ⓒ ⓓ	26.	ⓐ ⓑ ⓒ ⓓ	33.	ⓐ ⓑ ⓒ ⓓ	40.	ⓐ ⓑ ⓒ ⓓ
6.	ⓐ ⓑ ⓒ ⓓ	13.	ⓐ ⓑ ⓒ ⓓ	20.	ⓐ ⓑ ⓒ ⓓ	27.	ⓐ ⓑ ⓒ ⓓ	34.	ⓐ ⓑ ⓒ ⓓ	41.	ⓐ ⓑ ⓒ ⓓ
7.	ⓐ ⓑ ⓒ ⓓ	14.	ⓐ ⓑ ⓒ ⓓ	21.	ⓐ ⓑ ⓒ ⓓ	28.	ⓐ ⓑ ⓒ ⓓ	35.	ⓐ ⓑ ⓒ ⓓ	42.	ⓐ ⓑ ⓒ ⓓ

Chapter 05

Cell: The Basic Unit of Life

MCQs 1 Mark Questions

1. Which of the following option is true about cell theory?
   (a) It states that cells are fundamental and structural units of both plants and animals
   (b) It states that cells are the smallest unit of life that can replicate independently
   (c) It states that cells are not the smallest unit of life that can be used for replication
   (d) It states that cell active in protein synthesis will be rich in lysosomes

2. Which of the following represents the incorrect pair?

   (a)
   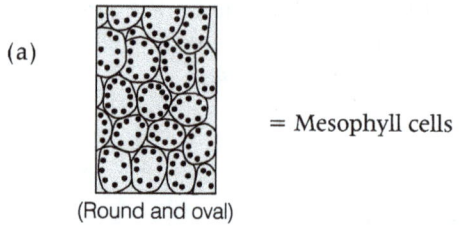
   = Mesophyll cells
   (Round and oval)

   (b)
   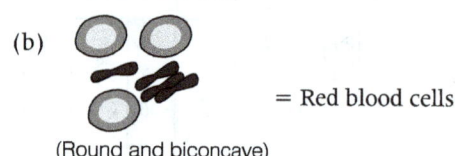
   = Red blood cells
   (Round and biconcave)

   (c)
   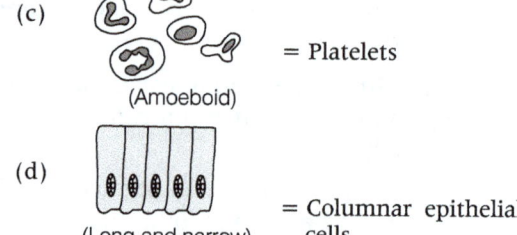
   (Amoeboid)
   = Platelets

   (d)
   (Long and narrow)
   = Columnar epithelial cells

3. Which combination of structures describes a prokaryotic cell?

	Nucleus	Membrane bound cell organelles	Ribosomes	Flagella
(a)	✗	✗	✓	✓
(b)	✗	✓	✗	✓
(c)	✓	✓	✗	✗
(d)	✓	✗	✓	✗

4. A cell has mitochondria, ribosomes, smooth ER and other organelles.

   From the above information, it could not be a
   (a) bacterium
   (b) cell from onion
   (c) cell from *Drosophila*
   (d) cell from *Neurospora*

5. Which one of the following is a correct option?
(a) Eukaryotes have more DNA than prokaryotes
(b) Eukaryotes are more complex because of DNA
(c) Both (a) and (b)
(d) Answer cannot be predicted

6. In a typical eukaryotic cell, the membrane across which the proton (H^+) gradient facilitates ATP synthesis is
(a) nuclear membrane
(b) plasma membrane
(c) mitochondrial membrane
(d) mitochondrial inner membrane

7. X and Y are two types of bacterial cell walls. X is a loose sheath while Y is thick and tough. Choose the correct option which represent X and Y.
(a) X-Capsule, Y-Slime layer
(b) X-Capsule, Y-Gell layer
(c) X-Huck, Y-Slime layer
(d) X-Slime layer, Y-Capsule

8. A special membrane structure X is formed by the extensions of plasma membrane into the cell. These extensions are in the form of vesicles, tubules and lamellae. Which of the following is best suitable for X?
(a) Ribosome　　　(b) Mesosome
(c) Lysosome　　　(d) Glycosome

9. Consider the following functions.
I. They help in respiration.
II. They help in DNA replication.
III. They help in cell wall formation.
IV. They increase surface area of plasma membrane.

Which of the following prokaryotic structure has all the above functions?
(a) Lysosome　　　(b) Mesosome
(c) Ribosome　　　(d) Chromosome

10. Which of the following option is correct about plant cell?
(a) Bigger vacuole with rigid cell wall
(b) Centriole take part in cell division
(c) Centriole are inactive in non-dividing cell
(d) Absence of cell membrane

11. How many of the following organelles are found only in plant cells?

Plastids, Chloroplast, Vacuole, Ribosomes, Lysosomes, Mitochondria.

(a) Two　　(b) Three　　(c) Four　　(d) Five

12. A few statements about plant and animal cells are made. Which of the following statement is true?
(a) Reserve food is usually starch for plant cell and glycogen for animal cell and fat is common in both
(b) Plant cell is usually smaller in size than animal cell
(c) Mitochondria are generally more in plant cell than in animal cell
(d) None of the above

13. Given below is the diagram of a plant cell with its labelled parts A to C.

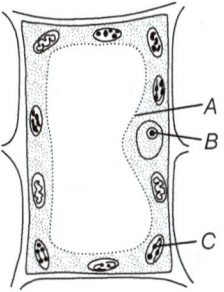

Choose the correct option for the labels A to C.

	A	B	C
(a)	Food storage	DNA material	Traps sunlight
(b)	DNA material	Food storage	Traps sunlight

| (c) | Traps sunlight | DNA material | Food storage |
| (d) | Food storage | Traps sunlight | DNA material |

14. Given below is the diagram of an animal cell with its labelled parts *A* to *D*.

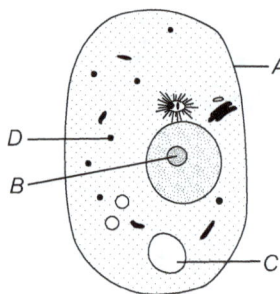

Which of the following part contain DNA?

(a) *B*   (b) *C*   (c) *A*   (d) *D*

15. Which of the following is the characteristic of phospholipids of plasma membrane?
    (a) One non-polar head and two polar tails
    (b) One polar head and two non-polar tails
    (c) Two non-polar heads and one polar tail
    (d) Two polar heads and one non-polar tail

16. Which of the following organelles does not contain RNA?
    (a) Nucleolus   (b) Chromosome
    (c) Plasmalemma   (d) Ribosome

17. Why tails of lipids in the cell membrane are towards inner-part?
    (a) The tail is non-polar hydrocarbon and so protected with an aqueous environment
    (b) The tail is polar hydrocarbon and so is protected from aqueous environment

(c) The non-polar or hydrophobic hydrocarbon tails of lipid, being on inner side ensure their protection from aqueous environment
(d) The tail is hydrophilic, so it tends to be located in the aqueous inner side of membrane

18. Choose the odd one out with respect to the composition of plant cell wall.
    (a) Cellulose
    (b) Galactans
    (c) Pectins and proteins
    (d) Hemicellulose

19. The innermost portion of a mature plant cell wall possesses
    (a) primary cell wall
    (b) plasma membrane
    (c) secondary cell wall
    (d) plasmodesmata

20. Which is not true about sphaerosomes?
    (a) Arise from ER
    (b) Related to fat
    (c) Single membrane-bound structure
    (d) Involved in photorespiration

21. The usual axonemal arrangement of microtubules is
    (a) 6 pairs of doublets radially arranged at periphery with a pair of centrally located microtubules
    (b) 6 pairs of doublets radially arranged at periphery with a single centrally located microtubule
    (c) 9 pairs of doublets radially arranged at periphery with a pair of centrally located microtubules
    (d) 9 pairs of doublets radially arranged at periphery with a single centrally located microtubule

22. The cytoplasmic bridges between adjacent cells formed in the area of pit fields in their walls is called
    (a) peptidoglycan   (b) microfibril
    (c) plasmodesmata   (d) suberin wall

23. The solid linear cytoskeletal elements having a diameter of 6 nm and made up of a single type of monomer are known as
    (a) lamina
    (b) microtubule
    (c) microfilaments
    (d) intermediate filaments

24. Study the following figure given below. Choose the correct option for the name of the organelle with its functions.

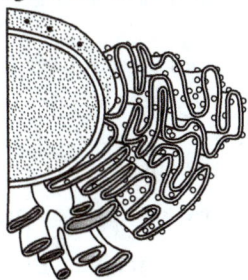

    (a) Golgi bodies, formation of glycolipids
    (b) Rough endoplasmic reticulum, protein synthesis
    (c) Golgi bodies, carbohydrate metabolism
    (d) Rough endoplasmic reticulum, pigment synthesis

25. In an experiment, the cells are broken down and sedimented by centrifugation. The new structures formed in one of the fraction is
    (a) microsomes
    (b) lysosomes
    (c) centrosomes
    (d) peroxisomes

26. An interconnecting membranous network of the cell composed of vesicles, flattened sacs and tubules is
    (a) nucleus
    (b) lysosome
    (c) mitochondria
    (d) endoplasmic reticulum

27. A cell organelle X is engaged for packaging of materials. It has thin membrane on its Y side. Identify X and Y.

    (a) X-mitochondria, Y-inner side
    (b) X-Golgi apparatus, Y-convex proximal side
    (c) X-mitochondria, Y-outer side
    (d) X-Golgi apparatus, Y-concave distal side

28. Consider two cell organelles X and Y. X digests cellular macromolecules and Y are responsible for protein assembly. Choose the correct option that represent X and Y.
    (a) X-microbodies, Y-lysosomes
    (b) X-centrioles, Y-mitochondria
    (c) X-lysosomes, Y-ribosomes
    (d) X-nucleus, Y-Golgi bodies

29. Lysosomes have acidic environment inside their vesicles due to the
    (a) production of carboxylate ions inside it
    (b) production of phosphate ions inside it
    (c) high pH compared to outside
    (d) None of the above

30. Small, spherical or large rosette-shaped particles occurring near SER in liver and muscle cells are called
    (a) starch grains
    (b) aleurone grains
    (c) phosphate granules
    (d) glycogen granules

31. Choose the incorrectly matched pair.
    (a) Sap vacuole - Stores mineral salts and nutrients
    (b) Food vacuole - Contains digestive enzymes
    (c) Air vacuole - Stores lipids
    (d) Contractile vacuole - Osmoregulation

32. Which of the following statement is not true about mitochondrial DNA?
    (a) It has its own cellular DNA
    (b) It is located in matrix attached to membranes
    (c) It contains several genes that produce enzymes used in oxidative metabolism
    (d) It is called autonomous organelles as it has its own protein synthesising machinery

33. Two membrane envelops is found in

(a) mitochondria, Golgi apparatus and chloroplast

(b) mitochondria, nucleus and chloroplast

(c) nucleus, Golgi apparatus and endoplasmic reticulum

(d) nucleus, ribosome and chloroplast

34. All plastids have similar structure because they can

(a) store starch, lipids and proteins

(b) get transformed from one type to another

(c) perform same function

(d) be present together

35. Given below are few types of plastids. How many plastids are used for storage purposes?

Rhodoplasts, Elaioplasts, Aleuroplasts, Phaeoplasts, Amyloplasts

(a) Two   (b) Three   (c) Four   (d) Five

36. Which of the following is not correctly matched?

(a) Chloroplasts - Green plastids

(b) Elaioplasts   - Yellow plastids

(c) Phaeoplasts - Brown plastids

(d) Rhodoplasts - Red plastids

37. Plastids differs from mitochondria on the basis of one of the following features. Choose the right answer.

(a) Presence of DNA

(b) Presence of ribosome

(c) Presence of chlorophyll

(d) Presence of two layers of membrane

38. Which of the following nucleic acid is present in an organism having 70S ribosomes only?

(a) Single-stranded DNA with protein coat

(b) Double-stranded circular naked DNA

(c) Double-stranded DNA enclosed in nuclear membrane

(d) Double-stranded circular DNA with histone proteins

39. Ribosomes are called as 'organelles within an organelle'. In which of the described organelles, ribosomes are not found within?

(a) Powerhouse of the cell

(b) Central unit of the cell

(c) Storage house of the cell

(d) Kitchen of the cell

40. Which of the following option is correct about ribosomes?

(a) Ribosomes are the largest organelles in the cell

(b) Ribosomes are bounded by membranes

(c) Ribosomes are the protein factories of the cell

(d) All of the above

41. Given below are few cell organelles.

Microtubules, Vacuoles, Endoplasmic reticulum, Peroxisomes, Mitochondria, Lysosomes

How many of the above organelles are considered as a part of endomembrane system?

(a) Two   (b) Three

(c) Four   (d) Five

42. Section of eukaryotic cilia or flagella shows.

	Peripheral microtubule	Radial spoke	Central sheath
(a)	9	7	2
(b)	9	9	1
(c)	7	9	2
(d)	7	7	1

43. The diagram given below shows a chromosome.

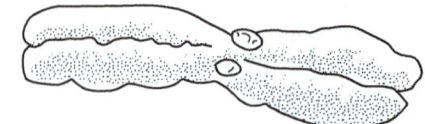

Which of the following table refers correctly to the chromosome?

	Number of centromere	Number of kinetochore	Number of arms
(a)	2	1	4
(b)	1	2	4
(c)	2	2	4
(d)	1	2	2

44. Choose the incorrectly matched pair.
(a) Alkaloids-Morphine
(b) Terpenoides- Codeine
(c) Lectins-Concavalin A
(d) Drugs-Vinblastin

45. In which of the following groups are all polysaccharides?
(a) Sucrose, glucose and fructose
(b) Maltose, lactose and fructose
(c) Glycogen, sucrose and maltose
(d) Glycogen, cellulose and starch

46. In a polysaccharide, the individual monosaccharides are linked by
(a) glycosidic bond
(b) peptide bond
(c) ester bond
(d) phosphodiester bond

47. Which of the following combination is not true for disaccharide?
(a) Sucrose = Glucose + Fructose
(b) Trehalose = Glucose + Glucose
(c) Maltose = Glucose + Galactose
(d) Lactose = Glucose + Galactose

48. Glycogen and inulin are reserve food material. These are the storage polysaccharides of plants and animals. A few statements about these polysaccharides are made. Choose the incorrect statement out of the following options.
(a) Glycogen is mainly stored inside liver and muscles
(b) Inulin is not metabolised in human body and is readily filtered through the kidney

(c) The polysaccharide gives yellow colour with iodine
(d) Glucose residues are arranged in a highly branched bush-like chains

49. Plant cell walls are made up of cellulose. Cellulose does not contain complex helices. Which of the following statement for cellulose molecule is true?
(a) $\beta - 1' - 4''$ linkage, branched
(b) $\beta - 1' - 4''$ linkage, unbranched
(c) $\beta - 1' - 6''$ linkage, branched
(d) $\beta - 1' - 6''$ linkage, unbranched

50. Which combination describes a phospholipid?

	Insoluble in water	Provides energy	Permeable in nature	Act as surfactants
(a)	✗	✗	✓	✓
(b)	✓	✓	✓	✓
(c)	✓	✓	✗	✗
(d)	✓	✗	✓	✓

51. Which is not consistent with double helical structure of DNA?
(a) A = T, C = G
(b) Density of DNA decreases on heating
(c) A + T/ C+G is not constant
(d) Both (a) and (b)

52. A segment of DNA has 120 adenine and 120 cytosine bases. The total number of nucleotides present in the segment is
(a) 120   (b) 240
(c) 60   (d) 480

53. Antiparallel strands of a DNA molecule means that
(a) one strand turns clockwise
(b) one strand turns anti-clockwise
(c) the phosphate group of two DNA strands, at their ends, share the same position
(d) the phosphate group at the start of two DNA strands are in opposite position (pole)

54. Consider the following properties.

I. It is hydrolyesd by RNase.

II. It helps in protein synthesis.

III. It is situated in cytoplasm, nucleoplasm and chromosomes.

Which of the following has all the above propertise?

(a) Only DNA   (b) Only RNA

(c) Both (a) and (b)   (d) None of these

55. Which of the following protein has antiparallel β-pleated secondary structure?

(a) Keratin   (b) Fibrin

(c) Fibroin   (d) Ribonuclease

56. Which of the following is not a conjugated protein?

(a) Peptone   (b) Lipoprotein

(c) Phosphoprotein   (d) Chromoprotein

57. The figure given below are few structures of protein.

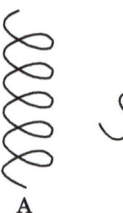  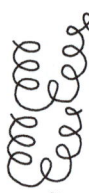

A   B   C

What is *A, B, C* ?

(a) *A*-2° structure, *B*-3° structure, *C*-4° structure

(b) *A*-1° structure, *B*-2° structure, *C*-4° structure

(c) *A*-4° structure, *B*-2° structure, *C*-3° structure

(d) *A*-3° structure, *B*-4° structure, *C*-2° structure

58. Choose the group of biological components that belong to fibrous protein.

(a) Hair, Muscles, Skin, Bones

(b) Blood, Skin, Nails, Hair

(c) Muscles, Skin, Blood, Nails

(d) Hair, Nails, Skin, Bones

59. Proteins perform many physiological functions. For example, some functions as enzymes. One of the following represents an additional function that some proteins discharge.

(a) Antibiotics

(b) Hormones

(c) Pigments conferring colour to skin

(d) Pigments making colours of flower

60. The energy content in kcal/g of carbohydrate : protein : triglycerol respectively is approximately in the ratio of

(a) 1 : 2 : 2   (b) 1 : 1 : 2

(c) 2 : 1 : 1   (d) 2 : 2 : 1

61. Among carbohydrates, proteins and fats, the energy yield in calories per gram is best represented by

(a) Fat > Protein = Carbohydrates

(b) Fat = Protein < Carbohydrates

(c) Protein > Carbohydrates > Fats

(d) Fat < Carbohydrates < Protein

62. An amino acid can stabilise protein structure by forming bonds. What is the amino acid and name the bond formed?

(a) Serine, hydrogen

(b) Cysteine, disulphide

(c) Tyrosine, covalent

(d) Proline, thioester

63. Given below is an analogy with respect to nature of amino acids.

Tyrosine : Methionine : : *A* : Non-polar

What is *A*?

(a) Positively charged

(b) Polar

(c) Neutral

(d) Negatively charged

64. Which of the following is incorrectly matched?

(a) Phospholipid - Hydrophilic head

(b) Enzyme - Biological catalysts

(c) Amino acid - Stores energy

(d) Collagen - Animal protein

65. Two amino acids X and Y. X is basic in nature and Y is ionisable in proteins. Identify X and Y.
(a) X-lycine, Y-leucine
(b) X-proline, Y-histidine
(c) X-glycine, Y-arginine
(d) X-leucine, Y-cysteine

66. Choose the incorrectly matched pair.
(a) Amino acid - Alanine
(b) Nucleotide - Adenylic acid
(c) Sugar - Palmitic acid
(d) Fatty acid - Linolenic acid

67.

Holoenzyme = Prosthetic group + Apoenzyme

Cofactor   Coenzyme

Which of the following statement is true about coenzyme?
(a) Ions like Ca^{2+}, Mg^{2+}
(b) Protein organic compounds
(c) Non-protein organic compounds like NAD, FMN, ATP, etc
(d) Ions like K^+, Na^+

68. Which of the following statement is incorrect regarding enzymatic activity?
(a) It is increases with increase in substrate concentration upto the saturation point
(b) It is highest at optimum pH value
(c) It is initially decreases with increase in pH value
(d) It is initially increases with increase in temperature and then decreases

69. Which of the following enzyme is involved in the following reaction?
$$A - X + B \leftrightarrow B X + A$$
(a) Lyase   (b) Transferase
(c) Hydrolase   (d) Ligases

70. An example of non-competitive inhibition is
(a) the inhibition of succinic dehydrogenase by malonate
(b) cyanide action on cytochrome oxidase
(c) sulpha drug on folic acid synthesising bacteria
(d) the inhibition of hexokinase by glucose 6-phosphate

71. A substance unrelated to the substrate that reversibly changes the activity of an enzyme by binding at a site other then the active site is known as
(a) allosteric modulator
(b) catalytic inhibitor
(c) competitive inhibitor
(d) non-competitive inhibitor

72. Which of the following does not occur in the interphase of eukaryotic cell division?
(a) Increase of ATP synthesis
(b) Increase of DNA synthesis
(c) Increase of RNA synthesis
(d) Reduction in cell size

73. Which of the following statement is not correct about cell cycle?
(a) During S-phase, each chromosome carries a duplicate set of genes
(b) In S-phase, a cell doubles the original diploid ($2n$) chromosome number
(c) During G_1-phase, cell grows physically and increases the volume of both protein and organelles
(d) During G_2-phase, a cell contains double amount of DNA present in the original diploid cell

74. Which of the following is the characteristic of pre-mitotic gap phase of the cell cycle?
(a) It is first substage of interphase
(b) Cell organelles increase in number
(c) It is longest phase of interphase
(d) Synthesis of DNA takes place in this stage

75. The cell cycle has many phases in which many events occurs in both mitosis and meiosis. Which one of the following event occurs only in meiosis?

(a) Formation of chromatid

(b) Nuclear membrane degradation

(c) Crossing-over

(d) Chromosome condensation

76. A cell divides in every one minute. At this rate of division it can fill a 100 mL of beaker in one hour. How much time does it take to fill a 50 mL beaker?

(a) 30 minutes   (b) 59 minutes

(c) 32 minutes   (d) 49 minutes

77. How many chromosomes will the cell have at G_1 after S and after M phase, respectively, if it has 14 chromosomes at interphase?

(a) 7, 7, 7   (b) 7, 14, 14

(c) 14, 14, 7   (d) 14, 14, 14

78. Mitotic anaphase differs from metaphase in possessing

(a) same number of chromosomes and same number of chromatids

(b) half number of chromosomes and half number of chromatids

(c) half number of chromosomes and same number of chromatids

(d) same number of chromosomes and half number of chromatids

79. The major event that occurs during the anaphase of mitosis, which brings about the equal distribution of chromosome is

(a) splitting of the chromatids

(b) splitting of the centromeres

(c) condensation of the chromatin

(d) replication of the genetic material

80. In an experiment, the students were provided with root-tips of onion and were asked to count the chromosomes. Which of the following stages would be most convenient to took into?

(a) Prophase   (b) Telophase

(c) Metaphase   (d) Anaphase

81. Given diagram indicates which of the following phase of mitosis? Choose the correct option.

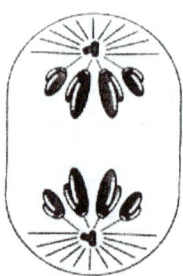

(a) Interphase

(b) Prophase

(c) Metaphase

(d) Anaphase

82. Choose the correct option at which stage of mitosis these following events occur.

	Breakdown of nuclear envelope	Arrangement of chromosome at centre	Spiralisation and condensation of DNA
(a)	Prophase	Metaphase	Prophase
(b)	Anaphase	Anaphase	Prophase
(c)	Prophase	Metaphase	Anaphase
(d)	Metaphase	Prophase	Anaphase

83. Choose the correct match.

	Phase	Ploidy	DNA content
(a)	S-phase	$2n$	4C
(b)	G_2-phase	n	2C
(c)	Prophase	$4n$	2C
(d)	Metaphase	$2n$	4C

84. Which one of the following is wrong for meiosis?

(a) It leads to formation of sister chromatids

(b) It occurs in diploid cell

(c) It occurs in haploid cell

(d) It occurs by splitting of centromeres and separation of sister chromatids

85. Cross-like configuration when non-sister chromatids of a bivalent come in contact during first meiotic division are
(a) bivalents
(b) chiasmata
(c) centromeres
(d) chromosomes

86. In which phase, the microtubules from opposite poles of the spindle get attached to the kinetochores of sister chromatids?
(a) Anaphase-II
(b) Prophase-II
(c) Metaphase-II
(d) None of the above

87. Name the stage in which the chromosomes present in a synaptonemal complex undergo crossing over after which individual chromosomes begin to become apparent.
(a) Zygotene
(b) Leptotene
(c) Pachytene
(d) Diplotene

88. Name the phase of meiosis when synaptonemal complex dissolves, chromatide becomes clear and bivalents are called tetrads.
(a) Pachytene
(b) Zygotene
(c) Diplotene
(d) Diakinesis

89. Choose the incorrectly matched pair.
(a) Zygotene - Synapsis of homologous chromosomes
(b) Pachytene - Recombination of genes
(c) Leptotene - Chiasmata move by terminalisation
(d) Diplotene - Chiasma formation

90. If a cell contains 36 chromosomes, what will be the number of chromosomes in each of the four daughter cells resulting from meiosis?
(a) 36
(b) 18
(c) 9
(d) 46

MCQs 2 Marks Questions

91. **Assertion** (A) Eukaryotic cells have membrane-bound organelles.

Reason (R) These occur in bacteria, blue-green algae, mycoplasma.

Choose the correct answer from the options given below.
(a) Both A and R are true and R is the correct explanation of A
(b) Both A and R are true, but R is not the correct explanation of A
(c) A is true, but R is false
(d) A is false, but R is true

92. Nucleus is a membranous cell organelle. It consists of nucleoplasm bound by membranes known as nuclear envelope. Which of the following statements are true for nucleus?
  I. It is found in both animal and plant cells.
 II. It is present in both prokaryotic and eukaryotic cells.
III. It controls all cellular activities.
(a) Only I is correct
(b) I and III are correct
(c) I and II are correct
(d) I, II and III are correct

93. Match the organelles with their systems.

	Organelles		Systems
A.	Chloroplast	1.	Light harvest system
B.	Mitochondria	2.	EMP system
C.	Peroxisome	3.	Storage system
D.	Vacuole	4.	Electron transport system
		5.	Photorespiratory system

Codes

	A	B	C	D			A	B	C	D
(a)	3	1	2	5		(b)	5	2	1	4
(c)	1	4	5	3		(d)	4	1	5	2

94. Following are few characteristics, which can be used to separate the following organelles.

Nucleus, Mitochondria, Ribosomes and Lysosomes

I. Inner membrane with stalked particles-*V*.

II. Composed of one unit - *Y*.

III. Membrane with definite pores - *W*.

IV. Composed of one large and one small subunit - *X*.

What are *V*, *W*, *X* and *Y* ?

	V	W	X	Y
(a)	Mitochondria	Nucleus	Ribosomes	Lysosomes
(b)	Nucleus	Mitochondria	Lysosomes	Ribosomes
(c)	Mitochondria	Ribosomes	Lysosomes	Nucleus
(d)	Lysosomes	Chloroplasts	Nucleus	Mitochondria

95. The diagram given below shows a ring-structure of glucose. Which form of glucose is shown and in which molecule is it present?

	Form of glucose	present in
(a)	α	Cellulose
(b)	β	Cellulose
(c)	α	Starch
(d)	β	Starch

96. In an experiment of carbohydrate test, following treatments were done as listed below. As a result the carbohydrates present were sucrose and starch. What kind of observations were seen?

Sample	Treatment	Observations
1.	Tested with Benedict's reagent	A
2.	Warmed with acid, neutralised and then tested with Benedict's reagent	B
3.	Treated with amylase solution and then tested with Benedict's reagent	C

(a) *A* – Brick red ppt., *B* – No colour change, *C* – Brick red ppt.

(b) *A* – No colour change, *B* – Brick red ppt. , *C* – Brick red ppt.

(c) *A* – Brick red ppt., *B* – Yellow ppt., *C* – No colour change.

(d) *A* – Yellow ppt., *B* – No colour change, *C* – Brick red ppt.

97. Different types of biomolecules, compounds and ions present in the cell is called cellular pool. It contains inorganic constituents occurring in the form of salts and ions. Iron is one of the element that our bodies need for many functions. Which of the following points shows its importance?

I. It is a constituent of haemoglobin.

II. It is a cofactor of certain enzymes.

III. It is required for maturation of chlorophyll.

(a) Only III   (b) I and II

(c) II and III   (d) I, II and III

98. In this diagrammatic representation of one of the categories of large molecular weight organic compounds. Identify the category shown and the one blank component '*X*' in it.

	Category	Component
(a)	Nucleotide	OH
(b)	Lipid	CH_3
(c)	Protein	NH_2
(d)	Amino acid	CH_2OH

99. Given below are the structural formulae of two organic compounds. Identify and choose the correct match along with its function.

        A   *B*

(a) *A* – Triglyceride – A type of fat found in blood

(b) *B* – Uracil – A component of DNA

(c) *A* – Lactose – A major source of energy

(d) *B* – Adenine – A nucleotide

100. Proteins are nitrogenous macromolecules composed of amino acids. They form the frame work of protoplasm. A few statements regarding proteins are given below.

  I. The function and shape of a protein is affected by sequence of 20 types of amino acids.

  II. Protein molecules are very large with high molecular weight ranging from 5000-25,000,00.

  III. Collagen is not only the most abundant protein in animals but also the whole biosphere.

  IV. Proteins are variously folded linear heteropolymers of amino acids.

Pick the combination of correct statements.

(a) I, II and III   (b) I and III

(c) I and IV   (d) I, II and IV

101. Assertion (A) Lysine, threonine and leucine should be compulsorily added in human diet.

Reason (R) Essential amino acids can not be synthesised in the human body.

Choose the correct answer from the options given below.

(a) Both A and R are true and R is the correct explanation of A

(b) Both A and R are true, but R is not the correct explanation of A

(c) A is true, but R is false

(d) A is false, but R is true

102. Match the following Column I with Column II and select the correct option from the codes given below.

	Column I		Column II
A.	Ascorbic acid	1.	Cellular respiration
B.	Phylloquinone	2.	Collagen synthesis
C.	Retinol	3.	Blood clotting
D.	Riboflavin (B_2)	4.	Normal vision
		5.	Amino acid metabolism

Codes

	A	B	C	D			A	B	C	D
(a)	2	3	4	1		(b)	3	4	5	1
(c)	4	1	5	2		(d)	2	4	3	5

103. Given below are the steps of catalytic action of an enzyme. Arrange the following steps accordingly.

  I. The substrate binds to the active site of the enzyme fitting into the active site.

  II. The enzyme releases the products of reaction and the enzyme is free to bind to another substrate.

  III. The active site of enzyme is in close proximity of the substrate and breaks the chemical bonds of the substrate.

  IV. The binding of substrate induces the enzyme to alter its shape fitting more tightly around the substrate.

(a) I → IV → III → II
(b) I → II → III → IV
(c) IV → III → II → I
(d) III → IV → II → I

104. How is the precise position of three amino acids is maintained in the structure of the enzyme chymotrypsin?

(a) By the folding of the chain

(b) By the binding of the substrate to the active site

(c) By the disulphide, ionic and hydrogen bonds

(d) By the distant placement of the three amino acids

105. Enzymes generally function in a narrow range of temperature and pH. Given below is a graph showing the relative activity of two different enzymes at various pH.

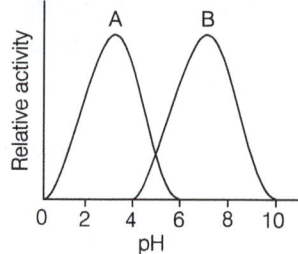

Determine the enzymes *A* and *B*.

(a) *A*-Pepsin, *B* - Lipase

(b) *A*-Pepsin, *B* - Arginase

(c) *A*-Arginase, *B* - Ribonuclease

(d) *A*-Lipase, *B* - Ribonuclease

106. The graph given below shows the effect of substrate concentration on the rate of reaction of an enzyme. What does the graph indicate?

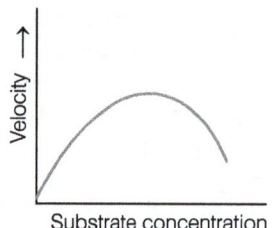

(a) Formation of an enzyme-substrate complex

(b) Presence of an enzyme inhibitor in the reaction mixture

(c) At higher substrate concentrate the pH increases

(d) The rate of enzyme reaction is directly proportional to the substrate concentration

107. Match the following enzymes with their primary functions.

Enzymes		Functions
A. Lyases	1.	Make large molecules, from small molecules
B. Synthase	2.	Cleaves bonds by elimination
C. Kinase	3.	Transfer phosphate group to biomolecules
D. Phosphatase	4.	Remove phosphate group from biomolecule

Codes

	A	B	C	D
(a)	3	2	4	1
(b)	2	1	4	3
(c)	4	3	2	1
(d)	2	1	3	4

108. Given are few statements of cell division.

i. Direct cell division by simple cleavage of nucleus.

ii. Does not form spindle or appearance of chromosomes.

iii. Daughter cells are not genetically identical.

What type of cell division it is?

(a) Mitosis   (b) Amitosis

(c) Meiosis I   (d) Meiosis II

109. Which of the following is correct for the figure given below.

	Number of homologous chromosomes	Number of chromatids	Phase of cell division
(a)	2	4	Telophase-I
(b)	4	8	Telophase
(c)	2	8	Telophase-II
(d)	4	2	Telophase

110. **Assertion** (A) Zygotic meiosis occurs just after fertilisation to produce haploid spores.

Reason (R) The spores divide by mitosis to produce a haploid adult generation.

Choose the correct answer from the options given below.

(a) Both A and R are true and R is the correct explanation of A

(b) Both A and R are true, but R is not the correct explanation of A

(c) A is true, but R is false

(d) A is false, but R is true

Darken your choice with HB Pencil

1.	ⓐ ⓑ ⓒ ⓓ	20.	ⓐ ⓑ ⓒ ⓓ	39.	ⓐ ⓑ ⓒ ⓓ	58.	ⓐ ⓑ ⓒ ⓓ	77.	ⓐ ⓑ ⓒ ⓓ	96.	ⓐ ⓑ ⓒ ⓓ
2.	ⓐ ⓑ ⓒ ⓓ	21.	ⓐ ⓑ ⓒ ⓓ	40.	ⓐ ⓑ ⓒ ⓓ	59.	ⓐ ⓑ ⓒ ⓓ	78.	ⓐ ⓑ ⓒ ⓓ	97.	ⓐ ⓑ ⓒ ⓓ
3.	ⓐ ⓑ ⓒ ⓓ	22.	ⓐ ⓑ ⓒ ⓓ	41.	ⓐ ⓑ ⓒ ⓓ	60.	ⓐ ⓑ ⓒ ⓓ	79.	ⓐ ⓑ ⓒ ⓓ	98.	ⓐ ⓑ ⓒ ⓓ
4.	ⓐ ⓑ ⓒ ⓓ	23.	ⓐ ⓑ ⓒ ⓓ	42.	ⓐ ⓑ ⓒ ⓓ	61.	ⓐ ⓑ ⓒ ⓓ	80.	ⓐ ⓑ ⓒ ⓓ	99.	ⓐ ⓑ ⓒ ⓓ
5.	ⓐ ⓑ ⓒ ⓓ	24.	ⓐ ⓑ ⓒ ⓓ	43.	ⓐ ⓑ ⓒ ⓓ	62.	ⓐ ⓑ ⓒ ⓓ	81.	ⓐ ⓑ ⓒ ⓓ	100.	ⓐ ⓑ ⓒ ⓓ
6.	ⓐ ⓑ ⓒ ⓓ	25.	ⓐ ⓑ ⓒ ⓓ	44.	ⓐ ⓑ ⓒ ⓓ	63.	ⓐ ⓑ ⓒ ⓓ	82.	ⓐ ⓑ ⓒ ⓓ	101.	ⓐ ⓑ ⓒ ⓓ
7.	ⓐ ⓑ ⓒ ⓓ	26.	ⓐ ⓑ ⓒ ⓓ	45.	ⓐ ⓑ ⓒ ⓓ	64.	ⓐ ⓑ ⓒ ⓓ	83.	ⓐ ⓑ ⓒ ⓓ	102.	ⓐ ⓑ ⓒ ⓓ
8.	ⓐ ⓑ ⓒ ⓓ	27.	ⓐ ⓑ ⓒ ⓓ	46.	ⓐ ⓑ ⓒ ⓓ	65.	ⓐ ⓑ ⓒ ⓓ	84.	ⓐ ⓑ ⓒ ⓓ	103.	ⓐ ⓑ ⓒ ⓓ
9.	ⓐ ⓑ ⓒ ⓓ	28.	ⓐ ⓑ ⓒ ⓓ	47.	ⓐ ⓑ ⓒ ⓓ	66.	ⓐ ⓑ ⓒ ⓓ	85.	ⓐ ⓑ ⓒ ⓓ	104.	ⓐ ⓑ ⓒ ⓓ
10.	ⓐ ⓑ ⓒ ⓓ	29.	ⓐ ⓑ ⓒ ⓓ	48.	ⓐ ⓑ ⓒ ⓓ	67.	ⓐ ⓑ ⓒ ⓓ	86.	ⓐ ⓑ ⓒ ⓓ	105.	ⓐ ⓑ ⓒ ⓓ
11.	ⓐ ⓑ ⓒ ⓓ	30.	ⓐ ⓑ ⓒ ⓓ	49.	ⓐ ⓑ ⓒ ⓓ	68.	ⓐ ⓑ ⓒ ⓓ	87.	ⓐ ⓑ ⓒ ⓓ	106.	ⓐ ⓑ ⓒ ⓓ
12.	ⓐ ⓑ ⓒ ⓓ	31.	ⓐ ⓑ ⓒ ⓓ	50.	ⓐ ⓑ ⓒ ⓓ	69.	ⓐ ⓑ ⓒ ⓓ	88.	ⓐ ⓑ ⓒ ⓓ	107.	ⓐ ⓑ ⓒ ⓓ
13.	ⓐ ⓑ ⓒ ⓓ	32.	ⓐ ⓑ ⓒ ⓓ	51.	ⓐ ⓑ ⓒ ⓓ	70.	ⓐ ⓑ ⓒ ⓓ	89.	ⓐ ⓑ ⓒ ⓓ	108.	ⓐ ⓑ ⓒ ⓓ
14.	ⓐ ⓑ ⓒ ⓓ	33.	ⓐ ⓑ ⓒ ⓓ	52.	ⓐ ⓑ ⓒ ⓓ	71.	ⓐ ⓑ ⓒ ⓓ	90.	ⓐ ⓑ ⓒ ⓓ	109.	ⓐ ⓑ ⓒ ⓓ
15.	ⓐ ⓑ ⓒ ⓓ	34.	ⓐ ⓑ ⓒ ⓓ	53.	ⓐ ⓑ ⓒ ⓓ	72.	ⓐ ⓑ ⓒ ⓓ	91.	ⓐ ⓑ ⓒ ⓓ	110.	ⓐ ⓑ ⓒ ⓓ
16.	ⓐ ⓑ ⓒ ⓓ	35.	ⓐ ⓑ ⓒ ⓓ	54.	ⓐ ⓑ ⓒ ⓓ	73.	ⓐ ⓑ ⓒ ⓓ	92.	ⓐ ⓑ ⓒ ⓓ		
17.	ⓐ ⓑ ⓒ ⓓ	36.	ⓐ ⓑ ⓒ ⓓ	55.	ⓐ ⓑ ⓒ ⓓ	74.	ⓐ ⓑ ⓒ ⓓ	93.	ⓐ ⓑ ⓒ ⓓ		
18.	ⓐ ⓑ ⓒ ⓓ	37.	ⓐ ⓑ ⓒ ⓓ	56.	ⓐ ⓑ ⓒ ⓓ	75.	ⓐ ⓑ ⓒ ⓓ	94.	ⓐ ⓑ ⓒ ⓓ		
19.	ⓐ ⓑ ⓒ ⓓ	38.	ⓐ ⓑ ⓒ ⓓ	57.	ⓐ ⓑ ⓒ ⓓ	76.	ⓐ ⓑ ⓒ ⓓ	95.	ⓐ ⓑ ⓒ ⓓ		

Photosynthesis in Higher Plants

MCQs 1 Mark Questions

1. Photosynthesis is the uphill process because
   (a) reactant O_2 is a strong electrolyte
   (b) reactant CO_2 is a strong electrolyte
   (c) reactant O_2 is a weak electrolyte
   (d) reactant CO_2 is a weak electrolyte

2. Which of the following experiment showed that CO_2 is essential for photosynthesis?
   (a) J. von Sach's experiment
   (b) Priestley's experiment
   (c) Moll's half leaf experiment
   (d) Variegated leaf experiment

3. Which of the following experiment confirmed essentiality of light in photosynthesis.
   (a) van Niel experiment
   (b) Mole's half leaf experiment
   (c) Ingenhousz experiment
   (d) Mayer experiment

4. Who demonstrated that photosynthesis is essentially a light dependent reaction in which hydrogen from a suitable oxidisable compound reduces carbon dioxide to carbohydrates?

   (a) Jan Ingenhousz
   (b) Julius von Sachs
   (c) TW Engelmann
   (d) Cornelis van Niel

5. Which of the following is not a Hill reagent?
   (a) DCPIP
   (b) Benzoquinone
   (c) Cardioline
   (d) Ferricyanide

6. The enhancement effect is due to
   (a) decline in quantum yield
   (b) synergistic effect
   (c) Hill's reagent
   (d) None of the above

7. The correct equation that would represent the overall process of photosynthesis is
   (a) $6CO_2 + 12H_2O \rightarrow C_6H_{12}O_6 + 7H_2O + 6CO_2$
   (b) $6CO_2 + 12H_2O \rightarrow C_6H_{12}O_6 + 6H_2O + 6O_2$
   (c) $6CO_2 + H_2O \rightarrow [CH_2O] + O_2$
   (d) $C_6H_{12}O_6 + 6O_2 \rightarrow 6CO_2 + 6H_2O$

8. A photosynthetic organism which does not release oxygen is
   (a) algal component of lichen
   (b) green alga
   (c) green sulphur bacterium
   (d) blue -green algae

9. Which of the following can photosynthesise at very low temperature?
   (a) Angiosperms   (b) Bacteria
   (c) Lichens   (d) Algae

10. Why photosynthesis is considered as the basis of life on earth?
    (a) Photosynthesis is the primary source of all food on earth
    (b) Photosynthesis is responsible for release of CO_2 into the atmosphere
    (c) Photosynthesis is responsible for release of O_2 into the atmosphere
    (d) Both (a) and (c)

11. The oxygen evolved during photosynthesis comes from water molecules. Which one of the following pairs of elements are involved in this reaction?
    (a) Magnesium and molybednum
    (b) Manganese and chlorine
    (c) Magnesium and chlorine
    (d) Manganese and potassium

12. During light reaction of photosynthesis which of the following phenomenon is observed during cyclic phosphorylation as well as non-cyclic phosphorylation?
    (a) Involvement of both PS-I and PS-II pigment system
    (b) Formation of ATP
    (c) Release of O_2
    (d) Formation of NADPH

13. Raw material required for light reactions are
    (a) ADP and $NADPH_2$
    (b) ATP and NADP
    (c) ADP, H_2O and NADP
    (d) ADP and H_2O

14. Which of the following statement is true about light reaction of photosynthesis?
    (a) PS-I produces strong oxidant while PS-II is a strong reductant
    (b) PS-I produces strong reductant NADPH while PS-II is a strong oxidant
    (c) PS-I produces ATP which is not formed by PS-II
    (d) PS-I produces ATP which is not formed by PS-II

15. Light harvesting complexes (LHC) are made up of hundreds of pigment molecules bound to proteins. In LHC, reaction centre is formed by
    (a) all pigments except one molecule of chlorophyll-a
    (b) a single chlorophyll-a molecule
    (c) carotenoids and chlorophyll-c
    (d) carotenoids and xanthophylls

16. Which of the following is not related to significance of carotenoid?
    (a) β- carotene is precursor of vitamin-A
    (b) It convert of atomic oxygen to molecular oxygen
    (c) Both (a) and (b)
    (d) None of the above

17. The basic structure of all chlorophyll comprises of
    (a) plastocyanin system
    (b) porphyrin ring
    (c) cytochrome system
    (d) flavoprotein

18. Chlorophyll molecule is asymmetrical and consists of two parts. Which of the following is correct for the same?
    (a) ◇   (b) ▭
    (c) ◇   (d) ◇▷

19. Main difference between chlorophyll-a and chlorophyll-b.
    (a) $-CH_3$ of chlorophyll-a is replaced by $-CHO$ in chlorophyll-b

(b) Chlorophyll-*a* is linear while chlorophyll-*b* is branched

(c) Chlorophyll-*a* has no Mg^{2+}

(d) All of the above

20. Which of the following pigment protects plants from photo-oxidation?
(a) Xanthophyll　　(b) Carotenoids
(c) Chlorophyll-*a*　(d) Chlorophyll-*b*

21. Which of the following pigment help in chromatic adaptation?
(a) Carotenoid　　(b) Chlorophyll
(c) Xanthophyll　(d) Phycobilins

22. Which of the following pigments is universally present in all green oxygenic plants?
(a) Chlorophyll-*a*　(b) Chlorophyll-*b*
(c) Chlorophyll-*c*　(d) Chlorophyll-*d*

23. Which of the following pigments are known as accessory pigments?
(a) Chlorophyll-*b*, xanthophyll
(b) Chlorophyll-*a*, chlorophyll-*b*
(c) Chlorophyll-*b*, carotenoids, xanthophylls
(d) Xanthophylls, chlorophyll-*a*, carotenoids

24. Most of the photosynthesis takes place in which of the following regions of the spectrum?
(a) Blue and yellow　(b) Red and yellow
(c) Blue and red　　(d) Yellow and black

25. Identify *X* and *Y* with respect to the given statement.
X-A curve obtained by plotting the amount of absorption of different wavelengths of light by a particular pigment.
Y-It is the number of photons required to produce one molecule of O_2 photons.

	X	Y
(a)	Quantum yield	Action spectrum
(b)	Action spectrum	Quantum requirement
(c)	Absorption spectrum	Quantum yield
(d)	Absorption spectrum	Quantum requirement

26. Identify *X* in the given graph of absorption spectra.

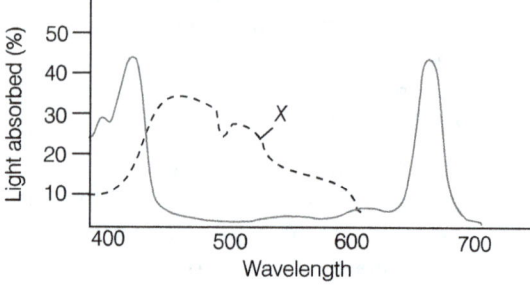

(a) Chlorophyll-*a*
(b) Chlorophyll-*b*
(c) β- carotene
(d) None of the above

27. The difference between pigment systems I and II given in tabular form. Identify the missing labelled part.

Pigment System I	Pigment System II
Situated on the outer surface of thylakoid membrane.	Situated on the inner surface of thylakoid membrane.
Reaction center is P_{700}.	Reaction center is P_{680}.
Concerned with $NADP^+$ reduction.	'*X*'

The *X* is
(a) concerned with photolysis of water
(b) concerned with decarboxylation
(c) concerned with NADPH reduction
(d) None of the above

28. Which of the following is inhibited by dichlorophenyl dimethyl urea?
(a) PS-I
(b) PS-II
(c) Both of the above
(d) None of the above

29. Photosynthesis occurs in two phases.

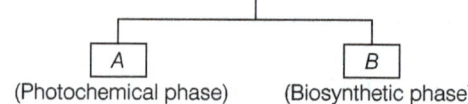

A (Photochemical phase)　　B (Biosynthetic phase)

Identify the labelled *A* and *B* in the above flowchart.

(a)	*A*-Dark reaction	*B*–Light reaction
(b)	*A*-Blackman's reaction	*B*–Hill reaction
(c)	*A*-Hill reaction	*B*–Blackman's reaction
(d)	None of the above	

30. Ferredoxin is a constituent of
   (a) P_{680} (b) photosystem - II
   (c) Hill reaction   (d) photosystem - I

31. '*X*' in excited state acts as very strong oxidising agent. It has a very strong affinity for electron. Identify '*X*'.
   (a) P_{700} (b) P_{680}
   (c) P_{890} (d) None of these

32. Red light of 680 nm wavelength carries 42 kcal energy per quantum. Thus, the total energy of sunlight used in synthesising a hexose molecule will be
   (a) 2017 kcal   (b) 2016 kcal
   (c) 2020 kcal   (d) 2018 kcal

33. 'During photolysis of water, ...*A*... molecules of water split to form ...*B*... mole of oxygen and ...*C*... using 8 quantum of light energy'.

   Complete the above passage by replacing *A*, *B* and *C* with correct option.
   (a) *A*-1   *B*-1   *C*-$2e^-$
   (b) *A*-3   *B*-2   *C*-$2e^-$
   (c) *A*-2   *B*-1   *C*-$4e^-$
   (d) *A*-2   *B*-2   *C*-$3e^-$

34. The water splitting complex is associated with the ...*X*... which itself is physically located on the ...*Y*... side of the membrane of the ...*Z*... .

   Complete the above passage by replacing *X*, *Y* and *Z* with correct option.
   (a) *X*-PS-I, *Y*- inner, *Z* - stroma lamella
   (b) *X*- PS-II, *Y* inner, *Z*- grana
   (c) *X*- PS-II, *Y*- inner, *Z*- thylakoid
   (d) *X*- PS-II, *Y*- outer, *Z*- thylakoid

35. Which of the following conditions are favourable for cyclic photophosphorylation?
   (a) Aerobic condition and optimum light
   (b) Aerobic condition and low light intensity
   (c) Anaerobic condition and optimum light
   (d) Anaerobic condition and low light intensity

36. In non-cyclic photophosphorylation, ATP synthesis takes place between which of the following electron carrier?
   (a) PQ and cyt - *f*
   (b) PS - II and Q
   (c) Cyt-b_6 and plastocyanin
   (d) PS - I and ferredoxin

37. "$NADP^+ \longrightarrow NADPH$". This reaction occurs at which labelled location.

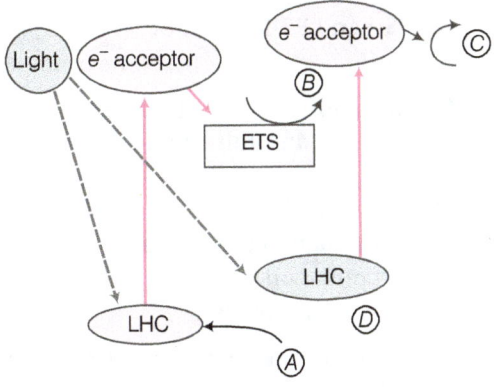

   (a) C   (b) A
   (c) B   (d) D

38. Which one of the following statement about the events of non-cyclic photophosphorylation is not correct?
   (a) ATP and NADPH are produced
   (b) Photolysis of water takes place
   (c) Only one photosystem participates
   (d) Oxygen is released

39. Which of the following statement is true about the chemiosmotic hypothesis of electron transfer?

(a) The chemiosmotic hypothesis explains mechanism of ADP synthesis

(b) Protons are accumulated inside the lumen of the membrane and this creates a proton gradient

(c) Carbon dioxide combines with RuBP and produces glucose

(d) Hill and Bendall explained this hypothesis

40. Based on your understanding of the process of photosynthesis, predict what will happen if ATP synthase is blocked?

(a) Synthesis of ATP is stopped

(b) Accumulation of proton within the lumen

(c) Both (a) and (b)

(d) None of the above

41. Which pigment system is inactivated in red drop?

(a) PS-I and PS-II   (b) PS-I

(c) PS-II   (d) None of these

42. Chemiosmotic theory of ATP synthesis in chloroplasts and mitochondria is based on

(a) proton gradient

(b) accumulation of Na ions

(c) accumulation of K ions

(d) membrane potential

43. Dark reaction in photosynthesis is called so because

(a) it can occur in dark alone

(b) it does not require direct light energy

(c) it cannot occur during daytime

(d) it occurs more rapidly in night

44. The path of CO_2 in the dark reaction of photosynthesis was successfully found by using

(a) centrifugation

(b) radioisotopes $^{14}CO_2$

(c) radioisotopes $^{12}CO_2$

(d) chromatography

45. Calvin cycle or C_3 pathway involves

(a) reductive decarboxylation

(b) oxidative carboxylation

(c) reductive carboxylation

(d) oxidative decarboxylation

46. Identify A and B in the given statement.

By using autoradiography ($^{14}CO_2$) and 'A', the sequence of Blackman reaction was determined in 'B' and *Scenedesmus*.

		A	B
(a)		Chromatography	*Chlorella*
(b)		Centrifugation	*Chlorella*
(c)		Chromatography	*Spirogyra*
(d)		Centrifugation	*Spirogyra*

47. Choose the correct reaction from the following options.

(a) $6CO_2 + 6RUBP + 18ATP + 12NADPH \rightarrow C_6H_{12}O_6 + 6RUBP + 18ADP + 12NADP$

(b) $6CO_2 + 6RUBP + 18ADP + 12NADPH \rightarrow C_6H_{12}O_6 + 6RUBP + 18ADP + 12NADPH$

(c) $6CO_2 + 6RUBP + 18ATP + 12NADP \rightarrow C_6H_{12}O_6 + 6RUBP + 18ADP + 12NADPH$

(d) $CO_2 + RUBP + ADP + NADP \rightarrow C_6H_{12}O_6 + RUBP + ATP + NADPH$

48. For fixing one molecule of CO_2 in Calvin cycle .... are required.

(a) $3 ATP + 1NADPH_2$

(b) $3 ATP + 2NADPH_2$

(c) $2 ATP + 3NADPH_2$

(d) $3 ATP + 3NADPH_2$

49. C_3-plants responds to higher CO_2 concentration by showing increased rate of photosynthesis leading to higher productivity. This phenomenon has been used for some greenhouse crops such as

(a) tomato and bell pepper

(b) tomato and black pepper

(c) tomato, lettuce and seedless cucumber

(d) beet and black pepper

50. How many PGAL would regenerate 15 RuBP?
(a) 30   (b) 25
(c) 15   (d) 20

51. Consider the following stages of Calvin cycle.
1. Reduction during which carbohydrate is formed at the expense of photochemically made ATP and NADPH.
2. Regeneration during which carbon dioxide acceptor 1, 5- RuBP is formed.
3. Carboxylation during which CO_2 combines with 1, 5 RuBP.

Identify the correct sequence from the options given below.
(a) 3, 1, 2   (b) 3, 2, 1
(c) 1, 2, 3   (d) 2, 1, 3

52. The first carbon dioxide acceptor in C_4-plants is
(a) phosphoenolpyruvate
(b) ribulose 1, 5- diphosphate
(c) oxaloacetic acid
(d) phosphoglyceric acid

53. Sugarcane shows high efficiency for CO_2 fixation because it performs
(a) Calvin cycle
(b) Hatch and Slack pathway
(c) EMP pathway
(d) TCA cycle

54. Source of CO_2 for photosynthesis during the day in CAM plants is
(a) malic acid
(b) 3 - PGA
(c) oxaloacetic acid
(d) pyruvate

55. In C_4-plants, synthesis of sugars/final CO_2-fixation occurs in
(a) spongy cells
(b) palisade cells
(c) undifferentiated mesophyll
(d) bundle sheath cells

56. In which of the following plants, malic acid formation during CO_2-fixation occurs in the cell of mesophyll ?
(a) C_3-plants   (b) C_4-plants
(c) CAM plants   (d) None of these

57. Bundle sheath around the vascular bundles in C_4-plants are characterised by
(a) few chloroplasts, thick cell walls and no intracellular spaces
(b) large number of chloroplasts, thin cell walls and no intracellular spaces
(c) large number of chloroplasts, thick cell walls and no intercellular spaces
(d) few chloroplasts, thick cell walls and intercellular spaces

58. Which of the following is incorrect about C_4-plants?
(a) These plants well adapted for hot or dry tropical climate
(b) They can photosynthesise from 6:00-6:30 am till 6 pm
(c) Mesophyll cells are much less in number than the bundle sheath cells
(d) These plants can continue their photosynthesis even if carbon dioxide level falls below 10 ppm

59. PEPcase has an advantage over RuBisCO. The advantage is
(a) RuBisCO combines with O_2, but PEPcase does not
(b) RuBisCO combines with NO_2, but PEPcase does not
(c) RuBisCO conserves energy, but PEPcase does not
(d) PEPcase is present in both mesophyll cells and bundle sheath cells, but RuBisCO is not

60. C_4-pathway is advantageous over C_3-pathway in plants, because it
(a) occurs in relatively low CO_2 concentration
(b) uses more amount of water
(c) occurs in relatively low O_2 concentration
(d) is less efficient in energy utilisation

61. Identify *A, B, C* and *D* in the given figure and choose the correct option accordingly.

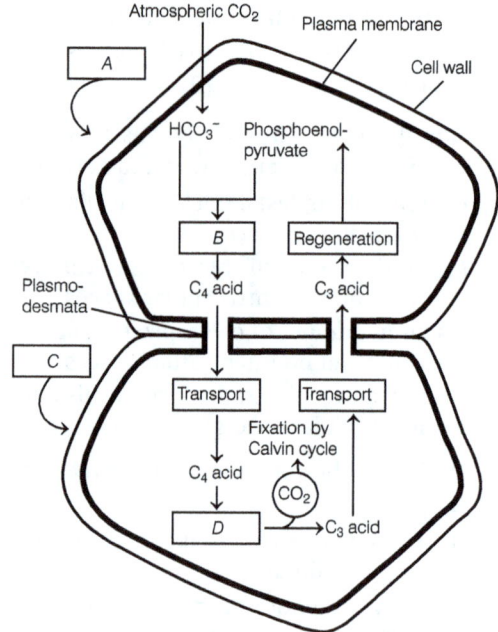

(a) *A*–Mesophyll cell, *B*–Fixation of CO_2
    C–Bundle sheath cell,
    D–Decarboxylation

(b) *A*–Mesophyll cell, *B*–Decarboxylation,
    C–Bundle sheath cell, *D*–Fixation of CO_2

(c) *A*–Chloroplast, *B*–Decarboxylation,
    C–Bundle sheath cell, *D*–Fixation of CO_2

(d) *A*–Chloroplast, *B*–Fixation of O_2,
    C–Bundle sheath cell, *D*–Fixation of CO_2

62. CAM plants do not show photorespiration due to the fact that they
(a) keep stomata closed during daytime
(b) use PEP carboxylase
(c) perform Calvin cycle at night
(d) fix CO_2 into organic acid in night, releasing CO_2 during day

63. During photorespiration, which reactions occurs in the stroma of chloroplast and peroxisomes?
(a) Oxygen consuming
(b) Oxygen producing
(c) Carbon dioxide consuming
(d) Carbon dioxide producing

64. Correct sequence of cell organelles during photorespiration.
(a) Chloroplast, vacuole, peroxisome
(b) Chloroplast, peroxisome, mitochondria
(c) Chloroplast, rough endoplasmic reticulum, dictyosomes
(d) Chloroplast, Golgi bodies, mitochondria

65. Which of the following is releases in photorespiration?
(a) PO_4 (b) SO_2
(c) NH_3 (d) All of these

66. Compensation point is the value of a factor where there is
(a) little photosynthesis
(b) beginning of photosynthesis
(c) photosynthesis equal to the rate of respiration
(d) neither photosynthesis nor respiration

67. I gave the law of limiting factors for explaining the role of various external factors in affecting rate of photosynthesis. Guess who am I?
(a) Robert Emerson   (b) F F Blackman
(c) Warburg   (d) Robert Hill

68. Which of the following would not be limiting factor in photosynthesis?
(a) Light   (b) CO_2
(c) O_2 (d) Chlorophyll

69. Study the following graph showing the effect of light intensity on the rate of photosynthesis. Which of the following option regarding this is correct?

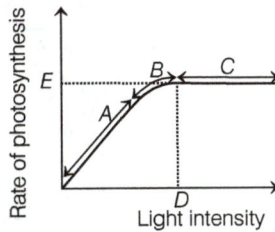

(a) Light is a limiting factor in the region *A*

(b) Region *C* represents that rate of photosynthesis is not increased further by increasing light intensity because some other factor becomes limited

(c) Point *D* represents the intensity of light at which some other factor becomes limiting

(d) All of the above

MCQs 2 Marks Questions

70. Given below are two statements.

Statement I Cyanobacteria synthesise starch as the byproduct of photosynthesis.

Statement II *Hydrilla* absorbs carbon dioxide from their entire body surface.

Choose the correct answer from the options given below.

(a) Both statement I and statement II are correct

(b) Both statement I and statement II are incorrect

(c) Statement I is correct, but statement II is incorrect

(d) Statement I is incorrect, but statement II is correct

71. Suggest why the rate of photosynthesis is low between 520 nm and 575 nm?

(a) The wavelengths of green light is least efficient for photosynthesis

(b) The green light is transmitted and reflected instead of being absorbed by the chlorophyll-*a* (green pigment)

(c) Both (a) and (b)

(d) None of the above

72. Given below are two statements.
Statement I Absorption spectrum is the curve that shows the amount of different wavelength of light absorbed by plant pigments.

Statement II Action spectrum

indicates the percentage of a particular wavelength of light absorbed during photosynthesis.

Choose the correct answer from the options given below.

(a) Both statement I and statement II are correct

(b) Both statement I and statement II are incorrect

(c) Statement I is correct, but statement II is incorrect

(d) Statement I is incorrect, but statement II is correct

73. Given below are two statements.

Statement I Redox potential of photosystem-II is greater than photosystem-I.

Statement II NADP and ADP produced on light reaction constitute assimilatory power.

Choose the correct answer from the options given below.

(a) Both statement I and statement II are correct

(b) Both statement I and statement II are incorrect

(c) Statement I is correct, but statement II is incorrect

(d) Statement I is incorrect, but statement II is correct

74. Based on your understanding of the process of photosynthesis.

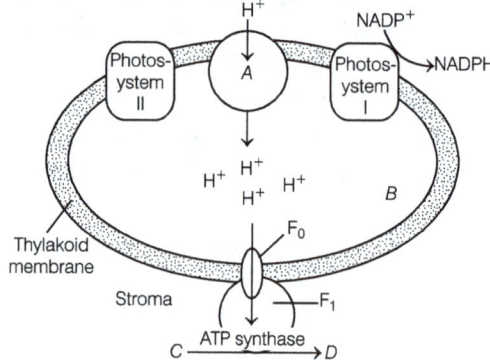

Select the incorrect match.

(a) A-Cytochrome-b and f

(b) B-Grana

(c) C-ADP

(d) D-ATP

75. A student conducted an experiment to know the rate of photosynthesis in aquatic plants. He added 'X' to water to accelerate the same.

What is X in the above experiment?

(a) KOH

(b) Soft drink

(c) NaCl

(d) Sugar solution

76. Refer to the diagram given below and answer the question that follow.

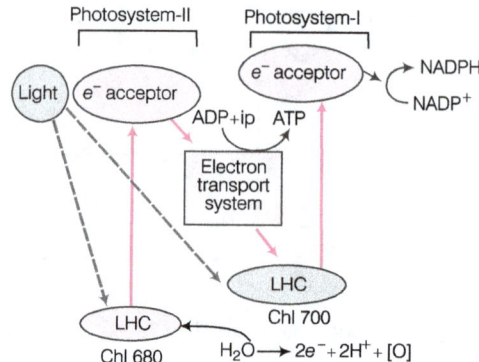

Which one will have highest redox potential in Z-scheme?

(a) P_{680}

(b) P_{700}

(c) $NADP^+$

(d) NADPH

Direction (Q. Nos. 77-79) Study the following passage and answer the questions that follow.

Mohan, who is a biology tutor was teaching photosynthesis in higher plants to the students at his place. While explaining the topic 'light reaction' said that two of three products of light reaction, ATP and NADPH are used to drive the reactions in biosynthesis/dark phase. It has been verified by the fact that immediately after light becomes unavailable, the biosynthetic phase continues for sometime and then stops, if light becomes available again, the process continues.

Students further asked the questions from of whole process for better understanding.

77. Why proton gradient is important in photosynthesis?
(a) It makes light available for photosynthesis
(b) It leads to the formation of ATP
(c) Proton gradient is directly proportional to light reaction
(d) Both (b) and (c)

78. During dark phase of photosynthesis which of the following products are oxidised or reduced?
(a) $NADPH_2$- reduced, CO_2-oxidised
(b) Only CO_2-oxidised
(c) CO_2-reduced, $NADP^+$-oxidised
(d) CO_2-reduced, $NADPH_2$-oxidised

79. The first stable product of dark reaction in photosynthesis is
(a) oxaloacetic acid
(b) dichlorophenyl dimethyl urea
(c) RuBP
(d) 3- Phosphoglyceric acid

80. Read the following statements and select the correct ones.
I. PS-I is involved in non-cyclic photophosphorylation only.
II. PS-II is involved in both cyclic and non-cyclic photophosphorylation.
III. Stroma lamellae membranes possess PS-I only, whereas grana lamellae membranes possess both PS-I and PS-II.
IV. Mesophyll cells possess both RuBisCO and PEPcase enzyme.
Codes
(a) I and II
(b) II and III
(c) Only III
(d) I, II, III and IV

81. Given below are two statements.

Statement I The granal fraction of isolated chloroplasts has the ability to synthesise ATP and $NADPH_2$, but not hexose sugar.

Statement II Stromal matrix has shown the ability of synthesise hexose sugar.

Choose the correct answer from the options given below.
(a) Both statement I and statement II are correct
(b) Both statement I and statement II are incorrect
(c) Statement I is correct, but statement II is incorrect
(d) Statement I is incorrect, but statement II is correct

82. Study the following statements.
I. Red light falling in the range of wavelength 660-760 nm is the most effective for photosynthesis.
II. Green light falling in the range of wavelength 500-580 nm is the least effective for photosynthesis.
III. Chlorophyll-a, chlorophyll-b, carotenes and xanthophylls are soluble in organic solvents.
IV. Phycobilins (phycocyanin, allophycocyanin and phycoerythrin) are soluble in water.

Which of the above statements is/are incorrect?
(a) II and III   (b) III and IV
(c) Only I   (d) None of these

83. Match the Column I with Column II and select the correct option from the codes given below.

Column I	Column II
A. C_3-plants	1. Reported in members of Liliaceae
B. Chlorophyll-a	2. Cyclic electron flow
C. PS-I	3. Occurs in chloroplast of bundle sheath
D. CAM	4. Methyl group attached with pyrrole ring

Codes

	A	B	C	D
(a)	4	3	1	2
(b)	3	4	2	1
(c)	1	2	3	4
(d)	2	3	4	1

84. Select the correct match.

(a)	Pigment soluble in hot water	Carotenoids
(b)	Plastids	Single-stranded circular DNA
(c)	Park and Biggins	Quantasomes
(d)	C_4 cycle	Chloroplast of bundle sheath

85. Assertion (A) Inhibition of photosynthesis occurs under increased level of oxygen.

Reason (R) This is mainly due to competitive inhibition of RuBisCO by increased level of oxygen.

Choose the correct answer from the options given below.

(a) Both A and R are true and R is the correct explanation of A

(b) Both A and R are true, but R is not the correct explanation of A

(c) A is true, but R is false

(d) A is false, but R is true

Darken your choice with HB Pencil

1.	ⓐ ⓑ ⓒ ⓓ	16.	ⓐ ⓑ ⓒ ⓓ	31.	ⓐ ⓑ ⓒ ⓓ	46.	ⓐ ⓑ ⓒ ⓓ	61.	ⓐ ⓑ ⓒ ⓓ	76.	ⓐ ⓑ ⓒ ⓓ
2.	ⓐ ⓑ ⓒ ⓓ	17.	ⓐ ⓑ ⓒ ⓓ	32.	ⓐ ⓑ ⓒ ⓓ	47.	ⓐ ⓑ ⓒ ⓓ	62.	ⓐ ⓑ ⓒ ⓓ	77.	ⓐ ⓑ ⓒ ⓓ
3.	ⓐ ⓑ ⓒ ⓓ	18.	ⓐ ⓑ ⓒ ⓓ	33.	ⓐ ⓑ ⓒ ⓓ	48.	ⓐ ⓑ ⓒ ⓓ	63.	ⓐ ⓑ ⓒ ⓓ	78.	ⓐ ⓑ ⓒ ⓓ
4.	ⓐ ⓑ ⓒ ⓓ	19.	ⓐ ⓑ ⓒ ⓓ	34.	ⓐ ⓑ ⓒ ⓓ	49.	ⓐ ⓑ ⓒ ⓓ	64.	ⓐ ⓑ ⓒ ⓓ	79.	ⓐ ⓑ ⓒ ⓓ
5.	ⓐ ⓑ ⓒ ⓓ	20.	ⓐ ⓑ ⓒ ⓓ	35.	ⓐ ⓑ ⓒ ⓓ	50.	ⓐ ⓑ ⓒ ⓓ	65.	ⓐ ⓑ ⓒ ⓓ	80.	ⓐ ⓑ ⓒ ⓓ
6.	ⓐ ⓑ ⓒ ⓓ	21.	ⓐ ⓑ ⓒ ⓓ	36.	ⓐ ⓑ ⓒ ⓓ	51.	ⓐ ⓑ ⓒ ⓓ	66.	ⓐ ⓑ ⓒ ⓓ	81.	ⓐ ⓑ ⓒ ⓓ
7.	ⓐ ⓑ ⓒ ⓓ	22.	ⓐ ⓑ ⓒ ⓓ	37.	ⓐ ⓑ ⓒ ⓓ	52.	ⓐ ⓑ ⓒ ⓓ	67.	ⓐ ⓑ ⓒ ⓓ	82.	ⓐ ⓑ ⓒ ⓓ
8.	ⓐ ⓑ ⓒ ⓓ	23.	ⓐ ⓑ ⓒ ⓓ	38.	ⓐ ⓑ ⓒ ⓓ	53.	ⓐ ⓑ ⓒ ⓓ	68.	ⓐ ⓑ ⓒ ⓓ	83.	ⓐ ⓑ ⓒ ⓓ
9.	ⓐ ⓑ ⓒ ⓓ	24.	ⓐ ⓑ ⓒ ⓓ	39.	ⓐ ⓑ ⓒ ⓓ	54.	ⓐ ⓑ ⓒ ⓓ	69.	ⓐ ⓑ ⓒ ⓓ	84.	ⓐ ⓑ ⓒ ⓓ
10.	ⓐ ⓑ ⓒ ⓓ	25.	ⓐ ⓑ ⓒ ⓓ	40.	ⓐ ⓑ ⓒ ⓓ	55.	ⓐ ⓑ ⓒ ⓓ	70.	ⓐ ⓑ ⓒ ⓓ	85.	ⓐ ⓑ ⓒ ⓓ
11.	ⓐ ⓑ ⓒ ⓓ	26.	ⓐ ⓑ ⓒ ⓓ	41.	ⓐ ⓑ ⓒ ⓓ	56.	ⓐ ⓑ ⓒ ⓓ	71.	ⓐ ⓑ ⓒ ⓓ		
12.	ⓐ ⓑ ⓒ ⓓ	27.	ⓐ ⓑ ⓒ ⓓ	42.	ⓐ ⓑ ⓒ ⓓ	57.	ⓐ ⓑ ⓒ ⓓ	72.	ⓐ ⓑ ⓒ ⓓ		
13.	ⓐ ⓑ ⓒ ⓓ	28.	ⓐ ⓑ ⓒ ⓓ	43.	ⓐ ⓑ ⓒ ⓓ	58.	ⓐ ⓑ ⓒ ⓓ	73.	ⓐ ⓑ ⓒ ⓓ		
14.	ⓐ ⓑ ⓒ ⓓ	29.	ⓐ ⓑ ⓒ ⓓ	44.	ⓐ ⓑ ⓒ ⓓ	59.	ⓐ ⓑ ⓒ ⓓ	74.	ⓐ ⓑ ⓒ ⓓ		
15.	ⓐ ⓑ ⓒ ⓓ	30.	ⓐ ⓑ ⓒ ⓓ	45.	ⓐ ⓑ ⓒ ⓓ	60.	ⓐ ⓑ ⓒ ⓓ	75.	ⓐ ⓑ ⓒ ⓓ		

Chapter 07

Respiration in Plants

MCQs 1 Mark Questions

1. Respiration differs from the process of combustion by the fact that
   (a) all energy stored in glucose is released at once due to combustion
   (b) all energy in glucose is gradually released due to combustion
   (c) comparatively large quantity of energy is produced due to combustion
   (d) the carbohydrates act as the combustion substance

2. The aerobic respiration yield
   (a) $10NADPH_2$, $2FADH_2$, $38ATP$
   (b) $10NADPH_2$, $2FADH_2$, $2GTP$, $2ATP$
   (c) $12NADPH_2$, $30 ATP$, H_2O
   (d) $8NADH_2$, $FADH_2$, $2ATP$

3. Complete the following equation by selecting the correct answer from the options given below.

   Adenosine diphosphate $+ A \xrightarrow[\text{(7.3kcal)}]{\text{Energy}} B$

(a)	$A\text{-}H_3PO_4$	B-Adenosine monophosphate
(b)	$A\text{-}H_3PO_4$	B-Adenosine triphosphate
(c)	$A\text{-}H_2PO_4$	B-Adenosine triphosphate
(d)	$A\text{-}H_3PO_4$	B-Adenosine

4. The structure of ATP is given below. Identify the high energy bond with respect to the same.

   (a) B (b) A (c) C (d) D

5. Which of the following statements is not correct with respect to ATP?
   (a) It is a raw material for activation of tRNA
   (b) It helps in passive absorption
   (c) It can be converted to heat energy, to light energy as per need
   (d) It is the source of energy for many metabolic processes

6. The number of ATP molecules formed by the complete oxidation of pyruvic acid is
   (a) 12   (b) 13   (c) 14   (d) 15

7. Connect the type of fermentation $(A\text{-}D)$ with organism involved in it.
   A-Pyruvic acid $\rightarrow$ Ethanol
   B-Pyruvic acid $\rightarrow$ Lactic acid
   C-Pyruvic acid $\rightarrow$ Acetic acid
   D-Pyruvic acid $\rightarrow$ Acetone

Which of the following option is correct?

(a) *Saccharomyces* $\rightarrow D$

(b) *Lactobacillus* $\rightarrow A$

(c) *Acetobacter* $\rightarrow C$

(d) *Clostridium* $\rightarrow B$

8. Observe the Venn diagram and identify the 'X' and 'Y'.

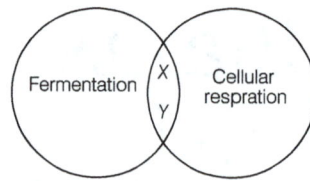

	(X) Reactant	(Y) Product
(a)	Glucose	Water
(b)	Lactose	Lactic acid
(c)	Glucose	CO_2
(d)	Oxygen	Ethanol

9. During cellulose fermentation by anaerobic bacteria in rumen and reticulum, cellulose is majorly converted into

(a) CO_2

(b) lactic acid

(c) ethyl alcohol

(d) volatile fatty acid

10. There is no change in oxidation state of carbon or H : C ratio in

(a) glycolysis

(b) ethanol fermentation

(c) lactic acid fermentation

(d) formation of acetyl Co-A

11. What will happen if fermentation is allowed to proceed in a closed vessel?

(a) No change will be there

(b) Vacuum will result

(c) Pressure will develop because of excessive CO_2

(d) Pressure will develop because of excessive O_2

12. Which of the following is correct with respect to the Pasteur effect?

(a) It decreases the rate of sugar breakdown

(b) It increases the evolution of Carbon-dioxide

(c) It inhibits ATP synthesis

(d) None of the above

13. Pasteur effect is concerned with shifting of environmental conditions from

(a) light to dark

(b) anaerobic to aerobic

(c) aerobic to anaerobic

(d) light to anaerobic

14. The increase of rate of glycolysis in absence of O_2 is due to

(a) availability of enzymes

(b) non-availability of enzymes

(c) toxic enzymes

(d) All of the above

15. After a hurdle race, an athlete feel pain, burning sensation, muscle fatigue and soreness in the leg muscle.

What is the possible reason for this condition?

(a) Accumulation of lactate

(b) Glycolysis

(c) Oxidative metabolism

(d) Performed ATP

16. 'X' is used in anaerobic respiration experiments because it does not react with CO_2. Identify X.

(a) Hydrogen   (b) Nitrogen

(c) Mercury   (d) None of these

17. Study the Venn diagram and identify the phase 'X'.

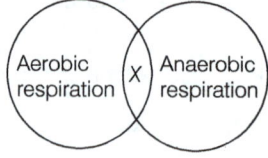

(a) Krebs' cycle   (b) Glycolysis

(c) Glycogenolysis   (d) ETS

18. Which of the following adversely affect the rate of respiration?
(a) High concentration of CO_2
(b) Absense of O_2
(c) Both of the above
(d) None of the above

19. Consider the given statements and complete it by selecting the correct option.

The ratio of CO_2 formation in aerobic and anaerobic respiration is 'A'.

The ratio of 'B' is aerobic and anaerobic respiration is 18 : 1.

	A	B
(a)	3 : 1	ATP
(b)	18 : 1	ADP
(c)	9 : 1	NADP
(d)	5 : 1	CO_2

20. Which of the following option is not true for glycolysis?
(a) Substrate level phosphorylation
(b) End product is CO_2, H_2O
(c) Expenditure of ATP
(d) Production of ATP

21. Which of the following minerals activate the enzymes involved in respiration?
(a) Copper and boron
(b) Nitrogen and phosphorous
(c) Sulphur and iron
(d) Magnesium and manganese

22. Consider the following statements and select the correct option in which carbon dioxide is not produced.
(a) During acetyl Co-A formation
(b) During formation of a α-ketoglutaric acid in Krebs' cycle
(c) During succinic acid formation in Krebs' cycle.
(d) During conversion of glucose-6-P to fructose-6-P

23. Pick out the reaction of glycolysis in which isomerisation takes place
(a) Glucose $\rightarrow$ Fructose-6-phosphate
(b) G–3–P $\rightarrow$ DHAP
(c) 3–phosphoglycerate $\rightarrow$ 2 phosphoglycerate
(d) Phosphoenol pyruvate $\rightarrow$ Pyruvate

24. Complete the reaction by identify 'X'.

2–phosphoglycerate $\overset{X}{\rightleftharpoons}$ 2 phosphoenol pyruvate
(a) Pyruvate kinase
(b) Enolase
(c) Phosphoglycerate kinase
(d) Addolase

25. Select the inappropriate feature of label 'A' from the options given below.

Fructose-6-phosphate + ATP $\xrightarrow[Mg^{++}]{'A'}$ Fructose-1, 6-diphosphate + ADP
(a) It is allosterically inhibited by ATP
(b) It is allosterically activated by AMP
(c) It exists as a pentamer and each subunit has two binding sites for ATP
(d) None of the above

26. Which of the following is incorrect with respect to realtends used and the end products during glycolysis?
(a) Glucose (1 mol) $\longrightarrow$ Pyruvic acid (2 moles)
(b) ADP(4) $\rightarrow$ ATP(4)
(c) $H_2O(2) \rightarrow H_2O_2(4)$
(d) $PO_4(2) \rightarrow PO_4(2)$

27. A scientist conducted an experiment to know the property of hexokinase in the process of glycolysis. He introduced more glucose-6-phosphate from external source to the process.

How would it effect on the enzyme activity?
(a) Enzyme activity will be inhibited
(b) Enzyme activity will be activated
(c) The activity will remain unchanged
(d) Result can not be predicted

28. Select the incorrectly matched pair.

(a) Glucose $\rightleftharpoons$ Glucose-6-phosphate — ATP is used

(b) 1, 3-diphosphoglyceraldehyde $\rightleftharpoons$ 1, 3-diphosphoglyceric acid — ATP direct synthesis

(c) 1, 3-diphosphoglyceric acid $\rightleftharpoons$ 3-phosphoglyceric acid — ATP direct synthesis

(d) Fructose-6-phosphate $\rightleftharpoons$ Fructose 1, 6-diphosphate—ATP is used

29. Consider the following statements with respect to pyruvic acid.

(i) Pyruvic acid is a type of acetic acid.

(ii) Pyruvic acid is oxidised to form succinyl coenzyme-A which is a raw material for synthesis of phytol chain of chlorophyll pigment.

Choose the correct answer from the option given below.

(a) I-True, II-False   (b) I-False, II-True

(c) I-False, II-False   (d) I-True, II-True

30. Observe the flow chart and complete it by missing the labelled part.

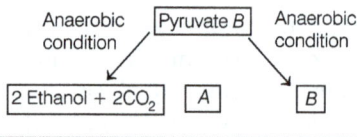

	A	B
(a)	2 Acetyl Co-A	g Lycolysis
(b)	Fermentation	Lactate
(c)	2Acetyl Co-A	2 Lactate
(d)	2 Lactate	2 Acetyl Co-A

31. Study the Venn diagram of respiratory substrates and identify the labelled part 'X'.

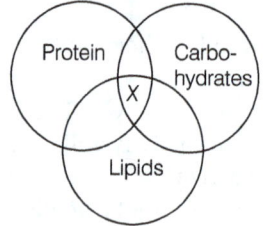

(a) Water   (b) ATP

(c) Acetyl Co-A   (d) Amino acids

32. Study the Venn diagram and identify the connecting link 'Y'.

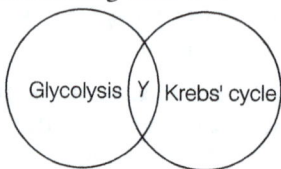

(a) Pyruvate   (b) Succinyl Co-A

(c) Acetyl Co-A   (d) None of these

33. The formation of acetyl coenzyme A from pyruvic acid is the result of its

(a) dehydration

(b) reduction

(c) oxidative decarboxylation

(d) dephosphorylation

34. Which of the following is often called substrate entrant of TCA cycle

(a) Pyruvic acid

(b) Acetyl coenzyme-A

(c) Succinyl Co-A

(d) Coenzyme-A

35. Degradation of sugar and fat to Acetyl Co-A will not take place, if the following organelle is not present in a eukaryotic cell.

(a) Mitochondria   (b) Golgi bodies

(c) Nucleus   (d) Ribosomes

36. When a molecule of pyruvic acid is subjected to anaerobic oxidation and forms lactic acid there is

(a) loss of 6 ATP molecules

(b) loss of 3 ATP molecules

(c) Gain of 4 ATP molecules

(d) Gain of 2 ATP molecules

37. All enzymes of TCA cycle are located in the mitochondrial matrix except one which islocated in the inner mitochondrial membranes in eukaryotes and in cytosol of prokaryotes. This enzymes is

(a) malate dehydrogenase
(b) lactate dehydrogenase
(c) isocitrate dehydrogenase
(d) succinate dehydrogenase

38. Largest amount of Phosphate bond energy is produced in the process of respiration during
(a) anaerobic respiration
(b) glycolysis
(c) Krebs' cycle
(d) None of the above

39. Identify enzyme A in the given reaction of Krebs' cycle.

Succinyl Co-A + GDP/ADP + H_3PO_4 $\xrightleftharpoons{A}$

Succinate + Co-A + GTP/ATP × 2
(a) Succinate dehydrogenase
(b) Succinyl Co-A synthetase
(c) Citrate synthetase
(d) Aconitase

40. In citric acid cycle, decarboxylation occurs when
(a) succinic acid converts to malic acid
(b) malic acid converts to oxaloacetic acid
(c) oxaloacetic acid converts to citric acid
(d) oxalosuccinic acid converts to α-ketoglutaric acid

41. In Krebs' cycle, the FAD participates as electron acceptor during conversion of
(a) α-ketoglutarate to succinyl Co-A
(b) succinyl Co-A to succinic acid
(c) succinic acid to fumaric acid
(d) fumaric acid to malic acid

42. In Krebs' cycle the hydrogen atoms removed at succinate level are accepted by 'Y'. Identify Y in the above statement.
(a) FAD   (b) ADP   (c) ATP   (d) NAD

43. In citric acid cycle substrate phosphorylation occurs during the conversion of
(a) malic acid → oxaloacetic acid
(b) succinyl Co-A → succinic acid
(c) succinic acid → fumaric acid
(d) pyruvic acid → acetyl Co-A

44. Which of the following reactions is not related to oxidative phosphorylation?
(a) Succinic acid → Fumaric acid
(b) Malic acid → Oxaloacetic acid
(c) Succinyl Co-A → Succinic acid
(d) Isocitric acid → Oxalosuccinic acid

45. Oxidative phosphorylation is
(a) Formation of ATP by transfer of phosphate group from a substrate to ADP
(b) Formation of ATP energy released from electrons removed during substrate oxidation
(c) Addition of phosphate group to ATP
(d) Oxidation of phosphate group in ATP

46. In oxidative photophosphorylation, the last 3 steps are as follows

$$Q \to C \to aa_3 \to O_2$$

(a) $aa_3 \to O_2 + H^+$ yielding site
(b) $Q \to C$ is H^+ absorbing site
(c) $Q \to C$ is H^+ yielding site and $aa_3 \to O_2$ is H^+ absorbing site
(d) NO H^+ is absorbed or released

47. Which of the following statements is/are incorrect about Electron Transport System (ETS)?
  I. It is essential for transfer of energy from low energy chemical bonds of ATP to high energy chemical bonds of respiratory substrates.
  II. It is located in the outer membrane of mitochondria.
(a) Only I   (b) I and II
(c) Only II   (d) None of these

48. Identify the labelled part 'A' in the given diagram.

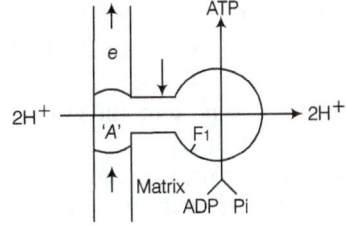

(a) F_1 (b) F_0
(c) ATP Synthase (d) None of the above

49. 'X' transfer electrons in electron transport system. Identify 'X'.
    (a) Phytochrome (b) Fe-S
    (c) F_1-particles (d) None of these

50. Identify the correct statement with respect to ATP, the energy molecule ATP is synthesised through ETS when
    (a) e^- is transferred from FAD to NAD
    (b) e^- is transferred from cyt-c_1 to cyt-b
    (c) e^- is transferred from cyt-a to cyt-a_3
    (d) None of the above

51. Cyanide resistant pathway is
    (a) anaerobic respiration
    (b) aerobic respiration
    (c) Both (a) and (b)
    (d) None of the above

52. Connect the inhibitors with their complexes.
    A. Malonate   B. Antimycin-A
    C. Rotenone

    Which of the following option is correct?
    (a) Complex I → Ⓐ B C
    (b) Complex II → A B Ⓒ
    (c) Complex III → A Ⓑ C
    (d) Complex IV → A B Ⓒ

53. Which of the following inhibits the oxidative phosphorylation?
    (a) Dinitrophenol (b) Oligomycin
    (c) Malonate (d) Antimycin -A

54. What kind of compound is F_1 particle and F_0 particle?
    (a) Peripheral protein and integral protein, respectively
    (b) Peripheral protein and embedded protein, respectively
    (c) Embedded protein and cutaneous protein, respectively
    (d) Cutaneous protein and integral protein, respectively

55. Study the table given below and balance the sheet of ATP.

	Stage	ATP
1.	Glycolysis	A
2.	Formation of Acetyl Co-A	B
3.	Krebs' cycle	C

    (a) A-3, B-6, C-24   (b) A-6, B-3, C-22
    (c) A-6, B-6, C-22   (d) A-6, B-6, C-24

56. If 7 NADH from Krebs' cycle and 3 NADH comes from the entry of acetyl coenzyme-A into the electron transport chain yield, how many ATP molecules will be produced?
    (a) 24 ATP   (b) 23 ATP
    (c) 30 ATP   (d) 36 ATP

57. Select the correct option by which energy efficiency can be calculated.
    (a) $\dfrac{\text{Energy stored in ATP produced} \times 100}{\text{Total energy content of } 1 \text{ g mole of glucose}}$

    (b) $\dfrac{\text{Energy stored in ATP produced}}{\text{Total energy content}}$

    (c) $\dfrac{\text{Energy stored in ATP produced} \times 100}{\text{Total energy content of } 100 \text{ g mole of glucose}}$

    (d) None of the above

58. Calculate the total energy gain through respiration per g mole of glucose when 1 ATP molecule contains 7.3 kcal energy.
    (a) 277.5 kcal
    (b) 277 kcal
    (c) 276 kcal
    (d) 277.4 kcal

59. Choose the incorrect statement with respect to Krebs' cycle.
    (a) α-ketoglutarate produces amino acid glutamate
    (b) Oxaloacetate produces amino acid serine
    (c) Succinyl Co-A takes part in the synthesis of chlorophyll
    (d) None of the above

60. Which of the following statement is not true?

(a) Oxaloacetate on amination produces aspartate

(b) α-ketoglutarate forms glutamate on amination

(c) Glycerol is phosphorylated and reduced to form glyceraldehyde-3-phosphate

(d) None of the above

61. The overall goal of glycolysis, Krebs' cycle and electron transport system is the formation of

(a) sugars

(b) ATP in small stepwise units

(c) ATP in one large oxidation reaction

(d) nucleic acids

62. The respiratory quotient during cellular respiration would depend on

(a) the nature of the substrate

(b) the nature of enzyme involved

(c) the amount of oxgyen utilised

(d) the amount of CO_2 released

63. Select the correct option for the statement given below.

"RQ is zero in case of"

(a) $C_6H_{12}O_6 + 6O_2 \longrightarrow 6CO_2 + 6H_2O + energy$

(b) $C_{54}H_{98}O_6 + 145O_2 \longrightarrow 102CO_2 + 98H_2O + energy$

(c) $C_6H_{12}O_6 + 3O_2 \longrightarrow 3C_4H_6O_5 + 3H_2O$

(d) $C_6H_{12}O_6 \longrightarrow 2C_2H_5O_2 + 2CO_2$

64. A mixture containing equal quantity of germinating maize and ground nut seeds are taken the RQ of this mixture would be

(a) one

(b) less than One

(c) more than One

(d) infinity

65. What is the possible reason for zero RQ of *Opuntia*?

(a) Stomata remains opened in day hours, exchange of gases take place

(b) Stomata might be dead

(c) Stomata remain closed in day hours thereby blocking gaseous exchange

(d) None of the above

66. Select the correct name of the figure given below.

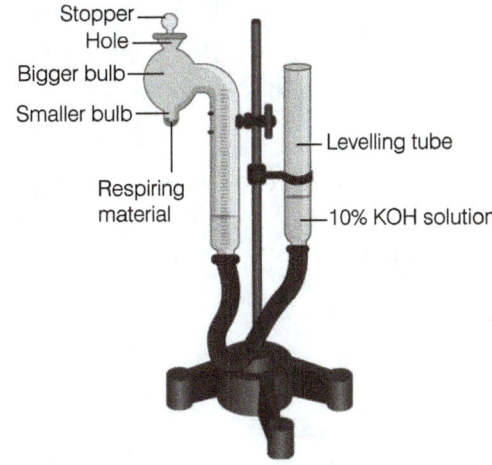

(a) Spirometer

(b) Ganong respirometer

(c) Wilmot bubbler

(d) Oxymeter

67. If the CO_2 content of atmosphere is as high as 300 parts per million

(a) the plants would not grow properly

(b) all plants will be killed

(c) the plant would thrive well

(d) plant would grow for sometime and then die

68. Potato grown on hills produces much larger tubers. Select the correct reason for the same.

(a) It exhibits an inverse correlation with rate of respiration

(b) On hills night experiences very low temperature and thus, rate of respiration is very low

(c) Oxygen is used in oxidation of respiratory substrate during aerobic respiration

(d) Rate of respiration is high in younger tissues

MCQs 2 Marks Questions

69. Identify the correct structure of labelled part '*A*' from the options given below.

NH$_2$

Low energy bond   High energy bonds

1500-1800 cal   7300 cal   7300 cal

(a)

(b)

(c)

(d)

70. **Assertion** (A) During hydrolysis of typical chemical bonds, about 3000 calories per mole are liberated.

Reason (R) ATP also yields about 3000 calories per mole after the release of any one of the two terminal phosphates.

Choose the correct answer from the options given below.

(a) Both A and R are true and R is the correct explanation of A

(b) Both A and R are true, but R is not the correct explanation of A

(c) A is true, but R is false

(d) A is false, but R is true

71. Study the given table and identify the process related to the same.

Used	Produced
1 Glucose	2 Pyruvic acid
4 ADP	4 ATP
4 Phosphate	2 Phosphate
2 ATP	2 ADP
2 NAD$^+$	2 NADH + 2H$^+$ + 2H$_2$O

(a) Glycolysis
(b) Krebs' cycle
(c) Fermentation
(d) Electron transport system

72. Study the given experimental setup and select the correct option with respect to the same.

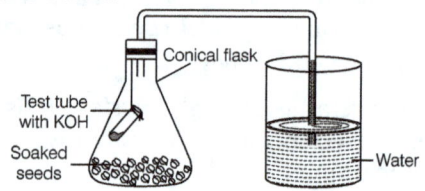

(a) Production of oxygen gas during respiration in conical flask

(b) Germinating seeds will die up

(c) Production of carbon dioxide gas during respiration in conical flask

(d) None of the above

73. Complete the following flowchart based on mechanism of respiration.

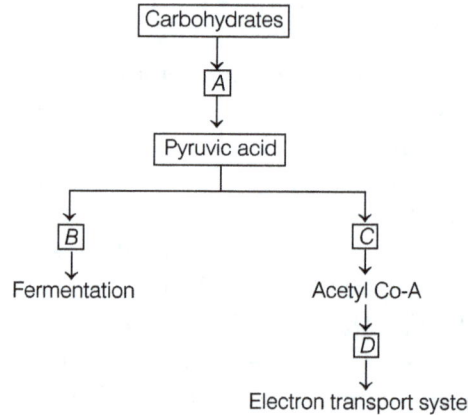

Choose the correct code from the option given below.

	A	B	C	D
(a)	Krebs' cycle	Aerobic respiration	Glycolysis	Anaerobic respiration
(b)	Glycolysis	Anaerobic respiration	Aerobic respiration	Glycogen
(c)	Glycolysis	Anaerobic respiration	Aerobic respiration	Krebs' cycle
(d)	Glycolysis	Aerobic respiration	Anaerobic respiration	Krebs' cycle

74. Identify the enzymes involved in the reaction A and B given below.

A. Glucose + ATP $\xrightarrow[\text{Mg}^{2+}]{}$

    Glucose-6-phosphate + ADP

B. Glucose-6-phosphate $\longrightarrow$

        Fructose-6-phosphate

(a)	A-Phosphofructokinase	B-Phosphohexo isomerase
(b)	A-Hexokinase	B-Phosphofructo-kinase
(c)	A-Hexokinase	B-Phosphohexois omerase
(d)	A-Phosphofructokinase	B-Hexokinase

75. Consider the flowchart given below regarding glycolysis pathway.

Glucose

$\downarrow (A)$

Glucose-6-phosphate

$\downarrow (B)$

Fructose 1, 6-diphosphate

$\downarrow$

3-phosphoglyceraldehyde

$\downarrow (C)$

1-3-bisphosphoglyceric acid

$\downarrow (D)$

3-phosphoglyceric acid

Choose the correct answer for the step that will release ATP from the options given below.

(a) B (b) D (c) C (d) A

76. With the reference to the given table of total input and output materials in glycolysis, identify the missing components. A, B and C by choosing the correct answer from the options given below.

	Total input	Total output
(1)	1 molecule of glucose	A
(2)	2 ATP	B
(3)	C	$2 \times \text{NADH} + 2\text{H}^+$

(a) A-2 molecules of pyruvate   B-4 ADP   C-2 × NAD$^+$

(b) A-4 molecules of pyruvate   B-No ATP   C-2 × NAD$^+$

(c) A-2 molecules of pyruvate   B-2 ATP   C-2 × NAD$^+$

(d) A-2 molecules of pyruvate   B-4 ATP   C-2 × NAD$^+$

77. Column I contains some enzymes and Column II contains reactions. Match them correctly by choose the right answer from the options given below.

	Column I		Column II
A.	Hexokinase	1.	Conversion of 1, 3-diphosphoglyceric aldehyde to 1,3-diphosphoglyceric acid
B.	Triosephosphate dehydrogenase	2.	Conversion of 3-phosphoglyceric acid to 2-phosphoglyceric acid
C.	Phosphoglycero-mutase	3.	Conversion of glucose to glucose-6 phosphate

Codes

    A B C   A B C

(a) 1 2 3   (b) 2 3 1

(c) 3 1 2   (d) 3 2 1

78. A scientist observed the process of glycolysis. In one experiment, he noticed that ATP was consumed but it was not produced.

What would be the possible reason for this condition?

(a) The cycle is reversible conditions are not favourable for production of ATP

(b) Phosphoglyceromutase enzyme is possible reason for inhibition of ATP production

(c) Diphosphoglyceraldehyde hydrogenase enzyme is a possible reason for inhibition of ATP production

(d) Pyruvate is causing hinderance in the production of ATP

79. With reference to the given Krebs' cycle, Answer the following questions.

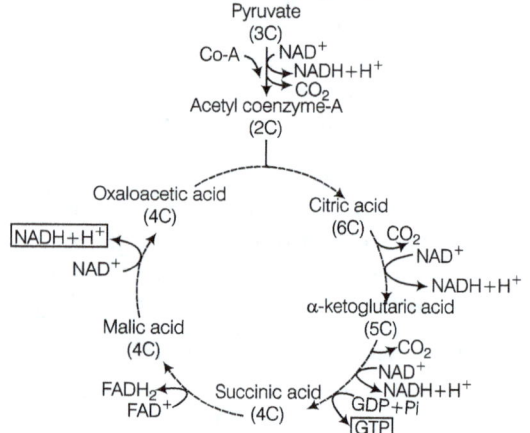

Tell, how many water molecules will be formed and the number of oxygen molecules required in Krebs' cycle.

(a)	Water molecules-12	Oxygen molecules-2
(b)	Water molecules-6	Oxygen molecules-5
(c)	Water molecules-12	Oxygen molecules-6
(d)	Water molecules-12	Oxygen molecules-5

80. Match Column I with Column II and choose the correct option from the codes given below.

	Column I		Column II
A.	4C compound	1.	Pyruvate
B.	5C compound	2.	Malic acid
C.	3C compound	3.	α-ketoglutaric acid

    Codes

	A	B	C		A	B	C
(a)	1	2	3	(b)	2	3	1
(c)	3	2	1	(d)	2	1	3

81. A scientist conducted an experiment to study the synthesis of ATP. He added an inhibitor 1, 2, 4-dinitrophenol to the same. Which process would be affected?
    (a) Glycolysis
    (b) Krebs' cycle
    (c) Pentose phosphate pathway
    (d) Oxidative phosphorylation

82. During anaerobic respiration for the conversion of pyruvate into acetaldehyde, along with coenzyme 'X', the cofactor 'Y' is from the options given below.

(a)	X-B-vitamins	Y-Zn^{++}
(b)	X-TPP	Y-Mg^{++}
(c)	X-TPP	Y-Zn^{++}
(d)	X-S-adenosyl methionine	Y-Fe^{++}

83. Identify the correct sequence of electron carriers of electron transport system.
    (a) NAD → FMN → Ubiquinone → FAD → cyt-a → cyt-a_3 → cyt-b → cyt-c → cyt-c_1
    (b) NAD → FMN → FAD → cyt-a → cyt-a_3 → cyt-b → cyt-c → Cyt-c_1 → Ubiquinone
    (c) NAD → FMN → FAD → Ubiquinone → cyt-b → cyt-c_1 → cyt-c → cyt-a → cyt-a_3
    (d) NAD → FMN → FADH → Ubiquinone → cyt-b → cyt-c_1 → cyt-c → cyt-a → cyt-a_1

84. Given below are two statements.

    Statement I In the electron transport system, the electrons tend to flow from electronegative to electropositive system.

    Statement II During electron transfer, the electron-donor gets reduced while electron-acceptor gets oxidised.

    Choose the correct answer from the options given below.

    (a) Both statement I and statement II are correct
    (b) Both statement I and statement II are incorrect
    (c) Statement I is correct, but statement II is incorrect
    (d) Statement I is incorrect, but statement II is correct

85. Match the Column I with Column II with respect to Respiratory quotient and choose the correct option from the codes given below.

	Column I		Column II
A.	Carbohydrates	1.	< 1
B.	Organic acid	2.	1
C.	Proteins	3.	0
D.	Succulents	4.	> 1

Codes

     A B C D
(a) 4 2 1 3
(b) 2 4 1 3
(c) 1 2 4 3
(d) 3 2 1 4

86. A scientist measured the RQ of rose petals and the reading was less than equal to 1.

Select the correct option which best describes the same.
(a) Due to synthesis of anthocyanin
(b) The respiratory substrates in petals is carbohydrate
(c) Both (a) and (b)
(d) None of the above

87. Select the incorrect match pair with respect to RQ
(a) Germinating barley seeds - 1
(b) Soybean - 0.9
(c) Castor seeds - 1.5
(d) Lemon - 0.4

Darken your choice with HB Pencil

1. ⓐⓑⓒⓓ	16. ⓐⓑⓒⓓ	31. ⓐⓑⓒⓓ	46. ⓐⓑⓒⓓ	61. ⓐⓑⓒⓓ	76. ⓐⓑⓒⓓ
2. ⓐⓑⓒⓓ	17. ⓐⓑⓒⓓ	32. ⓐⓑⓒⓓ	47. ⓐⓑⓒⓓ	62. ⓐⓑⓒⓓ	77. ⓐⓑⓒⓓ
3. ⓐⓑⓒⓓ	18. ⓐⓑⓒⓓ	33. ⓐⓑⓒⓓ	48. ⓐⓑⓒⓓ	63. ⓐⓑⓒⓓ	78. ⓐⓑⓒⓓ
4. ⓐⓑⓒⓓ	19. ⓐⓑⓒⓓ	34. ⓐⓑⓒⓓ	49. ⓐⓑⓒⓓ	64. ⓐⓑⓒⓓ	79. ⓐⓑⓒⓓ
5. ⓐⓑⓒⓓ	20. ⓐⓑⓒⓓ	35. ⓐⓑⓒⓓ	50. ⓐⓑⓒⓓ	65. ⓐⓑⓒⓓ	80. ⓐⓑⓒⓓ
6. ⓐⓑⓒⓓ	21. ⓐⓑⓒⓓ	36. ⓐⓑⓒⓓ	51. ⓐⓑⓒⓓ	66. ⓐⓑⓒⓓ	81. ⓐⓑⓒⓓ
7. ⓐⓑⓒⓓ	22. ⓐⓑⓒⓓ	37. ⓐⓑⓒⓓ	52. ⓐⓑⓒⓓ	67. ⓐⓑⓒⓓ	82. ⓐⓑⓒⓓ
8. ⓐⓑⓒⓓ	23. ⓐⓑⓒⓓ	38. ⓐⓑⓒⓓ	53. ⓐⓑⓒⓓ	68. ⓐⓑⓒⓓ	83. ⓐⓑⓒⓓ
9. ⓐⓑⓒⓓ	24. ⓐⓑⓒⓓ	39. ⓐⓑⓒⓓ	54. ⓐⓑⓒⓓ	69. ⓐⓑⓒⓓ	84. ⓐⓑⓒⓓ
10. ⓐⓑⓒⓓ	25. ⓐⓑⓒⓓ	40. ⓐⓑⓒⓓ	55. ⓐⓑⓒⓓ	70. ⓐⓑⓒⓓ	85. ⓐⓑⓒⓓ
11. ⓐⓑⓒⓓ	26. ⓐⓑⓒⓓ	41. ⓐⓑⓒⓓ	56. ⓐⓑⓒⓓ	71. ⓐⓑⓒⓓ	86. ⓐⓑⓒⓓ
12. ⓐⓑⓒⓓ	27. ⓐⓑⓒⓓ	42. ⓐⓑⓒⓓ	57. ⓐⓑⓒⓓ	72. ⓐⓑⓒⓓ	87. ⓐⓑⓒⓓ
13. ⓐⓑⓒⓓ	28. ⓐⓑⓒⓓ	43. ⓐⓑⓒⓓ	58. ⓐⓑⓒⓓ	73. ⓐⓑⓒⓓ	
14. ⓐⓑⓒⓓ	29. ⓐⓑⓒⓓ	44. ⓐⓑⓒⓓ	59. ⓐⓑⓒⓓ	74. ⓐⓑⓒⓓ	
15. ⓐⓑⓒⓓ	30. ⓐⓑⓒⓓ	45. ⓐⓑⓒⓓ	60. ⓐⓑⓒⓓ	75. ⓐⓑⓒⓓ	

Chapter 08

Plant Growth and Development

MCQs 1 Mark Questions

1. Choose the correct option for the characteristic of growth.
   (a) It is an irreversible permanent increase in size of an organ or its parts or even of an individual cell
   (b) It is accompanied by metabolic processes
   (c) It occurs at the expense of energy
   (d) All of the above

2. The type of growth where new cells are always being added to the plant body by the activity of meristem is called
   (a) closed form of growth
   (b) diffused form of growth
   (c) open form of growth
   (d) discontinuous form of growth

3. Identify A and B in the given figure and choose the correct option.

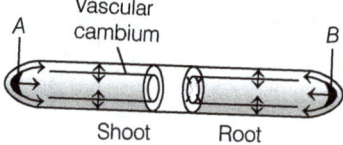

   (a) A–Root apical meristem; B–Shoot apical meristem
   (b) A–Shoot apical meristem; B–Root apical meristem
   (c) A–Permanent tissue; B–Radicle tissue
   (d) A–Radicle tissue; B–Apical tissue

4. In the diagram given below, what does A and B indicate?

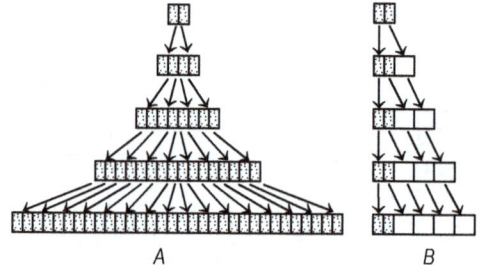

   Choose the correct option.
   (a) A–Mitosis; B–Meiosis
   (b) A–Arithmetic growth; B–Geometric growth
   (c) A–Geometric growth; B–Arithmetic growth
   (d) A–Multiplicative phase; B–Replicative growth

5. In expression, $L_t = L_0 + rt$ of arithmetic growth rate, L_t, L_0 and r represent

	L_t	L_0	r
(a)	Length at time zero	Length at time 't'	Elongation per unit time
(b)	Length at time 't'	Length at time zero	Elongation per unit time
(c)	Length at time 't'	Length at time zero	Growth rate
(d)	Both (b) and (c)		

6. The diagram of development process is shown below.

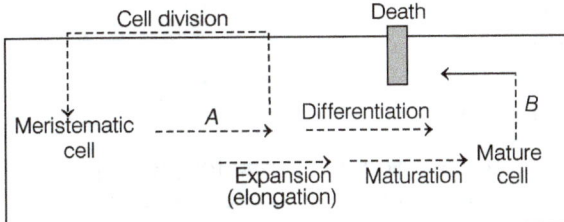

Choose the correct option that refers to A and B.

	A	B
(a)	Senescence-Ageing process	Plasmatic growth - Growth of cell size
(b)	Redifferentiation -Cells mature to perform functions	Dedifferentiation - Regain the ability of division
(c)	Plasmatic growth-Growth of all size	Senescence-Ageing process
(d)	Dedifferentiation - Regain the ability of division	Redifferentiation -Cells mature to perform functions

7. A farmer wants to increase sweetness of the fruits that he was growing in his field. Which of the plant growth hormone should he use?

(a) Cytokinin

(b) Auxin

(c) ABA

(d) Ethylene

8. You are given a tissue with its potential for differentiation in an artificial culture. Which of the following pair of hormones would you add to the medium to secure shoots as well as roots?

(a) IAA and gibberellin

(b) Auxin and cytokinin

(c) Auxin and abscisic acid

(d) Gibberellin and abscisic acid

9. Which of the following effects of auxins on plants is the basis for their commercial application?

(a) Callus formation

(b) Curvature of stem

(c) Induction of root formation in stem cuttings

(d) Induction of shoot formation

10. A farmer uses one of the plant growth hormone for increasing the length of the stem in sugarcane.

What is this plant growth hormone known as?

(a) Abscisic acid   (b) Ethylene

(c) Gibberellic acid (d) Cytokinin

11. Internodal elongation just prior to flowering in sugarbeet, cabbage and in many plants with rosette habit is called

(a) pruning   (b) bolting

(c) grafting   (d) cutting

12. Which of the following plant growth hormone is sprayed to conifers to attain early maturity?

(a) Ethylene   (b) Cytokinin

(c) Gibberellin   (d) ABA

13. Following are few functions.

I. Seed and bud germination.

II. Stem elongation.

III. Fruit development.

Which of the plant growth hormone have all the above functions?

(a) Abscisic acid   (b) Ethylene

(c) Gibberellin   (d) Brassinosteroids

14. Consider the following applications.

    I. Cut flowers can be made to remain fresh.

    II. Shelf life of fruits and vegetables can be prolonged.

    III. It is used in tissue culture.

    Which of the following plant growth hormone have all the above applications?
    (a) Auxin
    (b) Cytokinin
    (c) Gibberellin
    (d) Ethylene

15. Which of the following pair is not matched correctly?
    (a) 2, 4, 5-T – Cell wall elongation
    (b) Abscisic acid – Stomatal closure
    (c) Gibberellic acid–Delayed ripening in citrus
    (d) Ethylene – Epinasty

16. Plant growth hormone X is also called healing hormone and Y is known to increase resistance to infections. Identify X and Y.
    (a) X-auxin, Y-cytokinin
    (b) X-gibberellin, Y-ethylene
    (c) X-ethylene, Y-cytokinin
    (d) X-gibberellin, Y-auxin

17. A plant growth hormone X has 1AA as active form and tryptophan as precursor.

    Another plant growth hormone Y has trans-zeatin as active form and adenine as precursor. Identify X and Y.
    (a) X-gibberellin, Y-cytokinin
    (b) X-auxin, Y-abscisic acid
    (c) X-ethylene, Y-gibberellin
    (d) X-auxin, Y-cytokinin

18. A plant growth hormone on spraying over the leaves reduces transpiration as, it effects on partial closure of stomata. It is
    (a) ethylene   (b) auxin
    (c) ABA   (d) gibberellin

19. Abscisic acid (ABA) is called …A… hormone as in underwater condition, it influences the availability of …B… ions and therefore, the stomata are closed to reduce water loss.

    Complete the passage by replacing A and B with correct option.
    (a) A–plant, B–Ca^{2+} (b) A–stress, B–K^+
    (c) A–plant, B–Na^+ (d) A –stress, B– Mg^{2+}

20. Which of the following combination describes abscisic acid (ABA)?

	Stem growth	Seed dormancy	Abscission	Root growth
(a)	✓	✓	✗	✗
(b)	✗	✗	✓	✓
(c)	✗	✓	✓	✗
(d)	✓	✗	✗	✓

21. It takes very long time for pineapple plants to produce flowers. Which combination of hormones can be applied to artificially induce flowering in pineapple plants throughout the year to increase yield?
    (a) Gibberellin and cytokinin
    (b) Gibberellin and abscisic acid
    (c) Cytokinin and abscisic acid
    (d) Auxin and ethylene

22. Which of the following chemical is used in artificial ripening and degreening of citrus fruits?
    (a) IAA   (b) IBA
    (c) Ethephon   (d) ABA

23. In slight excess, a plant growth hormone has an adverse effect on blossoming of flowers. There is premature fading of flowers and the petals role inwardly and permanently close.

    The plant growth hormone is
    (a) Auxin
    (b) Ethylene
    (c) Cytokinin
    (d) Gibberellin

24. A farmer grows cucumber plants in his field. He wants to increase the number of female flowers in them. Which plant growth regulator can be applied to achieve this?

(a) ABA　　　　　　(b) Ethylene

(c) GA　　　　　　(d) Cytokinins

25. Which of the following is incorrectly matched?

(a)	Explant	–	Excised plant part used for callus formation
(b)	Cytokinin	–	Its high concentration causes root initiation in callus
(c)	Somatic embryo	–	Embryo produced from a vegetative cell
(d)	Anther culture	–	Haploid plants

MCQs 2 Marks Questions

26. **Assertion** (A) Both at the root apex and the shoot apex, the constantly dividing cells show the meristematic phase of growth.

Reason (R) The cells of this region have less protoplasm and lack nuclei.

(a) Both A and R true and R is the correct explanation of A

(b) Both A and R are true, but R is not the correct explanation of A

(c) A is true, but R is false

(d) A is false, but R is true

27. The Japanese biologist Kurosawa showed that the bakanae (foolish seedling) disease of rice was caused by a substance produced by the fungus *Gibberella fujikuroi*. The substance was named gibberellin. Which of the following statement about gibberellin is false?

(a) If gibberellin is applied to the stems of dwarf pea plants, the stems elongate, so that plant reach normal height

(b) The gibberellin produced by the fungus caused normal healthy rice plants to become usually tall

(c) Gibberellins stimulate stem growth in dwarf and rosette plants

(d) Dwarf plants would be expected to have higher levels of gibberellin in their stems than normal plants

Direction (Q. Nos. 28-30) Read the passage given below and answer the questions that are based on it.

Growth and development in plants is regulated by special chemical substances, identified as phytohormones. These are translocated to parts where required and induces a physiological response. These are classified as growth promoters and growth inhibitors based on their effect on plant growth.

28. In an appropriate concentration, auxin induces cell elongation in certain plant organs. However, some tissues responds differently to varying concentrations of auxins.

Which graph represents the best response of shoot and root to IAA application?

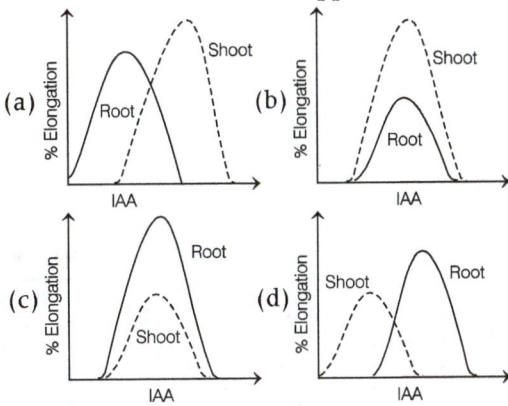

29. Consider the given flow chart.

X = More mitosis

↓

More mitosis = More cells

↓

More cells = Plant growth

Identify X.

(a) Ethylene   (b) Abscisic acid

(c) Cytokinin   (d) Auxin

30. The mutant varities of plants which are over producing ABA can be detected by thermal imaging. Such plants are warmer compared to their environment. This is because increased levels of ABA

(a) elevates metabolic rate

(b) raises optimum temperature of photosynthesis

(c) reduces evaporative cooling by inhibiting complete opening of stomata

(d) increases the rate of transpiration, causing drying of plant

31. Few observation made on root and shoot formation of tobacco pith cultures are given below.

Causes	Root formation	Shoot formation
1.	✓	
2.		✓
3.	✓	✓

What do the above case (1-3) tell us about the effect of changing ratio of cytokinin and auxin?

(a) 1-High $\dfrac{\text{Cytokinin}}{\text{Auxin}}$ ratio, 2-$\dfrac{\text{Low cytokinin}}{\text{Auxin}}$ ratio, 3-Intermediate $\dfrac{\text{Cytokinin}}{\text{Auxin}}$ ratio

(b) 1-Low $\dfrac{\text{Cytokinin}}{\text{Auxin}}$ ratio, 2-Intermediate $\dfrac{\text{Cytokinin}}{\text{Auxin}}$ ratio, 3-High $\dfrac{\text{Cytokinin}}{\text{Auxin}}$ ratio

(c) 1-Low $\dfrac{\text{Cytokinin}}{\text{Auxin}}$ ratio, 2-High $\dfrac{\text{Cytokinin}}{\text{Auxin}}$ ratio, 3-Intermediate $\dfrac{\text{Cytokinin}}{\text{Auxin}}$ ratio

(d) 1-Intermediate $\dfrac{\text{Cytokinin}}{\text{Auxin}}$ ratio, 2-High $\dfrac{\text{Cytokinin}}{\text{Auxin}}$ ratio, 3-Low $\dfrac{\text{Cytokinin}}{\text{Auxin}}$ ratio

32. Match the following natural hormones with their site of synthesis and their site of activation.

	Hormones	Synthesis		Activation
1.	Rhizocaline	A. Cotyledons	i.	Stem
2.	Caulocaline	B. Roots	ii.	Root
3.	Phyllocaline	C. Roots	iii.	Leaf

(a) 1-B-ii, 2-C-i, 3-A-iii

(b) 1-C-ii, 2-B-iii, 3-A-i

(c) 1-C-i, 2-A-iii, 3-B-ii

(d) 1-B-iii, 2-A-ii, 3-C-i

Darken your choice with HB Pencil

1.	ⓐ ⓑ ⓒ ⓓ	7.	ⓐ ⓑ ⓒ ⓓ	13.	ⓐ ⓑ ⓒ ⓓ	19.	ⓐ ⓑ ⓒ ⓓ	25.	ⓐ ⓑ ⓒ ⓓ	31.	ⓐ ⓑ ⓒ ⓓ
2.	ⓐ ⓑ ⓒ ⓓ	8.	ⓐ ⓑ ⓒ ⓓ	14.	ⓐ ⓑ ⓒ ⓓ	20.	ⓐ ⓑ ⓒ ⓓ	26.	ⓐ ⓑ ⓒ ⓓ	32.	ⓐ ⓑ ⓒ ⓓ
3.	ⓐ ⓑ ⓒ ⓓ	9.	ⓐ ⓑ ⓒ ⓓ	15.	ⓐ ⓑ ⓒ ⓓ	21.	ⓐ ⓑ ⓒ ⓓ	27.	ⓐ ⓑ ⓒ ⓓ		
4.	ⓐ ⓑ ⓒ ⓓ	10.	ⓐ ⓑ ⓒ ⓓ	16.	ⓐ ⓑ ⓒ ⓓ	22.	ⓐ ⓑ ⓒ ⓓ	28.	ⓐ ⓑ ⓒ ⓓ		
5.	ⓐ ⓑ ⓒ ⓓ	11.	ⓐ ⓑ ⓒ ⓓ	17.	ⓐ ⓑ ⓒ ⓓ	23.	ⓐ ⓑ ⓒ ⓓ	29.	ⓐ ⓑ ⓒ ⓓ		
6.	ⓐ ⓑ ⓒ ⓓ	12.	ⓐ ⓑ ⓒ ⓓ	18.	ⓐ ⓑ ⓒ ⓓ	24.	ⓐ ⓑ ⓒ ⓓ	30.	ⓐ ⓑ ⓒ ⓓ		

Breathing and Exchange of Gases

Chapter 09

MCQs 1 Mark Questions

1. Which of the following is a correct statement about respiration?
   (a) The respiratory system can alter blood pH by changing blood oxygen level
   (b) External respiration in the protists occurs through body wall
   (c) Gills are the gaseous exchange organs in aquatic animals
   (d) Book lungs are the respiratory organs in arthropods

2. Select the correct function of labelled part *A* from the options given below.

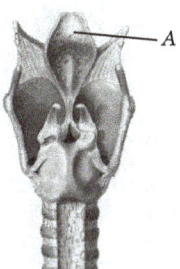

   (a) It helps in the movement of larynx
   (b) During swallowing it closes the glottis to check the entry of food into it
   (c) It provides passage to both air and food
   (d) All of the above

3. Two friends are eating together on a dining table. One of them suddenly starts coughing while swallowing some food. This coughing would have been due to the improper movement of
   (a) tongue
   (b) epiglottis
   (c) diaphragm
   (d) neck

4. The dorsal, ventral, lateral and lower side of thoracic chamber is bounded by
   (a) vertebral column, sternum, ribs, diaphragm
   (b) vertebral column, ribs, sternum, diaphragm
   (c) diaphragm, ribs, sternum, vertebral column
   (d) ribs, diaphragm, sternum, vertebral column

5. Select the incorrectly matched pair regarding cartilages of the larynx.

(a)	Epiglottis	– Leaf-shaped cartilage
(b)	Thyroid cartilage	– Smallest cartilage
(c)	Cricoid cartilage	– Signet ring-like cartilage
(d)	Arytenoid cartilage	– Small and two in number

6. Movement of foul air out of the lungs follows a certain pathway. Choose the correct answer from the options given below regarding the pathway.

   (a) Alveoli → alveolar duct → bronchioles → bronchi → larynx → trachea → pharynx → nasal cavities → outside

   (b) Alveoli → bronchi → larynx → trachea → pharynx → nasal cavities → outside

   (c) Alveoli → alveolar ducts → bronchioles → bronchi → trachea → larynx → glottis → pharynx → internal nares → nasal cavities → external nares → outside

   (d) None of the above

7. Observe the given diagrams *A* and *B*.

   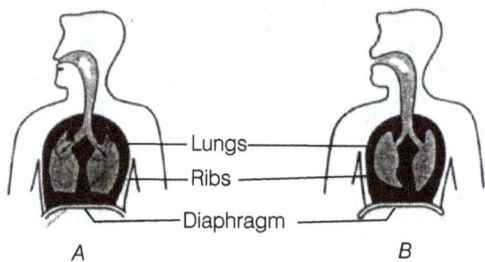

   Identify the correct processes occurring in diagram *A* and *B*, from the options given below.

   (a) *A*-Inspiration, *B*-Expiration

   (b) *A*-Expiration, *B*-Inspiration

   (c) *A*-Quiet breathing, *B*-Forced expiration

   (d) None of the above

8. Which changes occur as a person breathes in deeply?

	Diaphragm muscles	External intercoastal muscles
(a)	Contract	Contract
(b)	Contract	No change
(c)	Relaxe	Contract
(d)	Relaxes	Relax

9. Which of the following factors affect the rate of external respiration?
   I. Partial pressure differences of the gases.
   II. Surface area for gas exchange.
   III. Diffusion distance.
   IV. Solubility and molecular weight of the gases.
   V. Presence of bio-phosphoglycerate (BPG).

   (a) I, II and III   (b) II, IV and V
   (c) I, II, IV and V   (d) I, II, III and IV

10. Which of the following changes occurs in diaphragm and intercostal muscles when expiration of air takes place?

    (a) External intercostal muscles relax and diaphragm contracts

    (b) External intercostal muscles contract and diaphragm relaxes

    (c) External intercostal muscles and diaphragm relax

    (d) External intercostal muscles and diaphragm contract

11. Refer to the diagram given below, what changes occur in the thorax, ribcage and diaphragm?

    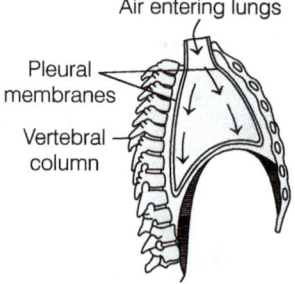

    Choose the correct option.

	Volume of thorax	Ribcage	Diaphragm
(a)	Decreased	Lowered	Relax
(b)	Increased	Lowered	Contract
(c)	Increased	Raised	Contract and lowered
(d)	Same	Raised	Lowered

12. Additional muscles which impact the ability of humans to increase the strength of inspiration and expiration are found in
    (a) chest   (b) diaphragm
    (c) abdomen   (d) lungs

13. Hyperpnea involves active inspiratory and expiratory movements. Which of the following best describes about forced expiration?
    (a) Internal intercostal muscle relaxes to reduce volume of thorax
    (b) Internal intercostal muscle contract to reduce volume of thorax
    (c) Internal intercostal muscle and accessory abdominal muscle contract to reduce the volume of thorax
    (d) None of the above

14. Match the Column I with Column II and choose the correct option from the codes given below.

	Column I		Column II
A.	Inspiratory capacity	1.	ERV+RV
B.	Functional residual capacity	2.	TV+IRV
C.	Vital capacity	3.	IC+FRC
D.	Total lung capacity	4.	IC+ERV

Codes
```
    A  B  C  D
(a) 1  4  3  2
(b) 3  1  2  4
(c) 2  1  4  3
(d) 1  2  3  4
```

15. Whether a child died after birth or died before birth, can be confirmed by measuring
    (a) residual volume of air
    (b) tidal volume
    (c) dead space air
    (d) weight of child

16. The sum of X and Y is equal to functional residual capacity. What is X and Y?

    (a) Residual volume and expiratory reserve volume
    (b) Tidal volume and vital capacity
    (c) Vital capacity and residual volume
    (d) Tidal volume and inspiratory reserve volume

17. Approximate volume of air, a healthy man can inspire or expire per minute is
    (a) 5000 to 6000 mL   (b) 6000 to 7000 mL
    (c) 6000 to 8000 mL   (d) 7000 to 9000 mL

18. Tidal volume and expiratory reserve volume of an athlete is 500 mL and 1000 mL, respectively. What will be his expiratory capacity if the residual volume is 1200 mL?
    (a) 1700 mL   (b) 2200 mL
    (c) 2700 mL   (d) 1500 mL

19. Additional volume of air, a person can inspire and expire by forcible inspiration and expiration, respectively is called
    (a) TV   (b) IRV and ERV
    (c) IC and EC   (d) FRC

20. Pulmonary capacities are the sum of two or more pulmonary volumes. On the basis of above statement which of the following option represents the inspiratory capacity?
    (a) 2400 mL   (b) 6000 mL
    (c) 3500 mL   (d) 4800 mL

21. After forceful inspiration, the amount of air that can be breathed out by maximum forced expiration is equal to
    (a) IRV + ERV + TV + RV
    (b) IRV + RV +ERV
    (c) IRV +TV + ERV
    (d) TV + RV + ERV

22. The partial pressure of oxygen in the alveoli of the lungs is
    (a) equal to that in the blood
    (b) more than that in the blood
    (c) less than that in the blood
    (d) less than that of carbodioxide

23.

Pressure of gases	Systemic veins	Systemic arteries
O_2	40 mm Hg	95 mm Hg
CO_2	A	B

Choose the correct option for A and B to complete the given data.
(a) A– 45 mm Hg; B– 40 mm Hg
(b) A– 45 mm Hg; B– 45 mm Hg
(c) A– 45 mm Hg; B– 50 mm Hg
(d) A– 45 mm Hg; B– 55 mm Hg

24. Partial pressure of O_2 and CO_2 in atmospheric air as compared to that in alveolar air is

	pO_2	pCO_2
(a)	Higher	Lower
(b)	Higher	Higher
(c)	Lower	Lower
(d)	Lower	Higher

25. In lungs, there is definite exchange of ions between RBC and plasma. Removal of CO_2 from blood involves
(a) influx of Cl^- into RBC
(b) efflux of Cl^- from plasma
(c) influx of HCO_3 ion in RBC
(d) efflux of HCO_3 from RBC

26. If under certain conditions, the P_{50} value of haemoglobin rises to 100 mm Hg, a person will die of O_2 deficiency, because the pigment
(a) is not loading enough oxygen in lungs
(b) can load enough oxygen in lungs, but cannot unload it in tissues
(c) can neither load nor unload oxygen
(d) suffers degradation

27. During exercise following changes occur inside the human body.
  I. During exercise, the O_2-dissociation curve is likely to shift to the right.
  II. After exercise, the curve is likely to shift to the left.

III. During exercise, the curve is likely to shift to the left.
IV. After exercise, the curve is likely to shift to the left.

Which of these changes are actually true and relate with the functioning of human body?

	I	II	III	IV
(a)	T	T	T	F
(b)	T	T	F	F
(c)	F	T	T	T
(d)	T	F	T	F

28. The oxygen dissociation curve is a graph that plots the proportion of haemoglobin its oxygen-laden saturated form on the vertical axis against the partial pressure of oxygen on horizontal axis.

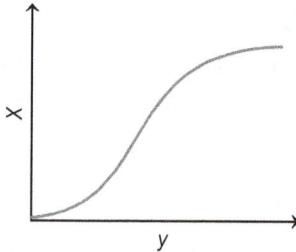

The graph indicates that binding of haemoglobin with oxygen is
(a) competitive   (b) non-competitive
(c) allosteric   (d) irreversible

29. Oxygen saturation curve of haemoglobin is shown in the graph given below.

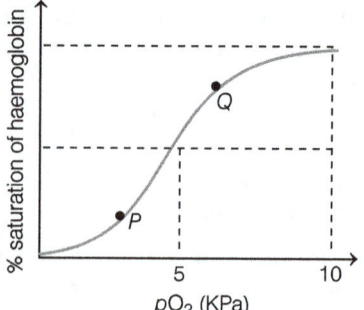

The correct representation of haemoglobin molecule at points P and Q is respectively,

(a) HbO_2 and HbO_4
(b) $HbCO$ and $HbCO_2$
(c) HbO_2 and HbO_8
(d) HbO_4 and HbO_6

30. Choose the combination of conditions in a tissue that would influence the most rapid dissociation of oxyhaemoglobin.

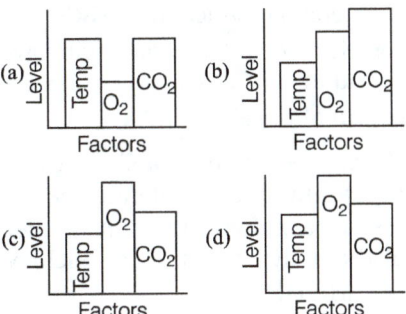

31. Blood carries the CO_2 in three forms. The correct percentages of CO_2 in these forms are

	As carbamino haemoglobin in RBC	As bicarbon-ates	Dissolved form in plasma
(a)	20–25%	70%	7%
(b)	70%	20–25%	7%
(c)	20–25%	7%	70%
(d)	7%	20–25%	70%

32. Which of the following equations is correct?

(a) $KHbO_2 + H^+ \underset{RBC}{\rightleftharpoons} Hb + K + H_2O$

(b) $Hb + O_2 \underset{\text{Dissociation in lungs}}{\overset{\text{Association in tissues}}{\rightleftharpoons}} HbO_2$

(c) $Na^+ + HCO_3^- \underset{\text{Erythrocyte}}{\rightleftharpoons} NaHCO_3$

(d) $HbO_2 \underset{\text{Association in lungs}}{\overset{\text{Dissociation in tissues}}{\rightleftharpoons}} Hb + O_2$

33. $CO_2 + H_2O \overset{A}{\rightleftharpoons} H_2CO_3 \overset{B}{\rightleftharpoons} HCO_3^- + H^+$

Name the enzymes A and B in the above equation.

(a) A–Carbonic anhydrase; B–Carbonic hydratase
(b) A–Carbonic hydratase; B–Carbonic anhydrase
(c) A–Carbonic anhydrase; B–Carbonic anhydrase
(d) A–Carbonic hydratase; B–Carbonic hydratase

34. People who have migrated from the planes to an area adjoining Rohtang pass about six months back

(a) have more RBCs and their haemoglobin has a lower binding affinity to O_2
(b) are not physically fit to play games like football
(c) suffer from altitude sickness with symptoms like nausea, fatigue, etc
(d) have the usual RBC count, but their haemoglobin has very high binding affinity to O_2

35. Which two of the following changes (i-iv) usually tend to occur in plain dwellers when they move to high altitudes (3500 or more)?

(i) Increase in red blood cell size.
(ii) Increase in RBC production.
(iii) Increased breathing rate.
(iv) Increase in thrombocyte count.

(a) (i) and (iv)   (b) (i) and (ii)
(c) (ii) and (iii)   (d) (iii) and (iv)

36. A person sitting at rest experiences a temporary cessation of breathing after forced deep breathing for a few minutes. This is due to

(a) too much CO_2 in the blood
(b) too much O_2 in the blood
(c) very little CO_2 in the blood
(d) Both high O_2 and very little CO_2 in the blood

37. A large proportion of oxygen is left unused in the human blood even after its uptake by the body tissues. This O_2
    (a) raises the pCO_2 of blood to 75 mm of Hg
    (b) is enough to keep oxyhaemoglobin
    (c) helps in releasing more O_2 to the epithelial tissues
    (d) acts as a reserve during muscular exercises

38. Read the following statements.
    I. Every 100 mL of deoxygenated blood delivers about 4mL of CO_2 to the alveoli.
    II. 30%-40% of CO_2 is transported to the alveoli as carbaminohaemoglobin.
    III. At respiratory surface CO_2 diffuses from venous blood into alveolar spaces.

    Choose the correct option.
    (a) I and II are correct statements
    (b) Only III is the correct statement
    (c) I and III are correct statements
    (d) All statements are correct

39. When you hold your breathe, which of the following gasesous changes in blood would first lead to the urge to breathe?
    (a) Falling O_2 concentration
    (b) Rising CO_2 concentration
    (c) Falling CO_2 concentration
    (d) Rising CO_2 and falling O_2 concentration

40. A person met with an accident and died instantly without any injury to heart, brain, stomach and kidney which one of the following is a reason for his death?
    (a) Intestine get twisted
    (b) RBCs became coagulated
    (c) Stomach stopped digestion
    (d) Diaphragm got punctured

41. When a man inhales air containing normal concentration of O_2 as well as CO, he suffers from suffocation because
    (a) CO reacts with O_2 reducing its % in air
    (b) Hb combines with CO instead of O_2 and form carboxyhaemoglobin

(c) CO affects diaphragm and intercostal muscles
(d) CO affects the nerves of the lungs

42. A person named Rajan from the sea coast goes to hill, few consequences of this case stated below. Which one of the following is incorrect?
    (a) His breathing rate and heart rate will increase
    (b) If he continues staying, the body will step up production of RBCs
    (c) His blood after 15 days will have less number of RBCs and less haemoglobin
    (d) All of the above

43. Human beings have a significant ability to maintain and moderate the respiratory rhythm to suit the demands of the body tissues. This is achieved by
    (a) arterial system
    (b) systemic vein system
    (c) neural system
    (d) cardiac system

44. Which of the following statement is incorrect?
    (a) DRG generate the basic respiratory rhythm, control external intercostal muscle and diaphragm
    (b) A chemosensitive area located close to the respiratory centre in medulla is highly sensitive to change in pH of blood
    (c) Pneumotaxic centre is located in the lower pons, it transmits inhibitory impulse to respiratory centre
    (d) VRG functions only during forced breathing

45. Name the pulmonary disease in which alveolar surface area involved in gas exchange is drastically reduced due to damage in alveolar walls.
    (a) Asthma
    (b) Pleurisy
    (c) Emphysema
    (d) Pneumonia

46. Tobacco smoking contains carbon monoxide which

(a) reduces the oxygen carrying capacity of blood

(b) causes gastric ulcer

(c) raises blood pressure

(d) weakens pumping of heart

47. Given in the box are certain disorders of human body?

> Asthma, Cyanosis, Blue body syndrome, Atelectasis, Jaundice, Anthracosis, Epilepsy, Asbestosis

How many disorders from the above are associated with human respiratory system?

(a) 3   (b) 4

(c) 5   (d) 6

48. Due to increasing air-borne allergens and pollutants, many people in urban areas are suffering from respiratory disorder causing wheezing due to

(a) inflammation of bronchi and bronchioles

(b) proliferation of fibrous tissues and damage of alveolar walls

(c) reduction in the secretion of surfactants by pneumocytes

(d) benign growth on mucous lining of nasal cavity

49. A person faces cancer major side effect in which fluid builds up in the space between the lung and chest wall. This condition will be named as

(a) pneumothorax   (b) pleural effusion

(c) pneumonia   (d) None of these

50. Select the incorrectly matched pair.

(a)	Apnea	Absence of breathing
(b)	Hypoxia	Condition of oxygen shortage in the tissue
(c)	Apneusis	Prolonging of respiration during expiration
(d)	Eupnea	Normal breathing

MCQs 2 Marks Questions

51. Match the Column I with Column II and choose the correct option from the codes given below.

	Column I		Column II
A.	Insects	1.	Branchial respiration
B.	Aquatic arthropods	2.	Pulmonary respiration
C.	Terrestrial molluscs	3.	Tracheal tubes

Codes

	A	B	C			A	B	C
(a)	1	2	3		(b)	2	1	3
(c)	3	1	2		(d)	3	2	1

52. The figure shows a diagrammatic view of human respiratory system with labels A, B, C and D. Select the option, which gives correct identification and main function and/or characteristic.

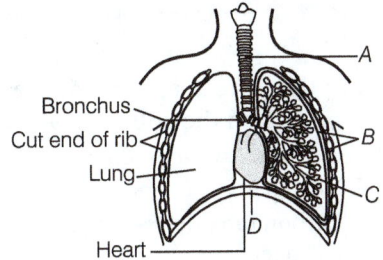

(a) A–Trachea–Long tube supported by complete cartilaginous rings for conducting inspired air

(b) B–Pleural membrane–Surround ribs on both sides to provide cushion against rubbing

(c) C–Alveoli–Thin-walled vascular bag-like structures for exchange of gases

(d) D–Lower end of lungs–Diaphragm pulls it down during inspiration

53. The graph illustrates change in air pressure taking place inside the lungs during complete cycle of breathing. Which position on the graph corresponds to the point at which the diaphragm gets lowered?

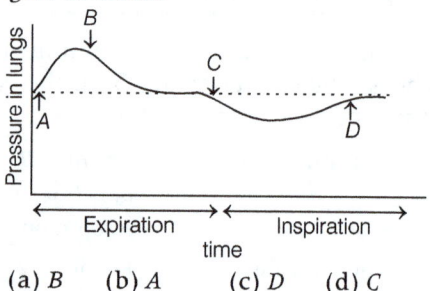

(a) B (b) A (c) D (d) C

54. Observe the graph given below, which indicates the percentage of different gases during breathing process.

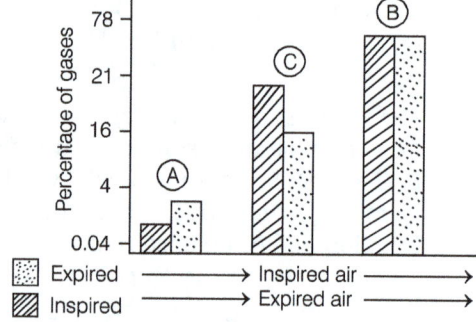

Choose the correct answer with respect to A, B and C from the options given below.

(a) A-Oxygen, B-Carbon dioxide, C-Nitrogen

(b) A-Carbon dioxide, B-Oxygen, C-Nitrogen

(c) A-Carbon dioxide, B-Nitrogen, C-Oxygen

(d) A-Nitrogen, B-Oxygen, C-Carbon dioxide

55. 'X' is a region on the medial surface of the lungs where structures such as bronchus, blood vessels, nerves and lymphatic vessels enter or exit the lung.

All the structures passing through X are referred to as the 'Y'. Identify the correct answer from the options given below.

(a) X-Hilum, Y-Oblique fissure

(b) X-Root of the lung, Y-Hilum

(c) X-Hilum, Y-Root of the lung

(d) X-Oblique fissure, Y-Root of the lung

56. Given below are two statements.

Statement I Type I alveolar cells are thin squamous epithelial cells that form 90% of the alveolar surface.

Statement II Type II alveolar cells also called surfactant, are abundant in number and scattered among squamous cell.

Choose the correct answer from the options given below.

(a) Both statement I and statement II are correct

(b) Both statement I and statement II are incorrect

(c) Statement I is correct, but statement II is incorrect

(d) Statement I is incorrect, but statement II is correct

57. **Assertion** (A) The wall of alveoli is highly vascularised in amphibians.

Reason (R) Alveoli are the primary sites for the exchange of gases.

Choose the correct answer from the options given below

(a) Both A and R are true and R is the correct explanation of A

(b) Both A and R are true, but R is not the correct explanation of A

(c) A is true, but R is false

(d) A is false, but R is true

Direction (Q.Nos. 58-60) consider the spirogram shown and answer the questions given below.

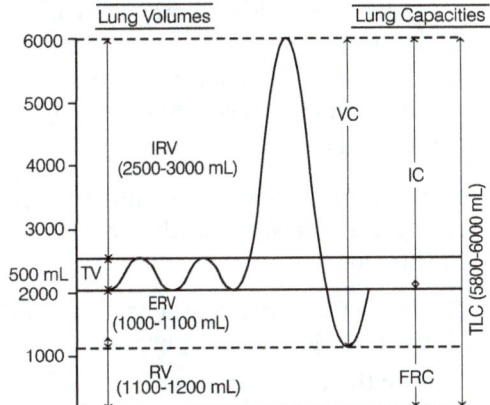

58. Observe the above given diagram and choose the correct answer with respect to the vital capacity from the options given below.

(a) 4000

(b) 4700

(c) 4500

(d) 3500

59. If total lung capacity (TLC) is 5800 mL, inspiratory reserve volume (IRV) is 2850 mL, expiratory reserve volume (ERV) is 1000 mL and tidal volume (TV) is 500 mL then what will be the value of residual volume (RV)?

(a) 2550 mL

(b) 1100 mL

(c) 1500 mL

(d) 1450 mL

60. Choose the correct statement from the options given below with respect to respiratory volume.

(a) The volume of air which normally passes in and out of the lungs during each cycle of quiet breathing is residual volume

(b) The volume of air that remains in the lung after most forceful expiration is tidal volume

(c) The amount of air we can expire over and above the residual volume by most forceful expiration

(d) The extra volume of air that can be inhaled in lungs during deepest possible inspiration is inspiratory reserve volume

61. Identify A to E in the given diagram and choose the correct option accordingly.

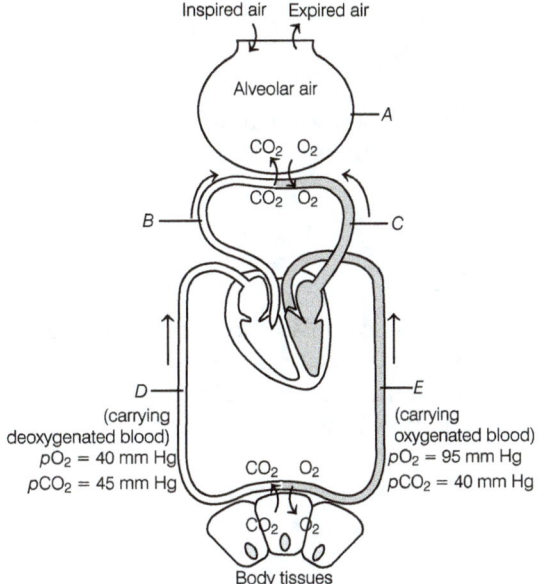

(a) A–Alveolus, B–Pulmonary artery, C–Pulmonary vein, D–Systemic vein, E–Systemic arteries

(b) A–Alveolus, B–Pulmonary vein, C–Pulmonary artery, D–Systemic vein, E–Systemic arteries

(c) A–Alveolus, B–Pulmonary vein, C–Pulmonary artery, D–Systemic arteries, E–Systemic vein

(d) A–Alveolus, B–Pulmonary vein, C–Pulmonary artery, D–Systemic arteries, E–Portal vein

62. Given below a venn diagram, depicting three processes diffusion, evaporation and muscle action.

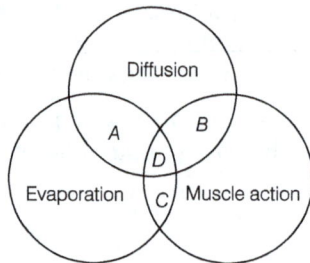

Which processes help the excretion of CO_2 from the lungs?

(a) A

(b) B

(c) C

(d) D

63. Ram has complaint of chest pain. He visited the doctor and was diagnosed with punctured pleural cavity. It is the condition in which

(a) blood, air or both cannot enter the pleural cavity

(b) air or blood rushes into the space in order to equalise the pressure with atmosphere

(c) the fluid is disrupted and two membranes can adhere to each other

(d) All of the above

64. **Assertion** (A) The partial pressure of nitrogen is the same in the alveoli as it is in the blood.

Reason (R) Nitrogen as a gas is used up by the body for various purpose.

Choose the correct answer from the options given below.

(a) Both A and R are true and R is the correct explanation of A

(b) Both A and R are true, but R is not the correct explanation of A

(c) A is true, but R is false

(d) A is false, but R is true

Darken your choice with HB Pencil

1. ⓐ ⓑ ⓒ ⓓ	12. ⓐ ⓑ ⓒ ⓓ	23. ⓐ ⓑ ⓒ ⓓ	34. ⓐ ⓑ ⓒ ⓓ	45. ⓐ ⓑ ⓒ ⓓ	56. ⓐ ⓑ ⓒ ⓓ
2. ⓐ ⓑ ⓒ ⓓ	13. ⓐ ⓑ ⓒ ⓓ	24. ⓐ ⓑ ⓒ ⓓ	35. ⓐ ⓑ ⓒ ⓓ	46. ⓐ ⓑ ⓒ ⓓ	57. ⓐ ⓑ ⓒ ⓓ
3. ⓐ ⓑ ⓒ ⓓ	14. ⓐ ⓑ ⓒ ⓓ	25. ⓐ ⓑ ⓒ ⓓ	36. ⓐ ⓑ ⓒ ⓓ	47. ⓐ ⓑ ⓒ ⓓ	58. ⓐ ⓑ ⓒ ⓓ
4. ⓐ ⓑ ⓒ ⓓ	15. ⓐ ⓑ ⓒ ⓓ	26. ⓐ ⓑ ⓒ ⓓ	37. ⓐ ⓑ ⓒ ⓓ	48. ⓐ ⓑ ⓒ ⓓ	59. ⓐ ⓑ ⓒ ⓓ
5. ⓐ ⓑ ⓒ ⓓ	16. ⓐ ⓑ ⓒ ⓓ	27. ⓐ ⓑ ⓒ ⓓ	38. ⓐ ⓑ ⓒ ⓓ	49. ⓐ ⓑ ⓒ ⓓ	60. ⓐ ⓑ ⓒ ⓓ
6. ⓐ ⓑ ⓒ ⓓ	17. ⓐ ⓑ ⓒ ⓓ	28. ⓐ ⓑ ⓒ ⓓ	39. ⓐ ⓑ ⓒ ⓓ	50. ⓐ ⓑ ⓒ ⓓ	61. ⓐ ⓑ ⓒ ⓓ
7. ⓐ ⓑ ⓒ ⓓ	18. ⓐ ⓑ ⓒ ⓓ	29. ⓐ ⓑ ⓒ ⓓ	40. ⓐ ⓑ ⓒ ⓓ	51. ⓐ ⓑ ⓒ ⓓ	62. ⓐ ⓑ ⓒ ⓓ
8. ⓐ ⓑ ⓒ ⓓ	19. ⓐ ⓑ ⓒ ⓓ	30. ⓐ ⓑ ⓒ ⓓ	41. ⓐ ⓑ ⓒ ⓓ	52. ⓐ ⓑ ⓒ ⓓ	63. ⓐ ⓑ ⓒ ⓓ
9. ⓐ ⓑ ⓒ ⓓ	20. ⓐ ⓑ ⓒ ⓓ	31. ⓐ ⓑ ⓒ ⓓ	42. ⓐ ⓑ ⓒ ⓓ	53. ⓐ ⓑ ⓒ ⓓ	64. ⓐ ⓑ ⓒ ⓓ
10. ⓐ ⓑ ⓒ ⓓ	21. ⓐ ⓑ ⓒ ⓓ	32. ⓐ ⓑ ⓒ ⓓ	43. ⓐ ⓑ ⓒ ⓓ	54. ⓐ ⓑ ⓒ ⓓ	
11. ⓐ ⓑ ⓒ ⓓ	22. ⓐ ⓑ ⓒ ⓓ	33. ⓐ ⓑ ⓒ ⓓ	44. ⓐ ⓑ ⓒ ⓓ	55. ⓐ ⓑ ⓒ ⓓ	

Chapter
10

Body Fluids and Circulation

MCQs 1 Mark Questions

1. Which of the following correctly identifies where the carbon dioxide and oxygen are transported in blood?

	CO_2	O_2
(a)	Plasma	Plasma
(b)	Plasma	RBC
(c)	RBC	Plasma
(d)	RBC	RBC

2. In which of the following cell, the surface area to volume ratio of the cell most important to its function?
   (a) Red blood cell   (b) Bone marrow cell
   (c) Platelet   (d) White blood cell

3. Select the option which incorrectly describes a structural feature and how it helps in the functional aspects of RBCs.
   (a) Elastic membrane permits squeezing through narrow lumen of capillaries
   (b) Thin membrane for efficient diffusion
   (c) Haemoglobin pigment for oxygen transport
   (d) Enucleated for reduced cell division

4. Blood cells that increase in number during allergic condition (asthma) and worm infection respectively are

	Asthma	Worm infection
(a)	neutrophils	lymphocytes
(b)	lymphocytes	basophils
(c)	eosinophils	eosinophils
(d)	basophils	lymphocytes

5. Which of these characteristics is not related to platelets?
   (a) These are tiny fragment of cytoplasm
   (b) Enucleated with granular cytoplasm
   (c) Formation in bone marrow from certain large cells
   (d) Biconcave shape for increased surface area to volume ratio

6. The phenomenon shown below is
   (i) known as X
   (ii) performed by Y cells

   Select the option which correctly identifies X and Y.
   (a) Diapedesis, Platelets
   (b) Pinocytosis, RBCs
   (c) Phagocytosis, Leucocytes
   (d) Exocytosis, WBCs

7. A certain road accident patient with unknown blood group needs immediate blood transfusion. His one doctor friend at once offers his blood. What was the blood group of the donor?

(a) Blood group B   (b) Blood group AB

(c) Blood group O   (d) Blood group A

8. Which of the given option is correct about blood groups and donor compatibility?

(a) 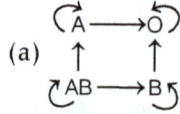   (b)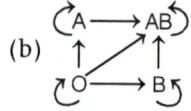

(c) 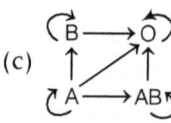   (d)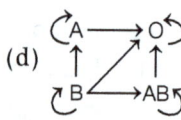

9. During blood transfusion, if blood groups of recipient and donor are not correctly matched, it will result in clumping of RBCs due to

(a) antigen- antibody reaction

(b) antigen - antigen reaction

(c) antibody - antibody reaction

(d) None of the above

10. What will happen if a Rh^- person's blood is exposed to the Rh^+ person?

(a) Antigen formation takes place

(b) Negative and positive Rh antigen cancel out each other

(c) Nothing will happen

(d) Antibody will be produced

11. Donor X and recipient Y belong to same blood group. Transfusion has led to RBCs agglutination because

(a) X is Rh^+, Y is Rh^-

(b) X is Rh^-, Y is Rh^+

(c) Both are Rh^+

(d) Both are Rh^-

12. A fat soluble component X is required for the activation of Y, directly involved with blood clotting.

Which order of description is correct with respect to this molecule?

(a) X is vitamin-E , Y is fibrin

(b) X is vitamin-K, Y is prothrombin

(c) X is factor VIII, Y is prothrombin

(d) X is thromboplastin, Y is vitamin-K

13. Heparin, a natural anticoagulant that inhibits the working of following clotting factors.

(a) II, IX

(b) X, XI and XIII

(c) II, IX, X, and XII

(d) I, III, IX and XI

14. A new chemical P has been discovered that can catalyse the conversion of Fibrin $\rightarrow$ Fibrinogen.

Which of the following would become the most useful application of this chemical?

(a) Treatment of haemophilia

(b) Removal of embolisms

(c) Repair of damaged blood vessels

(d) Supervised vasodilation

15. When compared to blood, lymph is different with respect to

(a) plasma without proteins

(b) more WBCs

(c) more RBCS

(d) less WBCs

16. Given below is a list of some organisms, which one have open circulatory system.

1. *Ascidia*	2. Cockroach	3. Earthworm
4. Prawn	5. Silver fish	6. Snail 7. *Squid*

(a) 1, 2, 6, 7

(b) 3, 4, 5, 7

(c) 1, 3, 4, 6

(d) 2, 4, 5, 6

17. The heart of fish is 2 chambered with 1 auricle and 1 ventricle. The type of blood flows through the heart of fish is venous blood, whereas in case of frog heart is 3 chambered and the type of blood flow is
    (a) mixed blood
    (b) auricle has venous blood and ventricles has atrial blood
    (c) venous blood
    (d) atrial blood

18. Identify the correct option with respect to description of circulatory system in four different animals.

Animal groups	Chambers in heart	Types of circulatory circuit	Sites of blood oxygenation
(a) Pigeon	4	Double, complete	Lungs
(c) Scorpion	3	Incomplete, double	Skin / lungs / gills
(c) Cockroach	2	Single	Gills
(d) Fish	1	Single	Skin/gills

19.

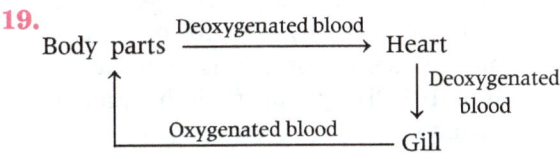

    Given diagram depicts the circulation in
    (a) fishes   (b) mammals
    (c) reptiles   (d) amphibians

20. In reptiles and amphibians, there is no clear cut separation of oxygenated and deoxygenated blood because they have
    (a) one atrium
    (b) one ventricle
    (c) incomplete double circulation
    (d) Both (b) and (c)

21. Which of the following structures is present in 4-chambered heart but absent in 3-chambered heart?

(a) Aorta
(b) Bicuspid valve
(c) Median-septum
(d) Tricuspid valve

22. Among the labelled vessels (A, B, C and D) which carries blood from the head, neck, arms and chest to the heart.

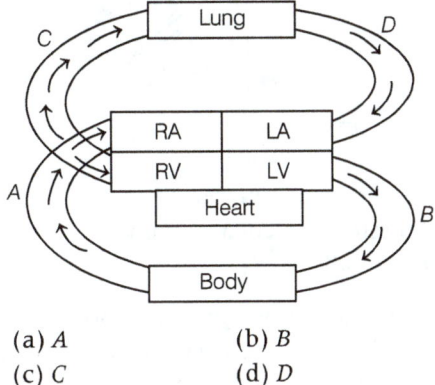

(a) A   (b) B
(c) C   (d) D

23. The lower left heart chamber called left ventricle generate relatively high pressure can be due to
    (a) thicker wall and strong valves
    (b) denser reticulum of Purkinje fibre
    (c) greater volume of blood received by it
    (d) stepwise pressure difference generated between right and left chambers of heart

24. Heart valves function to
    (a) slow down blood flow as it passes through the heart
    (b) keep blood moving forward through the heart
    (c) mix blood thoroughly as it passes through the heart
    (d) control the amount of blood pumped by the heart

25. Opening of the right ventricle into the pulmonary artery and that of left ventricle into the aorta is provided with
    (a) bicuspid valve   (b) tricuspid valve
    (c) semilunar valve (d) mitral valve

26. In figure given below, *C* is the structure involved in the initiation and transmission of impulses generated in it.

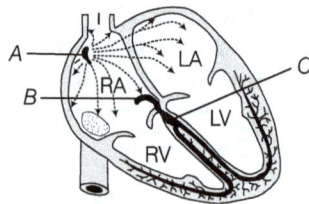

Structure 'C' is
(a) sinoatrial node
(b) atrioventricular node
(c) interventricular septum
(d) bundle of His

27. If due to some injury the chordae tendineae of the tricuspid valve of the human heart is partially non-functional, what will be the immediate effect?
(a) The SA node will become non-functional
(b) Back flow of blood will occur in the left atrium
(c) The flow of blood into the pulmonary artery will be reduced
(d) The flow of blood into aorta reduces

28. All the components of the nodal tissue are autoexcitable. Why does the SA node act as the normal pacemaker ?
(a) SA node has the lowest rate of depolarisation
(b) SA node is the only component to generate the threshold potential
(c) Only SA node can convey the action potential to the other components
(d) SA node has the highest rate of depolarisation

29. What will happen when pacemaker becomes non-functional?

(a) Only the auricle will contract rhythmically
(b) The cardiac muscles will not contract in a coordinated manner rhythmically
(c) Only ventricles will contract rhythmically
(d) Cardiac muscles will contract in a coordinated manner

30. A 70 year old man was admitted to hospital since his heartbeat dropped to 40 beats per minute (a condition called bardycardia). Thus, doctor implanted artificial pacemaker, as his natural pacemaker started to dysfunction. Choose the incorrect statement regarding pacemaker.
(a) SA node is natural pacemaker of heart
(b) The pacemaker electrically stimulates the contractile heart walls
(c) Heart pacemaker is a life saving device when the normal heart rate of 72-80 drops 30-40 due to some disease
(d) SA node acting as natural pacemaker generates lowest number of action potentials in conducting system

31. The cardiac pacemaker in a patient fails to function normally. The doctors find that an artificial pacemaker is to grafted in him. It is likely that it will be grafted out at the site of
(a) AV bundle
(b) AV node
(c) Purkinje system
(d) SA node

32. If the stroke volume of heart increases, but the total volume of blood remains the same, the heart beats per minute will turn out to
(a) decrease in number
(b) be unaffected
(c) increase in number
(d) be erratic

33. The given figure indicates three stages in the cardiac cycle.

  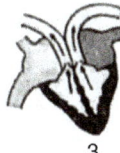

1   2   3

Choose the correct sequence.
(a) 3, 2, 1   (b) 2, 1, 3
(c) 1, 2, 3   (d) 2, 3, 1

34. The cardiac cycle is a defined sequence of alternating contraction and relaxation of atria and ventricles. In this cycle, blood pressure is maximum when
(a) the atria are contracting during systole
(b) the atria are contracting during diastole
(c) the ventricles are contracting during systole
(d) the ventricles are relaxing during diastole

35. The production of 'lub' sound in a heartbeat is due to
(a) opening of AV valve
(b) closing of AV valve
(c) opening of semilunar valves of aorta and pulmonary artery
(d) closing of semilunar valves of aorta and pulmonary artery

36. An event taking place in the heart during the cardiac cycle is shown below.

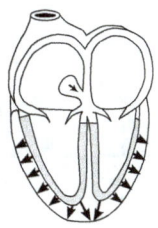

In the corresponding ECG, this event is depicted by
(a) P-wave
(b) QRS wave
(c) T-wave
(d) It cannot be studied in the ECG

37. What prevents the atria and ventricles from contracting at the same time?
(a) It takes time for epinephrine to diffuse from atria to ventricles to trigger contraction
(b) The electrical signal generated in right atrium is delayed at AV node before passing to the ventricles
(c) The Na^+ channels responsible for initiating ventricular contraction are inactivated
(d) Calcium ions released from endoplasmic reticulum are responsible for this

38. To obtain a standard ECG, the patient is connected to the machine with three electrical leads. These three electrical lead are connected to
(a) chest and each wrist
(b) each ankle and wrist
(c) thigh and chest ankle
(d) each wrist and left ankle

39. Given below is the diagrammatic representation of standard Electrocardiogram (ECG). Identify the figure which is the correct one.

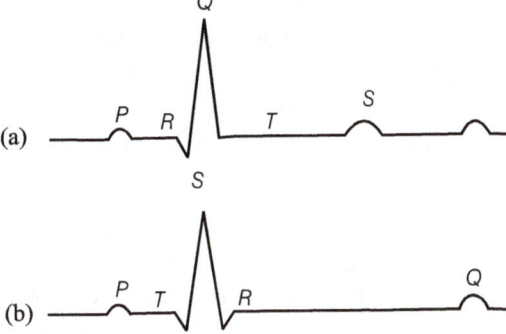

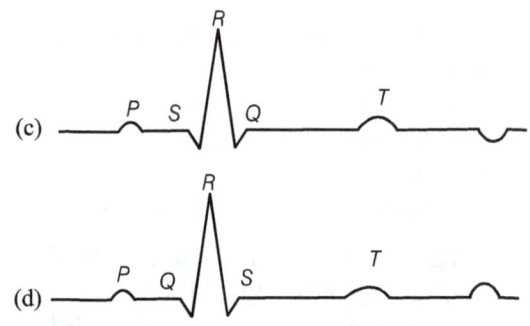

(c)

(d)

40. A heart specialist while listening to a patient's heart discovered the sound 'siss-dupp, siss-dupp' instead of the normal lub-dupp heart sound. The doctor said to patient, I think it's something to worry because there may be a problem in
    (a) the aorta
    (b) your pacemaker
    (c) one of coronary arteries
    (d) the atrioventricular valve

41. Given below is the schematic diagram of heart.

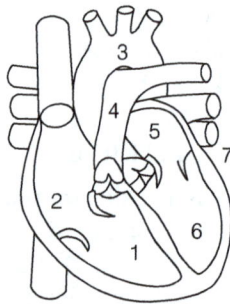

Which of the following option is the correct sequence of blood flow?
(a) 2-1-4- Systemic -3-6-5-7 lungs
(b) 3-6-5-7 Systemic -4-1-2- lungs
(c) 4- lungs -7-5-6-3 systemic-2-1
(d) 6-4- lungs -3- systemic-2-1-5-7

42. Blood vessels include veins, artries and capillaries. These vessels circulate blood throughout our body and help deliver oxygen to vital organs and tissues, and also remove waste products. Which one of following graphs best describe the blood pressure change when blood moves from aorta to capillaries.

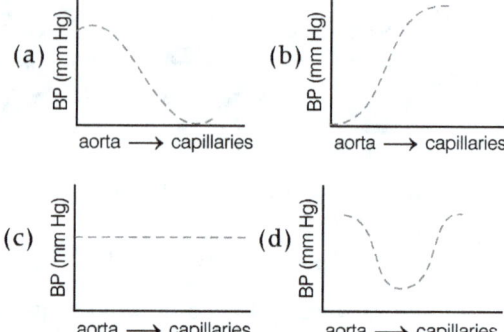

43. If the diameter of a blood vessel, is reduced to half, the rate of blood flow through it decrease to .... of the original rate.
    (a) 1/2   (b) 1/4
    (c) 1/6   (d) 1/8

44. The blood flows more slowly in the arterioles in comparison to that in arteries because the arterioles
    (a) must provide an opportunity for exchange with interstitial fluid
    (b) contains channels to venules that often remain closed
    (c) collectively have a larger cross-sectional area
    (d) Both (a) and (c)

45. The graph shown below highlight the relative thickness of the main layers of walls in blood vessels.

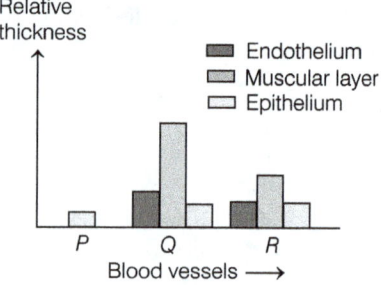

Blood vessels *P, Q* and *R* could be respectively

(a) arteries, veins, capillaries

(b) venules, capillaries, arterioles

(c) capillaries, arteries, veins

(d) arterioles, venules, capillaries

46. Identify the component of the venous system formed by the fusion of two brachiocephalic veins.

(a) Superior vena cava

(b) Inferior vena cava

(c) Ascending aorta

(d) Descending aorta

47. The inferior vena cava is formed by the union of

(a) two brachiocephalic veins

(b) two common iliac veins

(c) a brachiocephalic and iliac veins

(d) carotid artery and iliac vein

48. Identify *A, B* and *C* in the given diagram.

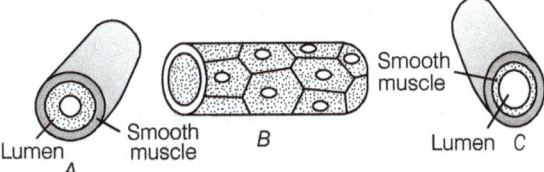

(a) *A*–Artery, *B*–Capillary, *C*–Vein

(b) *A*–Artery, *B*–Vein, *C*–Capillary

(c) *A*–Vein, *B*–Artery, *C*–Capillary

(d) *A*–Capillary, *B*–Artery, *C*–Vein

49. Pulmonary circulation is

(a) Left auricle $\xrightarrow[\text{blood}]{\text{Oxygenated}}$ Lungs $\xrightarrow[\text{blood}]{\text{Deoxygenated}}$ Right ventricle

(b) Left auricle $\xrightarrow[\text{blood}]{\text{Deoxygenated}}$ Lungs $\xrightarrow[\text{blood}]{\text{Oxygenated}}$ Right ventricle

(c) Right ventricle $\xrightarrow[\text{blood}]{\text{Deoxygenated}}$ Lungs $\xrightarrow[\text{blood}]{\text{Oxygenated}}$ Left auricle

(d) Right ventricle $\xrightarrow[\text{blood}]{\text{Oxygenated}}$ Lungs $\xrightarrow[\text{blood}]{\text{Deoxygenated}}$ Left auricle

50. What will be the effect of cutting the sympathetic nerve fibres to the heart?

(a) Decreased heartbeats

(b) Decreased length of diastolic phase

(c) Decreased length of systolic phase

(d) Decreased stroke volume

51. Which statement is true for hepatic portal vein?

(a) It is an artery carries blood to liver

(b) It is hepatic vein transports blood from liver

(c) It is the vein carries blood from major digestive organs to liver

(d) It connects liver to the gut

52. Which of the following statement best defines a portal system?

(a) The arteries subdivide into large number of branches of capillaries and again join with another artery

(b) A system of blood supply between heart and liver

(c) A system of veins which begins and ends with a bed of capillaries

(d) Part of the lymphatic circulatory system where blood from organ is forwarded to open sinus through a network of capillaries

53. 'At rest, the blood flow to body organs varies'. From the statements given below identify the one which are in favour of above observation.

(a) In cool weather, at rest, blood supply to skin is greater

(b) At rest, blood flow to liver will be greater than the heart

(c) Both are correct

(d) Both are incorrect

54. The amount of blood flow to skeletal muscles get greatly enhanced during exercise. This redirection of blood into muscles is achieved due to

(a) contraction of muscles in arterial wall

(b) opening of valves in arteries

(c) relaxation of muscles in wall of arterioles

(d) opening of valves in veins

55. Epinephrine is both neurotransmitter and a hormone. Administration of a local anaesthetic with epinephrine will most likely produce which of the following cardiovascular effect?

(a) Increased heart rate

(b) Decreased heart rate

(c) Increased diastolic blood pressure

(d) Decreased systolic blood pressure

56. Neural centre in medulla oblongata can moderate the cardiac function through

(a) ANS (Autonomic Nervous System)

(b) sympathetic nervous system

(c) parasympathetic nervous system

(d) somatic nervous system

57. In mammals, the parasympathetic nervous system regulates the heartbeat by transmitting impulses through the vagus nerve. To achieve this, the vagus nerve will connect to the heart at which site and what will be its effect on the heart rate? Select the correct option.

	Sites in heart where vagus is connected	Effects on heart rate
(a)	AVN	Decrease
(b)	SAN	Decrease
(c)	AVN	Increase
(d)	SAN	Increase

58. A specialised nodal tissue embedded in the lower corner of the right atrium, close to atrio-ventricular septum, delays the spreading of impulses to heart apex for about 0.1 sec. The delay allows

(a) blood to enter in aorta

(b) the ventricles to empty completely

(c) blood to enter pulmonary arteries

(d) the atria to empty completely

59. Bicuspid valve guards the passage of blood between the chambers on left side of the heart. What is going to happen if this valve becomes leaky due to certain medical condition?

(a) A heart attack

(b) Reduced blood pressure in aorta

(c) Irregularities in heart beats

(d) Blood leaving aorta would be less oxygenated

60. The figure below shows a section of coronary artery of 52 year old man.

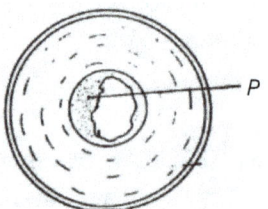

P represents the condition where deposition of fatty acids take place in the lumen and along the muscular wall of an artery.

Which of the following represents the possible effect of *P* on this individual's health?

(a) Low blood cholesterol level

(b) Increased risk of heart attack

(c) Increased blood pressure in the blood pumping arteries to body parts

(d) No blood clotting

61. The main symptom of congestive heart failure is

(a) hypertension

(b) impared heart valve

(c) congestion in lungs

(d) blockage in pulmonary artery

62. A patient brought to a hospital with myocardial infarction is normally immediately given

(a) penicillin   (b) streptokinase

(c) cyclosporin-A   (d) statins

63. In human beings, the blood pressure is 120/80/40, where 120 represents systolic pressure, 80 is diastolic and 40 is the pulse pressure. If in a patient, the pressure picture comes out to be 140/110/30, it suggests that there is
(a) an increase in resistance from arteries
(b) a decrease in resistance from arteries
(c) an increase in resistance from veins
(d) a decrease in resistance from veins

64. Various cardiovascular disorders, body parts affected and their major causes are listed below. Select the correct match.

Column I	Column II		Column III
(a) Coronary heart disease	(i) Arteries	I.	Narrowing of arteries
(b) Arteriosclerosis	(ii) Heart muscles	II.	Slowing or stopping of contractions in.
(c) Coronary thrombosis	(iii) Arteries	III.	Blood clot in arteries
(d) Hypertension	(iv) Veins	IV.	Reduced blood transport to body parts

MCQs 2 Marks Questions

65. Identify the names in box which can be associated with descriptions (P-S).

P. Most numerous circulating leucocytes.

Q. Circulating cells responsible for plugging leaks in vessel systems.

R. Plasma without clotting factors.

S. Fluid circulating in cockroach.

> 1. Thrombocytes, 2. Serum 3. Blood
> 4. Neutrophils 5. Haemolymph 6. Lymph

Select the correct option.

	P	Q	R	S			P	Q	R	S
(a)	1	2	3	4		(b)	4	1	2	5
(c)	2	4	6	3		(d)	6	3	1	4

66. When a blood sample is spun in a high speed centrifuge, it separates into 2 layers, described below.

1. Upper layer is pale coloured.

2. Lower layer is dark coloured.

The components given below will be segregated into which categories.

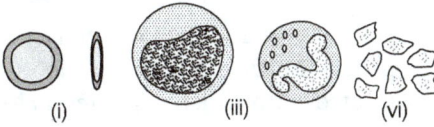

(i)   (iii)   (vi)

(ii) Inorganic salts   (iv) Water   (v) Proteins

	1	**2**
(a)	i, ii and iii	iv, v and vi
(b)	ii, iv and iv	i, iii and v
(c)	ii, iii and vi	i, iv and v
(d)	ii, iv and v	i, iii and vi

Direction (Q. Nos. 67-68) Read the passage given below and answer the questions that are based on it.

The blood cells constitute the formed elements (40-45%) of blood.
Mainly three types of cellular elements are present in blood, i.e. erythrocytes, leucocytes and thrombocytes. These cells help to the blood in performing all of its major functions like nutrient exchange, transport, homeostasis, etc.

67. Observe the Venn diagram given below.

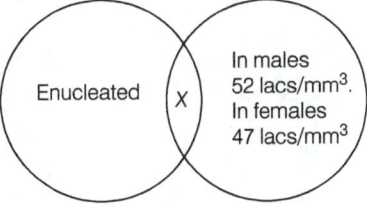

Given below are some functions which may/may not be performed by X.

(i) Transport of O_2 and nutrients.

(ii) Develops hypersensitivity to allergens.

(iii) Coagulation.

(iv) Antibody production.

How many of these are functions of X?

(a) 2   (b) 1

(c) 4   (d) 3

68. Select the option which correctly identifies the figures (I-V) of blood cells associated with functions listed below.

(i) Phagocytic.

(ii) Blood clotting.

(iii) Allergic reactions.

(iv) Secretion of histamine and serotonin.

  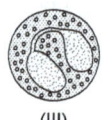  

(I)   (II)   (III)   (IV)   (V)

Codes

(a) (i)–I, (ii)–II, (iii)–III, (iv)–IV, V

(b) (i)–IV, (ii)–III, (iii)–II, V, (iv)–I

(c) (i)–II, IV, (ii)–V, (iii)–III, (iv)–I

(d) (i)–III, (ii)–IV, V, (iii)–I, (iv)–II

69. Depending on the nature of antigens on RBCs, blood groups were named as shown in table below.

Phenotypes (Their percentage in human population)	Genotypes	Antigens on RBC membrane
A(40%)	$I^A I^A$ or $I^A I^O$	A
B(10%)	$I^B I^B$ or $I^B I^O$	B
AB(4%)	$I^A I^B$	A and B antigen
O(46%)	$I^O I^O$	No

For a patient severely bleeding, the nurse 'says not to worry' even though blood is in short supply.

Select a reason from the options below.

(a) Patient is AB blood type

(b) Patient is O blood type

(c) Lot of donors are present at the time

(d) Patient is B blood type

70. Agglutination is a clumping reaction, occurring when RBCs carrying an antigen gets exposed to their corresponding antibodies.

Agglutination reactions for three blood samples P, Q and R are depicted below.

What type of antibodies will be found in the plasma of a person Q and R?

(a) A, AB   (b) O, AB

(c) B, AB   (d) AB, O

71. Assertion (A) The blood does not clot inside the body.

Reason (R) Blood naturally contain heparin.

Choose the correct answer from the options given below.

(a) Both A and R are true and R is the correct explanation of A

(b) Both A and R are true, but R is not the correct explanation of A

(c) A is true, but R is false

(d) A is false, but R is true

72. Read the statements given below.

Erythroblastosis foetalis occurs when,

I. Mother is Rh negative and child is Rh positive.

II. Mother and child are Rh positive, but father is Rh negative.

III. Mother is Rh positive, but child is Rh negative.

Select the correct option.

	I	II	III
(a)	✗	✓	✓
(b)	✓	✓	✗
(c)	✗	✗	✓
(d)	✓	✗	✗

73. Structure aspects of circulation in animals *A-C* are described below.

Characteristics	*A*	*B*	*C*
Heart's activity	Neurogenic and pulsatile	Neurogenic	Myogenic
Blood vessels	✓	✗	✓
Respiratory pigment in circulation	Intracellular	Extra cellular	Intra cellular

Choose the appropriate category of animals to which *A, B* and *C* can belong from the box and select the correct option.

1. Fish 2. Amphibians 3. Arthropoda
4. Annelids 5. Reptiles 6. Echinoderms

	A	*B*	*C*
(a)	4	3	2
(b)	3	2	6
(c)	1	5	6
(d)	2	1	4

74. Events in a heartbeat are tabulated below.

	Diastole	Atrial systole	Ventricular systole
Muscles	Atria and ventricle relax	Both atria contract Both ventricles relax	Both ventricles relax
Blood flow	Into ventricles	Into ventricles	Into pulmonary vein
Bicuspid and tricuspid valves	P	Q	R
Atrial valves	S	T	U

To identify the condition of valves, use the terms,

(i) opened

(ii) closed

for each phase of diastole/systole and select the correct option.

(a) (i)- S, T, U, (ii)-P, Q, R

(b) (i)-P, T, R, (ii)-S, Q, U

(c) (i)-Q, R, T, (ii)-P, S, U

(d) (i)-P, Q, R, (ii)-S, T, U

75. If a molecule of CO_2 released into the blood in the food of a human foetus is exhaled through the mouth of the mother, it will not travel through the

(a) left venticle of mother

(b) left venticle of foetus

(c) right autrium of mother

(d) right atrium of foetus

76. Consider the following graph representing the heart activity in heart cycle. *X*, *Y* and *Z* are some points marked in the graph.

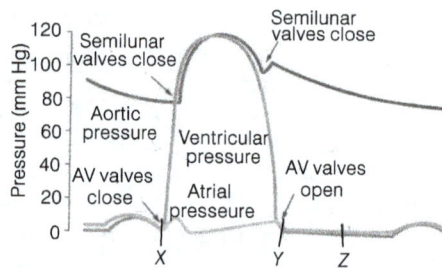

At which of the above labellings (*X*, *Y* and *Z*) are lub and dub sounds observed?

	Iub	Dub
(a)	Y	Z
(b)	Z	X
(c)	Y	X
(d)	X	Y

77. Read the statement given below.

(i) At what point '*P*' does the bicuspid valves open up during the cardiac cycle?

(ii) This opening provides passage for blood from point *Q-R*.

The correct option for *P, Q, R* respectively is

	P	*Q*	*R*
(a)	Atrial systole	Ventricle	Atrium
(b)	Atrial diastole	Ventricle	Atrium
(c)	Ventricular diastole	Atrium	Ventricle
(d)	Atrial systole	Atrium	Ventricle

78. Refer to the information given below related to ECG.

(i) In an ECG, P wave represents atrial contraction.

(ii) QRS wave represents ventricular contraction.

(iii) T-wave represents ventricular relaxation.

If a blockage appears in the region lying between AV node and atrioventricular bundle, what changes will we observe in an ECG report?

(a) The number of QRS waves will be more than P

(b) The number of P waves will be increase

(c) P-R internal would become smaller

(d) QRS intervals would become longer

79. Some people are born with structural defects in/of the heart or its associated blood vessels. Such defects are identified as congenital heart diseases. In the figure of heart shown below, the dotted circles indicate the areas that can get affected by congenital diseases.

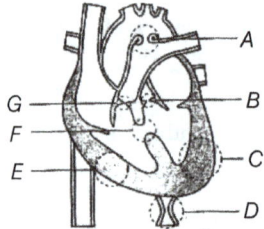

A description of structural defects associated with 2 types of congenital diseases is given below. Match the dotted areas (*A-G*) with diseases and select the correct option.

I. Patent ductus arteriosus - failure in closure of an opening between pulmonary artery and the aorta after birth.

II. Ventricular septal-defect - a hole in the septum between the ventricles.

Codes

(a) I (*A*), II-(*F*)   (b) I (*B*), II-(*F*)

(c) I (*C*), II-(*E*)   (d) I (*D*), II-(*A*)

80. A condition of cardiovascular system wherein,
    (i) The heart is not pumping blood effectively to meet the O_2 needs of body.
    (ii) Arteries are atherosclerotic.
    (iii) Cessation of blood supply to heart.
    (iv) Heart may suddenly stop working.
    (v) Hypercholesterolemia.

    These conditions are indicative of
    (a) arteriosclerosis
    (b) congestive heart failure
    (c) myocardial infarction
    (d) hypertension

81. What would happen if ventricles are unable to receive atrial impulse?
    I. Ventricular escape.
    II. Irregularity in heart rhythm.
    III. Arteriosclerosis.
    (a) I and III
    (b) II and III
    (c) I and II
    (d) Only I

Darken your choice with HB Pencil

1. ⓐⓑⓒⓓ	15. ⓐⓑⓒⓓ	29. ⓐⓑⓒⓓ	43. ⓐⓑⓒⓓ	57. ⓐⓑⓒⓓ	71. ⓐⓑⓒⓓ
2. ⓐⓑⓒⓓ	16. ⓐⓑⓒⓓ	30. ⓐⓑⓒⓓ	44. ⓐⓑⓒⓓ	58. ⓐⓑⓒⓓ	72. ⓐⓑⓒⓓ
3. ⓐⓑⓒⓓ	17. ⓐⓑⓒⓓ	31. ⓐⓑⓒⓓ	45. ⓐⓑⓒⓓ	59. ⓐⓑⓒⓓ	73. ⓐⓑⓒⓓ
4. ⓐⓑⓒⓓ	18. ⓐⓑⓒⓓ	32. ⓐⓑⓒⓓ	46. ⓐⓑⓒⓓ	60. ⓐⓑⓒⓓ	74. ⓐⓑⓒⓓ
5. ⓐⓑⓒⓓ	19. ⓐⓑⓒⓓ	33. ⓐⓑⓒⓓ	47. ⓐⓑⓒⓓ	61. ⓐⓑⓒⓓ	75. ⓐⓑⓒⓓ
6. ⓐⓑⓒⓓ	20. ⓐⓑⓒⓓ	34. ⓐⓑⓒⓓ	48. ⓐⓑⓒⓓ	62. ⓐⓑⓒⓓ	76. ⓐⓑⓒⓓ
7. ⓐⓑⓒⓓ	21. ⓐⓑⓒⓓ	35. ⓐⓑⓒⓓ	49. ⓐⓑⓒⓓ	63. ⓐⓑⓒⓓ	77. ⓐⓑⓒⓓ
8. ⓐⓑⓒⓓ	22. ⓐⓑⓒⓓ	36. ⓐⓑⓒⓓ	50. ⓐⓑⓒⓓ	64. ⓐⓑⓒⓓ	78. ⓐⓑⓒⓓ
9. ⓐⓑⓒⓓ	23. ⓐⓑⓒⓓ	37. ⓐⓑⓒⓓ	51. ⓐⓑⓒⓓ	65. ⓐⓑⓒⓓ	79. ⓐⓑⓒⓓ
10. ⓐⓑⓒⓓ	24. ⓐⓑⓒⓓ	38. ⓐⓑⓒⓓ	52. ⓐⓑⓒⓓ	66. ⓐⓑⓒⓓ	80. ⓐⓑⓒⓓ
11. ⓐⓑⓒⓓ	25. ⓐⓑⓒⓓ	39. ⓐⓑⓒⓓ	53. ⓐⓑⓒⓓ	67. ⓐⓑⓒⓓ	81. ⓐⓑⓒⓓ
12. ⓐⓑⓒⓓ	26. ⓐⓑⓒⓓ	40. ⓐⓑⓒⓓ	54. ⓐⓑⓒⓓ	68. ⓐⓑⓒⓓ	
13. ⓐⓑⓒⓓ	27. ⓐⓑⓒⓓ	41. ⓐⓑⓒⓓ	55. ⓐⓑⓒⓓ	69. ⓐⓑⓒⓓ	
14. ⓐⓑⓒⓓ	28. ⓐⓑⓒⓓ	42. ⓐⓑⓒⓓ	56. ⓐⓑⓒⓓ	70. ⓐⓑⓒⓓ	

Chapter
11

Excretory Products and Their Elimination

MCQs 1 Mark Questions

1. The process of osmoregulation maintains a constant osmotic pressure in fluids of organisms. It is helpful to
   (a) control the concentration of water and salt in the body
   (b) retain excess salt and water
   (c) maintain the properties of cell membrane
   (d) prevents the excess flow of water

2. Listed below are few characteristics of substance. Which of the following characteristics is shared by urea, uric acid and ammonia?
   i. They are nitrogenous waste.
   ii. They are equally toxic.
   iii. They are produced in the kidneys.
   iv. They all need very large amount of water for excretion.
   (a) i and ii   (b) Only i
   (c) Only iv   (d) i, ii and iii

3. Which of the following option best describes ureotelic product?

	Toxicity	Solubility in water	Habitat of animals
(a)	High	Moderate	Aquatic
(b)	Moderate	Moderate	Aquatic and land
(c)	Low	High	Aquatic and land
(d)	Low	Moderate	Aquatic

4. Uric acid is the nitrogenous waste excreted by birds, insects and many reptiles. What is the advantage and disadvantage of excreting uric acid?
   (a) Save energy; highly toxic
   (b) Less toxic; waste a lot of water
   (c) Save water; costs energy
   (d) Soluble in water, cost energy

5. Some animals perform dual excretion. Like for example *A* and *B* live in water they are normally *C* but they become *D* when they lie immobile in moist air or mud during summer.

Complete the above paragraph with the correct option.

	A	B	C	D
(a)	Lung fish	African toad	Ammonotelic	Ureotelic
(b)	Earthworm	Lung fish	Ureotelic	Ammonotelic
(c)	African toad	Crocodiles	Ammonotelic	Ureotelic
(d)	Earthworm	Crocodiles	Ureotelic	Ammonotelic

6. Freshwater fish produces enormous quantity of dilute urine. Whereas marine bony fish produces very little urine. What will happen when freshwater fish is kept in salt water?
   (a) They will lose water from their bodies due to the hypertonic environment
   (b) They will have excess water in their bodies due to hypotonic environment
   (c) They will lose water from their bodies due to hypotonic environment
   (d) They will have excess water in their bodies due to hypertonic environment

7. Most aquatic animals excrete ammonia, while land animals excrete urea or uric acid. What can be the most possible reason for this?
   (a) Ammonia is very toxic and it takes a lot of water to dilute it
   (b) Land animals can get the energy needed to make urea or uric acid
   (c) Land animals cannot get enough energy to make ammonia
   (d) They have different diet

8. Fishes like sharks, rays and skates are oldest surviving jawed vertebrates. How do they protect themselves in hypertonic sea water?
   (a) By accumulating excess of uric acid in their bodies
   (b) By accumulating excess of urea in their bodies
   (c) By secreting excess of urea in the sea water
   (d) By accumulating excess of ammonia in their body

9. Almost all the aquatic animals excrete ammonia as nitrogenous waste product. Which of the following statement is not in an agreement with this situation?
   (a) Ammonia is released from the body in gaseous state
   (b) Ammonia is easily soluble in water
   (c) Ammonia gets converted into a less toxic form called urea
   (d) Ammonia is highly toxic and needs to be eliminated

10. Which of the following structures help in the removal of nitrogenous waste as well as concerned with osmoregulation?
   (a) Protonephridia
   (b) Nephridia
   (c) Malpighian tubules
   (d) All of the above

11. Few difference about kidney of frog and kidney of man are listed below. Choose the incorrect option.
   (a) Human have metanephric type of kidney and frog have mesonephric type of kidney
   (b) Human have Malpighian corpuscle while frog lacks it

(c) Bidder's canal is absent in human kidney while it is present in frog's kidney

(d) Henle's loop is present in human kidney while it is absent in frog's kidney

12. The graph given below depicts the concentration of enzymes involved in urea synthesis in a developing tadpole. It indicates a transition from

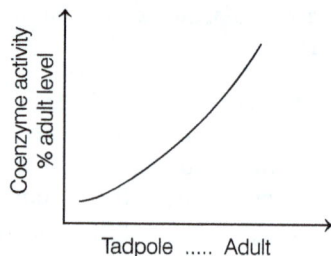

(a) ammonotelism to uricotelism

(b) ammonotelism to ureotelism

(c) uricotelism to ureotelism

(d) ureotelism to uricotelism

13. Most reptiles excrete uric acid, but X excrete ammonia in addition to uric acid.

Y excrete both urea and ammonia.

	X	Y
(a)	Aquatic turtles	Crocodiles
(b)	Crocodiles	Aquatic turtles
(c)	Birds	Fish
(d)	Crocodiles	Birds

14. Part of the kidney through which the ureter, blood vessels and nerves enter into it is

(a) renal cortex

(b) renal medulla

(c) hilum

(d) urethra

15. The diagram given below shows the structures of kidney.

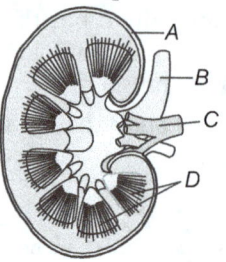

Which labelled part is the site of secretion of a hormone named erythropoietin?

(a) A (b) D (c) C (d) B

16. The diagram given below shows the LS of human kidney.

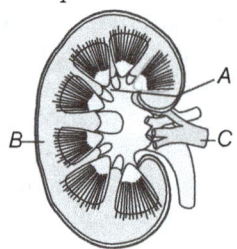

Choose the correct option for the parts A to C.

	A	**B**	**C**
(a)	Renal vein	Cortex	Calyx
(b)	Cortex	Renal vein	Calyx
(c)	Calyx	Cortex	Renal vein
(d)	Cortex	Calyx	Renal vein

17. The diagram given below shows LS of Malpighian corpuscle. Choose the correct option for the parts A-C.

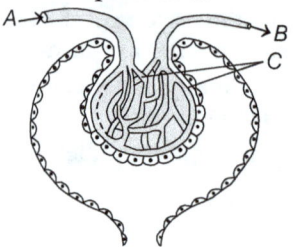

	A	*B*	*C*
(a)	Efferent arteriole	Afferent arteriole	Glomerulus
(b)	Glomerular capsule	Afferent arteriole	Efferent arteriole
(c)	Glomerulus	Efferent arteriole	Afferent arteriole
(d)	Afferent arteriole	Efferent arteriole	Glomerulus

18. The structures from which the collecting duct receives the filtrate and the structure into which it pours the filtrates, respectively are
    (a) PCT and urinary bladder
    (b) DCT and renal pelvis
    (c) Henle's loop and Bowman's capsule
    (d) Glomerulus and efferent arteriole

19. The majority of nephrons in which , the loop of Henle found is too short and extend very little into the medulla are
    (a) cortical nephrons
    (b) medullary nephrons
    (c) juxta-medullary nephrons
    (d) peritubular nephrons

20. Which of the following sections of the mammalian nephron is incorrectly paired with its function?
    (a) Descending limb of loop of Henle- diffusion of urea out of filtrate
    (b) Ascending limb of loop of Henle - diffusion and pumping of NaCl out of filtrate
    (c) Proximal tubule - secretion of ammonia and H^+ ions and transport of glucose and amino acids
    (d) Bowman's capsule and glomerulus - filtration of blood

21. A large quantity of fluid is filtered everyday by the nephrons in the kidneys. But only about 1% of it is excreted as urine and the remaining 99% is not excreted. What happens to the rest 99% of the fluid?
    (a) It is lost as sweat
    (b) It is stored in the urinary bladder
    (c) It gets collected in the renal pelvis
    (d) It gets reabsorbed in the blood

22. Proximal convoluted tubule (PCT) is made up of .... It has microvilli so it is known as brush border epithelium. It is most important site for selective reabsorption.
    (a) squamous epithelium
    (b) unspecialised squamous epithelium
    (c) simple cuboidal epithelium
    (d) endothelium

23. The correct order of processes that occur in urine formation.
    (a) Glomerular filtration → Tubular secretion → Reabsorption
    (b) Tubular secretion → Glomerular filtration → Reabsorption
    (c) Glomerular filtration → Reabsorption → Tubular secretion
    (d) Tubular secretion → Reabsorption → Glomerular filtration

24. The following figure given below shows the parts of nephron.

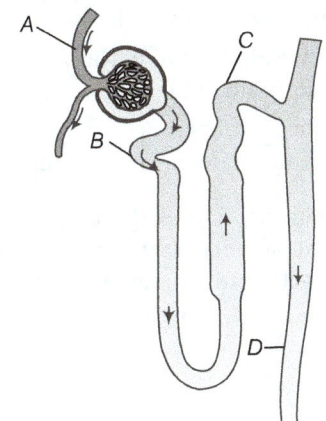

Which among the following part has highest concentration of protein?

(a) B   (b) C   (c) A   (d) D

25. The diagram given below shows the reabsorption and secretion at different parts of nephron. Which of the following parts of nephron is least permeable to water?

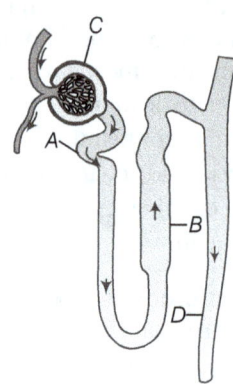

(a) A   (b) B   (c) C   (d) D

26. During the process of urine formation, a high osmotic pressure is maintained in the uriniferous tubule. Which of the following process aids to it?

(a) Active absorption of Cl^-, followed by absorption of Na^+

(b) Active secretion of Na^+ into efferent arteriole followed by absorption of Cl^- into efferent arteriole

(c) Active absorption of Na^+, followed by absorption of Cl^-

(d) Active secretion of Cl^- and absorption of Na^+ into efferent renal arteriole

27. The reabsorption of the maximum amount of electrolytes and water (70-80 per cent) from the glomerular filtrate takes place in which part of the nephron?

(a) Ascending limb of loop of Henle
(b) Descending limb of loop of Henle
(c) Distal convoluted tubule
(d) Proximal convoluted tubule

28. Choose the correct option for the reabsorption in descending and ascending limbs of Henle's loop.

	Descending limb	Ascending limb
(a)	Permeable to water	Active and passive transport of electrolytes
(b)	Impermeable to water	Permeable to water
(c)	Permeable to electrolyte	Impermeable to electrolytes
(d)	Active and passive transport of electrolytes	Impermeable to water

29. How much percentage of the filtrate is reabsorbed in the renal tubules if volume of filtrate formed per day is 180 L and urine released is 1.5 L?

(a) 5%   (b) 25%
(c) 90%   (d) 99%

30. Concerning water reabsorption by the proximal tubule

(a) main driving forces for water absorption in the proximal tubule are solute uptake and oncotic pressure

(b) a significant amount of water uptake in the proximal tubule is dependent on sodium uptake by the Na^+/H^+ antiports present in their luminal membrane.

(c) aquaporin- I are abundantly present in the cellular membranes of proximal tubule cells

(d) All are correct

31. The below given graph shows reabsorption of some of the constituents of glomerular filtrate in different parts of mammalian nephron.

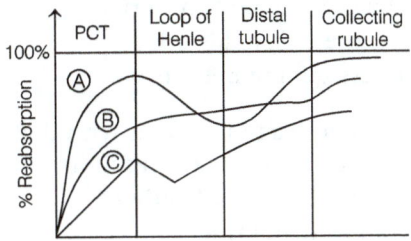

Which of the following option is correct regarding A, B and C?
(a) $A \rightarrow Na^+$, $B \rightarrow$ Water, $C \rightarrow$ Urea
(b) $A \rightarrow$ Urea, $B \rightarrow Na^+$, $C \rightarrow$ Water
(c) $A \rightarrow$ Water, $B \rightarrow Na^+$, $C \rightarrow$ Urea
(d) $A \rightarrow Na^+$, $B \rightarrow$ Urea, $C \rightarrow$ Water

32. Removal of proximal convoluted tubule from the nephron will result in
(a) more diluted urine
(b) more concentrated urine
(c) no change in quality and quantity of urine
(d) no urine formation

33. Choose the correct option for the composition of urine.

	pH	Solution
(a)	2.2 – 3.8	Isotonic
(b)	7.5 – 9.5	Hypotonic
(c)	3.8 – 4.8	Isotonic
(d)	4.8 – 8.2	Hypertonic

34. Choose the correct option for the route of blood flow in kidney.
   I. Renal vein
   II. Renal artery
   III. Peritubular capillary and vasa recta
   IV. Glomerulus
   V. Afferent arteriole

(a) II → V → IV → III → I
(b) II → III → IV → V → I
(c) III → V → IV → I → II
(d) II → III → V → I → IV

35. Counter-current mechanism helps to maintain a concentration gradient. This gradient helps in
(a) easy passage of water from medulla to collecting tubule and thereby concentrating urine
(b) easy passage of water from collecting tubule to interstitial fluid and thereby concentrating urine
(c) easy passage of water from medullary interstitial fluid to collecting tubule and thereby diluting urine
(d) inhibition of passage of water between the collecting tubule and medulla and so isotonic urine is formed

36. The distal tubule and collecting duct is permeable to water. This permeability is under the control of which hormone?
(a) Aldosterone   (b) Vasopressin
(c) Renin   (d) Glucose

37. An increase excretion of rennin would be expected to have what effect on sodium extraction and potassium excretion in urine?
(a) Increase in Na^+ excretion and increase K^+ excretion
(b) Increase in Na^+ excretion and decrease K^+ excretion
(c) Decrease in Na^+ excretion and increase K^+ excretion
(d) Decrease in Na^+ excretion and decrease K^+ excretion

38. Drinking which of the following would lead to the highest rate of ADH secretion and release?
(a) 2 L of distilled water
(b) 2 L of sea water
(c) 2 L of iso-osmotic saline
(d) 2 L of human plasma

39. If for any season, the release of antidiuretic hormone is inhibited, how will this affect the volume and concentration of the urine produced?

	Volume	Concentration
(a)	Large	Hypotonic
(b)	Small	Hypotonic
(c)	Large	Hypertonic
(d)	Small	Hypertonic

40. The release of hormone X inhibits ADH (Antidiuretic hormone) secretions which contributes to the loss of sodium and water. What is X and what is the reason behind the release of this hormone?

(a) Natriuretic hormone, decreased atrial stretch

(b) Steroid hormone, increased renal excretion

(c) Natriuretic hormone, increased atrial stretch

(d) Steroids hormone, decreased renal excretion

41. Which of the following statement about micturition is incorrect?

(a) Nerve impulses are sent to spinal cord when the bladder becomes full

(b) The internal urethral sphincter regulates involuntary control of urine flow

(c) The external urethral sphincter provides voluntary control of urine flow

(d) Both the internal and external urethral sphincter provides involuntary control of urine flow

42. Human skin has two types of glands, i.e. sudoriferous glands and sebaceous glands. Sudoriferous glands secretes an aqueous fluid called A. It consists of B, C, etc.

(a) A = Sebum, B = NaCl, C = Lactic acids

(b) A = Sweat, B = NaCl, C = Urea

(c) A = Sebum, B = Urea, C = Glucose

(d) A = Sweat, B = Fatty acids, C = Glucose

43. A person was not drinking water for several hours. He was feeling dizzy and tired. This person will have

(a) less urea in his urine

(b) more glucose in his urine

(c) more urea in his urine

(d) less sodium in his urine

44. A patient was diagnosed with diabetes mellitus. What following indications or sign were observed earlier?

(a) Glucose in urine

(b) Insulin in urine

(c) Glucose in blood

(d) Insulin in blood

45. A man visits the hospital for a problem of frequent urination. After test, what possible disease showed up and what was the reason behind it?

(a) Diabetes insipidus, low level of antidiuretic hormone

(b) Diabetes insipidus, high level of antidiuretic hormone

(c) Diabetes mellitus, high level of glucose

(d) Diabetes mellitus, low level of glucose

46. A person is highly involved in fitness. His trainer advised him to take protein rich diet. After following the diet, which major substance will be eliminated off in his urine?

(a) Creatinins   (b) Glucose

(c) Urea   (d) Creatine

47. In a lab, urine test was conducted, where the odour of one sample was sweet and fruity. It indicates the presence of which substance and the patient was diagnosed with which disease thereafter?

(a) Acetone, Cystitis

(b) Ammonia, Diabetes

(c) Carbonate, Cystitis

(d) Sugar, Diabetes

48. If due to some reason, the neurohypophysis gets destructed or hampered, what impact will this have on kidney (A) and name the disease (B) caused due to this condition?
    (a) $A \rightarrow$ reduced renal reabsorption, $B \rightarrow$ diabetes insipidus
    (b) $A \rightarrow$ increased renal reabsorption, $B \rightarrow$ diabetes insipidus
    (c) $A \rightarrow$ reduced renal reabsorption, $B \rightarrow$ diabetes mellitus
    (d) $A \rightarrow$ increased renal reabsorption, $B \rightarrow$ diabetes mellitus

49. An X-ray of lower abdomen shows a shadow in the region of ureter suspected to be a ureteric calculus. A possible clinical symptom would be
    (a) Acute renal failure
    (b) Anuria and hematuria
    (c) Motor aphasia
    (d) Chronic acute failure

50. A patient suffering from dehydration comes to the hospital. On examined he told that he is a worker in deep mines. What could be the reason of dehydration?
    (a) more sweating
    (b) less sweating
    (c) no sweating at all
    (d) failure of sweat to evaporate due to excessive humidity

51. Why did the coach of an athlete advise him not to drink lots of water after heavy exercise?
    I. During heavy exercise, excessive sweating occurs and the body loses lot of salts along with water.
    II. Drinking lots of water after sweating causes dilution of tissues fluids and electrolytic in balance in the body.

Codes
(a) Only I   (b) Only II
(c) Both I and II   (d) None

52. Glomerulonephritis is an inflammation of glomerulus. In severe cases the renal functions may fail completely. Which of the following might not be the possible reason for this disease?
    (a) It is due to a type of bacterial infection
    (b) It is due to accumulation of excess water
    (c) It is due to some tubular injury
    (d) It is due to the result of drug reaction

53. A person was having high fever with chills, and also his skin and eyes turned yellow. Later, he visited the doctor and gone for a urine test. What did his test reports say?
    (a) High level of bilirubin
    (b) Low level of bilirubin
    (c) High level of creatinine
    (d) Low level of creatinine

54. A person was suffering with a disease called renal calculi where he suffered from severe pain in the abdomen or pain during urinate on. It is not formed due to the accumulation of which substance?
    (a) Calcium phosphate
    (b) Cholesterol
    (c) Calcium oxalate
    (d) Calcium oxide

55. Certain substances such as calcium oxlate, phosphates and uric acid are formed in kidney which leads to severe pain. What are these called?
    (a) Cystitis
    (b) Gout
    (c) Uremia
    (d) Renal calculi

56. Kidney dialysis machine is a great substitute for those having kidney failure. What is the similarity between human kidney and kidney dialysis machine?

(a) It deaminates amino acids to urea

(b) It removes large molecules from the blood

(c) It takes sugar molecules out of the blood

(d) It regulates the concentration of the blood

57. The process of haemodialysis is given below. Arrange the following steps accordingly.

I. Nitrogenous waste are removed from the blood.

II. Blood is passed through a coiled membrane of tube bathing in dialysis fluid.

III. Blood is drained from artery and anticoagulant (heparin) is added.

IV. Blood is mixed with antiheparin and passed into vein.

(a) I → II → III → IV

(b) III → II → I → IV

(c) I → III → II → IV

(d) IV → I → III → II

58. Diuretic also called as water pill is a drug that elevates the rate of bodily urine excretion. It is used to treat heart failure, liver cirrhosis, hypertension, etc. What is the reason that it is used in heart failure?

(a) It helps kidneys get rid of unneeded water and salt

(b) It helps kidneys to accumulate more water

(c) It helps kidneys to secretes more salts

(d) It helps kidneys to remove drugs from the system

59. A patient with advanced renal failure is waiting for suitable kidney donor for a transplantation operation. His blood urea, nitrogen level is high and he is developing some of the signs of uraemia. What method can you adopt to keep this patient alive until a suitable donor can be found?

(a) Duretics to flush out urea

(b) Haemodialysis

(c) Only transplant can help

(d) Give normal saline to the patient

60. Before a kidney transplantation, donor selection is done by following certain measures. Which of the following is not true?

(a) Donor should be free from hypertension and diabetes

(b) Donor should not have any problem with renal function

(c) Donor should maintain a healthy diet

(d) Donor should have a good emotional stability

MCQs 2 Marks Questions

61. Match the following animals with their main excretory organs.

	Animals		Excretory organs
A.	Protozoa	1.	Flame cells
B.	Platyhelminthes	2.	Malpighian tubules
C.	Insects	3.	Green glands
D.	Crustacea	4.	Contractile vacuole

	A	B	C	D			A	B	C	D
(a)	2	3	1	4		(b)	4	1	2	3
(c)	2	3	1	4		(d)	3	1	4	2

62. Given below are few pairs of animals with their organs of excretion. Find out the incorrect match.

(a) Arachnida   - Coxal glands

(b) *Mollusca*   - Keber's organ

(c) Earthworm   - Malpighian tubules

(d) Aschelminthes - Renette cell

63. Assertion (A) Kidneys maintain the osmotic concentration of the blood.

Reason (R) Kidneys eliminate either hypotonic or hypertonic urine according to the need of the body.

(a) Both A and R are true and R is the correct explanation of A

(b) Both A and R are true, but R is not the correct explanation of A

(c) A is true, but R is false

(d) A is false, but R is true

64. Match the following excretory organs with their excretory products.

	Excretory organ		Excretory products
A.	Kidney	1.	Amino acids
B.	Lungs	2.	Urea
C.	Liver	3.	Iron, magnesium
D.	Intestine	4.	CO_2 and water

Codes

	A	B	C	D
(a)	2	4	1	3
(b)	4	2	3	1
(c)	2	3	1	4
(d)	3	1	4	2

65. The graph slows the effect of liver and kidney in an individual on the amount of urea present in the blood. Two points P and Q on the graph, shows the time when both organs were removed. Which mark show the removal of which organ.

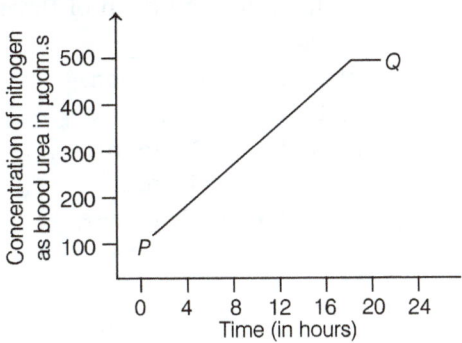

(a) P stands for removal of liver and Q for the removal of kidney

(b) P stands for the removal of kidney and Q for the removal of liver

(c) The given data is incomplete

(d) Any point in between P and Q can be taken as the time of removal of kidney or liver

66. Urea is produced in one organ, filtered from the blood by a second organ and stored inside a third organ before being expelled from the body. Which organs carry out these functions?

	Production	Filtration	Storage
(a)	Kidney	bladder	liver
(b)	Kidney	liver	bladder
(c)	Liver	bladder	kidney
(d)	Liver	kidney	bladder

67. Figure given below shows the human urinary system with structures labelled *A-D*. Select option, which correctly identifies them and gives their characteristics and/of functions?

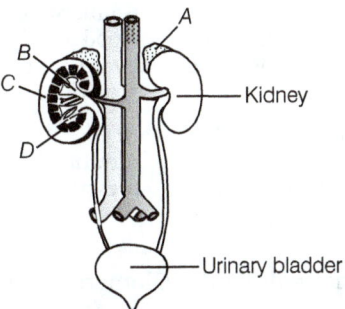

(a) *A*–Adrenal gland–located at the anterior part of kidney, secretes catecholamines, which stimulate glycogen breakdown

(b) *B*–Pelvis-broad funnel–shaped space inner to hilum, directly connected to loop of Henle

(c) *C*–Medulla–inner zone of kidney and contains complete nephrons

(d) *D*–Cortex–outer part of kidney and does not contain any part of nephrons

68. The diagram given below shows the ultrafiltration in Malpighian body. What does *A-D* indicate?

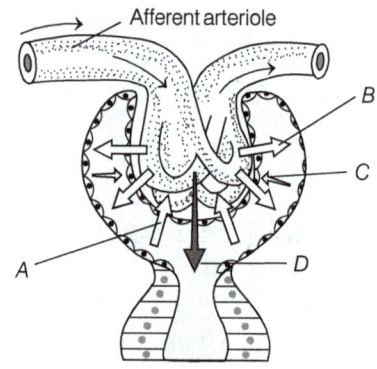

Afferent arteriole

	A	B	C	D
(a)	Capsular hydrostatic pressure	Glomerular blood hydrostatic pressure	Blood colloid osmotic pressure	Net filtration pressure
(b)	Glomerular blood hydrostatic pressure	Blood colloid osmotic pressure	Capsular hydrostatic pressure	Net filtration pressure
(c)	Capsular hydrostatic pressure	Net filtration pressure	Glomerular blood hydrostatic pressure	Blood colloid osmotic pressure
(d)	Glomerular blood hydrostatic pressure	Blood colloid osmotic pressure	Net filtration pressure	Capsular hydrostatic pressure

69. What will be the Glomerular Filtration Pressure (GFP) if Glomerular Hydrostatic Pressure (GHP) is 60 mm Hg, Blood Colloidal Osmotic Pressure (BCOP) is 30 mm Hg and Capsular Hydrostatic Pressure (CHP) is 20 mmHg?
(a) 50 mm Hg   (b) 30 mm Hg
(c) 70 mm Hg   (d) 10 mm Hg

70. Suppose a calculus is blocking a major calyx, What effect might this have on capsular Hydrostatic pressure (CHP) and thus, on Net Filtration Pressure (NFP)?

	CHP	NFP
(a)	↓	↑
(b)	↑	↑
(c)	↓	↓
(d)	↑	↓

71. Identify the correct statements and choose the appropriate option accordingly.
  I. Bowman's capsule is single-layered structure at the end of Henle's loop.
  II. Vasa recta, peritubular capillaries and glomerulus, all have blood.
  III. Glomerular filtration rate is amount of filtrate formed by the kidneys per minute.
  IV. Vasa recta runs parallel to the Henle's loop in the juxta-medullary nephron.

Choose the correct option.
(a) I, II and III   (b) I, II and IV
(c) I, III and IV   (d) II, III and IV

72. Consider the following statements.
  I. Filtration slits are minute spaces between the podocytes of Bowman's capsule.
  II. All the constituents of plasma except proteins can pass through filtration slits into the lumen of Bowman's capsule.

Select the correct option.
(a) I is true, II is false
(b) Both I and II are true
(c) I is false, II is true
(d) Both I and II are false

73. Consider the following statements.

  I. Renin is released by the podocytes of Bowman's capsule.

  II. Renin inhibits glomerular blood flow and thus, decreases GFR.

  III. Glucose, Na^+ ions and amino acids are actively reabsorbed by the nephrons.

  IV. Nephron reabsorbs nitrogenous waste through carrier transport.

  Select the option containing correct statements.

  (a) I, II and IV   (b) II, III and IV

  (c) I, III and IV   (d) I, II and III

74. Which of the following is/are correct statements?

  I. Angiotensin-II, being a powerful vasoconstrictor, increases glomerular pressure and thereby GFR.

  II. Angiotensin-II activates the adrenal cortex to release aldosterone.

  III. Aldosterone promotes reabsorption of Na^+ and water from the DCT leading to an increase in blood pressure and GFR.

  IV. ANF causes vasoconstriction.

  Select correct combination.

  (a) I, II and III   (b) I, II and IV

  (c) I, III and IV   (d) II, III and IV

75. Label the parts A, B, C and D with respect to reabsorption and secretion at different parts of nephron.

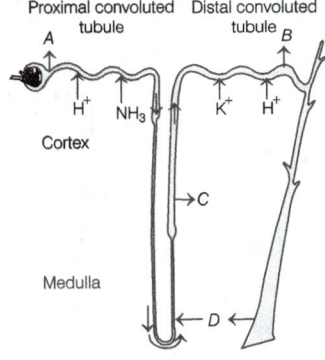

	A	B	C	D
(a)	HCO_3^-	HCO_3^-	NaCl	Urea
(b)	HCO_3^-	NaCl	Urea	NH_3
(c)	NaCl	Urea	NH_3	HCO_3^-
(d)	NH_3	NaCl	HCO_3^-	Urea

76. Read the following statements given below.

  I. It secretes variable amounts of H^+ to help regulate the pH of extracellular fluid.

  II. It control the intracellular fluid volume by regulating blood volume and blood pressure.

  III. It regulates the concentration of major ions such as Na^+, Cl^-, HCO_3^-, etc.

  Which of the following statement is not true about kidney?

  (a) I and II   (b) Only II

  (c) Only I   (d) II and III

77. Select the correct options that shows how various substances are reabsorbed in Proximal Convoluted Tubule (PCT).

	Simple diffusion	Facilitated diffusion
(a)	K^+ and Glucose	Glucose and urea
(b)	Cl^- and urea	Glucose and amino acids
(c)	HCO_3^- and amino acids	Cl^- and HCO_3^-
(d)	Urea and glucose	HCO_3^- and amino acids

78. Match the following processes given in Column I with their related location given in Column II and choose the correct option from the codes given below.

	Column I		Column II
A.	Transport of urine	1.	Malpighian corpuscle
B.	Storage of urine	2.	Henle's loop
C.	Ultrafiltration	3.	Ureter
D.	Concentration of urine	4.	Urinary bladder
		5.	Proximal convoluted tubule

Codes

	A	B	C	D		A	B	C	D
(a)	3	4	1	2	(b)	2	4	1	3
(c)	4	5	2	3	(d)	3	1	2	5

79. **Assertion** (A) The antidiuretic hormone (ADH) increases the water permeability of distal convoluted tubule.

Reason (R) In the absence of antidiuretic hormone, water reabsorption is considerably reduced.

(a) Both A and R are true and R is the correct explanation of A

(b) Both A and R are true, but R is not the correct explanation of A

(c) A is true, but R is false

(d) A is false, but R is true

80. **Assertion** (A) During micturition, urine is prevented from flowing back into the ureter.

Reason (R) Urethral sphincters relax during micturition.

(a) Both A and R are true and R is the correct explanation of A

(b) Both A and R are true, but R is not the correct explanation of A

(c) A is true, but R is false

(d) A is false, but R is true

81. Haemodialysis works on the same principle as the real kidney. _A_ is added to the blood to prevent clotting. It removes waste products from blood especially _B_ and excess of _C_. Complete the passage by correct option for *A* to *C*.

(a) A = Heparin, B = uric acid, C = K^+ and Ca^{2+}

(b) A = Aspirin, B = urea, C = K^+ and Ca^{2+}

(c) A = Heparin, B = urea, C = Na^+ and K^+

(d) A = Aspirin, B = uric acid, C = K^+ and Ca^{2+}

Darken your choice with HB Pencil

1.	(a) (b) (c) (d)	15.	(a) (b) (c) (d)	29.	(a) (b) (c) (d)	43.	(a) (b) (c) (d)	57.	(a) (b) (c) (d)	71.	(a) (b) (c) (d)
2.	(a) (b) (c) (d)	16.	(a) (b) (c) (d)	30.	(a) (b) (c) (d)	44.	(a) (b) (c) (d)	58.	(a) (b) (c) (d)	72.	(a) (b) (c) (d)
3.	(a) (b) (c) (d)	17.	(a) (b) (c) (d)	31.	(a) (b) (c) (d)	45.	(a) (b) (c) (d)	59.	(a) (b) (c) (d)	73.	(a) (b) (c) (d)
4.	(a) (b) (c) (d)	18.	(a) (b) (c) (d)	32.	(a) (b) (c) (d)	46.	(a) (b) (c) (d)	60.	(a) (b) (c) (d)	74.	(a) (b) (c) (d)
5.	(a) (b) (c) (d)	19.	(a) (b) (c) (d)	33.	(a) (b) (c) (d)	47.	(a) (b) (c) (d)	61.	(a) (b) (c) (d)	75.	(a) (b) (c) (d)
6.	(a) (b) (c) (d)	20.	(a) (b) (c) (d)	34.	(a) (b) (c) (d)	48.	(a) (b) (c) (d)	62.	(a) (b) (c) (d)	76.	(a) (b) (c) (d)
7.	(a) (b) (c) (d)	21.	(a) (b) (c) (d)	35.	(a) (b) (c) (d)	49.	(a) (b) (c) (d)	63.	(a) (b) (c) (d)	77.	(a) (b) (c) (d)
8.	(a) (b) (c) (d)	22.	(a) (b) (c) (d)	36.	(a) (b) (c) (d)	50.	(a) (b) (c) (d)	64.	(a) (b) (c) (d)	78.	(a) (b) (c) (d)
9.	(a) (b) (c) (d)	23.	(a) (b) (c) (d)	37.	(a) (b) (c) (d)	51.	(a) (b) (c) (d)	65.	(a) (b) (c) (d)	79.	(a) (b) (c) (d)
10.	(a) (b) (c) (d)	24.	(a) (b) (c) (d)	38.	(a) (b) (c) (d)	52.	(a) (b) (c) (d)	66.	(a) (b) (c) (d)	80.	(a) (b) (c) (d)
11.	(a) (b) (c) (d)	25.	(a) (b) (c) (d)	39.	(a) (b) (c) (d)	53.	(a) (b) (c) (d)	67.	(a) (b) (c) (d)	81.	(a) (b) (c) (d)
12.	(a) (b) (c) (d)	26.	(a) (b) (c) (d)	40.	(a) (b) (c) (d)	54.	(a) (b) (c) (d)	68.	(a) (b) (c) (d)		
13.	(a) (b) (c) (d)	27.	(a) (b) (c) (d)	41.	(a) (b) (c) (d)	55.	(a) (b) (c) (d)	69.	(a) (b) (c) (d)		
14.	(a) (b) (c) (d)	28.	(a) (b) (c) (d)	42.	(a) (b) (c) (d)	56.	(a) (b) (c) (d)	70.	(a) (b) (c) (d)		

Chapter 12

Locomotion and Movement

MCQs 1 Mark Questions

1. Movement is one of the major characteristic of living beings. It can occur at the cellular level, e.g. $\boxed{X}$ and at organ level, e.g. $\boxed{Y}$.

   Choose the correct examples from the options given below.
   (a) X-Movement of muscles, Y-Movement of limbs
   (b) X-Movement of limbs, Y-Cytoplasmic streaming
   (c) X-Cytoplasmic streaming, Y-Movement of limbs
   (d) X-Cytoplasmic streaming, Y-Movement of muscles

2. Select the incorrectly matched pair.
   (a) Amoeboid movement - *Amoeba*
   (b) Flagellar movement - *Euglena*
   (c) Ciliary movement - *Amoeba*
   (d) None of the above

3. Which of the following statement is incorrect about muscles?
   (a) Muscle is a specialised tissue of mesodermal origin
   (b) Phosphorus is the most abundant mineral element in muscles
   (c) Muscles store glycogen
   (d) Visceral muscles are found in posterior part of oesophagus

4. Study the table given below and identify A and B with respect to muscles from the options given below.

A	1. Found in limbs, body wall, tongue and pharynx.
	2. These muscles are under control of animals will.
B	1. Found in posterior part of the oesophagus, stomach, lungs.
	2. These muscles are controlled by autonomic nervous system.

   (a) A-Striated muscle, B- Cardiac muscle
   (b) A-Cardiac muscle, B- Visceral muscle
   (c) A-Striated muscle, B-Visceral muscle
   (d) A-Visceral muscle, B-Striated muscle

5. Identify the correct statement with respect to the given diagram.

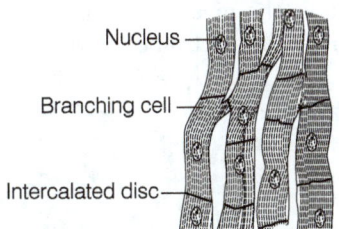

   (a) These muscles are found in the wall of pulmonary veins and superior vena cava
   (b) Sarcolemma is absent
   (c) The muscles are under the control of animal's will
   (d) All of the above

6. Complete the following statement by identifying labels *A* and *B* correctly from the options given below.

Each skeletal muscle in our body is made up of a number of *A* held together by a common collagenous connective tissue layer called *B*.

(a) *A*-Myofibril, *B*-Sarcoplasm

(b) *A*-Muscle bundles, *B*-Fascicles

(c) *A*-Fascia, *B*-Fascicles

(d) *A*-Fascicles, *B*-Fascia

7. Choose the incorrect statement about the skeletal muscles.

(a) Their activities are under the voluntary control of the nervous system

(b) They are known as unstriated muscles

(c) They are primarily involved in locomotory actions and changes of body postures

(d) They are found close to skeletal components of body-like bones

8. A person's medical report revealed that his sarcoplasmic reticulum is damaged. This damage will result in

(a) impaired calcium release

(b) fatigue in isolated skeletal muscle fibres

(c) Both (a) and (b)

(d) None of the above

9. Observe the given diagram of muscle and identify the part labelled *A*.

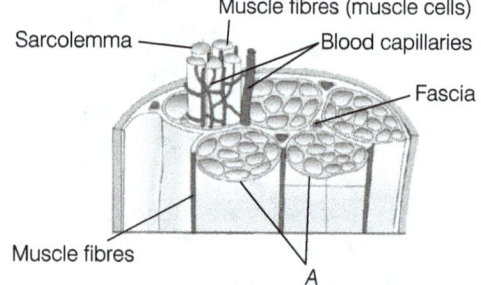

(a) Myofibrils   (b) Fascicles

(c) Sarcolemma   (d) Fascia

10. Which of the following component in the given figure blocks the active sites of actin and prevents myosin from binding to it, when a muscle fibre is relaxed?

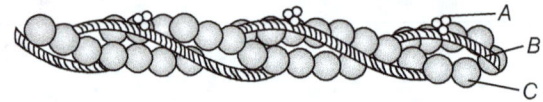

Choose the correct answer from the options given below.

(a) *A*   (b) *B*

(c) *C*   (d) None of these

11. Observe the given stages in cross-bridge formation.

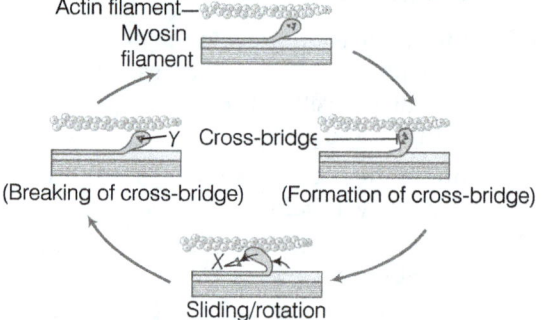

Choose the correct answer with respect to components *X* and *Y* from the options given below.

(a) *X* - ATP, *Y*- ADP

(b) *X* - ADP, *Y*- ATP

(c) *X* - ADP + P, *Y* - ATP

(d) None of the above

12. Which of the following diagram given below is the correct representation of the structure of skeletal muscle?

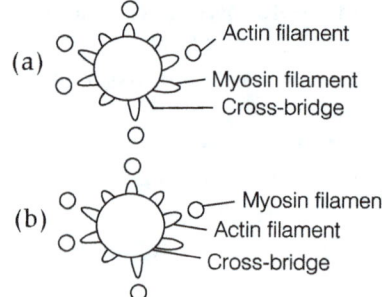

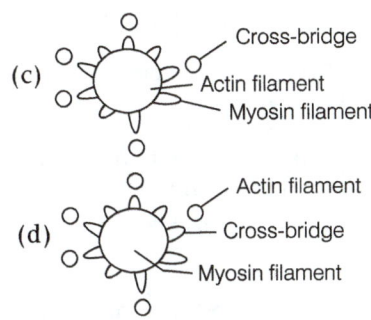

13. Given below is the figure of a sarcomere. Identify the parts labelled as *A* to *D* and select the correct option.

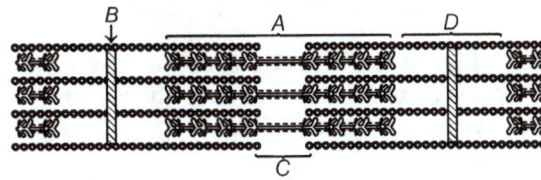

	A	B	C	D
(a)	A-band	Z-line	H-zone	I-band
(b)	A-band	H-line	Z-zone	I-band
(c)	I-band	H-line	Z-zone	A-band
(d)	I-band	Z-line	H-zone	A-band

14. Electron microscopic studies of the sarcomeres have revealed that during muscle contraction

    I. the width of A-band remains constant.

    II. the width of the I-band increases.

    Choose the correct answer from the options given below. Where T denotes true and F denotes false.

    (a) I - T, II - F   (b) I - F, II - T
    (c) I - T, II - T   (d) I - F, II - F

15. Name the ion responsible for unmasking of active sites for myosin for cross-bridge activity during muscle contraction.

    (a) Calcium   (b) Magnesium
    (c) Sodium   (d) Potassium

16. Calcium is important in skeletal muscle contraction because it

    (a) detaches the myosin head from the actin filament

    (b) activates the myosin ATPase by binding to it

    (c) binds to troponin to remove the masking of active sites on actin for myosin

    (d) prevents the formation of bonds between the myosin cross-bridges and the actin filament

17. Identify the state of sarcomere in the diagram and choose the correct option accordingly.

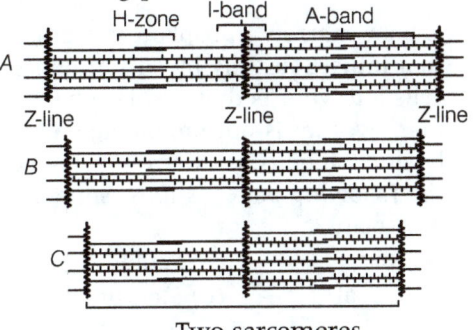

Two sarcomeres

    (a) *A*–Contracting, *B*–Relaxed, *C*–Maximally contracted

    (b) *A*–Relaxed, *B*–Contracting, *C*–Maximally contracted

    (c) *A*–Maximally contracted, *B*–Contracting, *C*–Relaxed

    (d) *A*–Relaxed, *B*–Maximally contracted, *C*–Contracting

18. For how long, contraction of the muscles continues in sliding filament theory?

    (a) Till ATP binds to myosin head

    (b) Till ADP binds to myosin head

    (c) Till Ca^{2+} is present in sarcoplasm

    (d) Till polymerisation of myosin head is going on

19. A scientist conducted an experiment to know the property of bone.

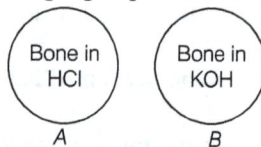

What happens to bone in both the cases *A* and *B* after sometime?

(a) *A* - Dissolved completely, *B* - Break

(b) *A* - Break, *B* - Remain unchanged

(c) *A* - Starts to dissolve, *B*- Remain unchanged

(d) *A*- Remain unchanged, *B* - Dissolved incompletely

20. A bone marrow transplant is a procedure that infuses healthy blood forming stem cells into your body to replace bone marrow, that is not producing enough healthy blood cells. Marrow for which of the following bones is most suitable for transplant?

(a) Ribs   (b) Femur

(c) Carpal   (d) Sternum

21. Find out the correct order of number of bones in the human skull (i.e. cranial bone, facial bone, hyoid bone and middle ear bone, respectively).

(a) 14, 8, 1 and 3   (b) 6, 8, 14 and 1

(c) 14, 8, 3 and 1   (d) 8, 14, 1 and 6

22. Which of the following is made up of a single bone in a mammal?

(a) Carpals   (b) Hyoid

(c) Upper jaw   (d) All of these

23. Which of the following bone is found embedded within a muscle or tendon near joint surfaces, existing as focal areas of ossification and functioning as pulley to alleviate stress on that muscle or tendon?

(a) Patella   (b) Femur

(c) Humerus   (d) Skull

24. Given below is a list of skull bones.

Frontal, Occipital, Sphenoid, Nasals, Zygomatic, Vomer. ,

How many of the above bones take part in the formation of brain box?

(a) 4   (b) 5

(c) 3   (d) 2

25. Phalangeal formula for human hand is

(a) 0, 2, 3,3, 3

(b) 2, 0, 3, 2, 3

(c) 3, 3, 2, 3, 3

(d) 2, 3, 3, 3, 3

26. Identify *A*, *B*, *C* and *D* in the given diagram of human skull, choose the correct option.

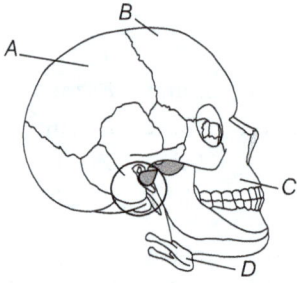

(a) *A*–Hyoid bone, *B*–Maxilla, *C*–Frontal bone, *D*–Parietal bone

(b) *A*–Hyoid bone, *B*–Maxilla, *C*–Parietal bone, *D*–Frontal bone

(c) *A*–Maxilla, *B*–Hyoid bone, *C*–Parietal bone, *D*–Frontal bone

(d) *A*–Parietal bone, *B*–Frontal bone, *C*–Maxilla, *D*–Hyoid bone

27. Which is correct description?

(a) First vertebrae is axis, which articulates with occipital condyles

(b) Parietal bone and temporal bone of skull are jointed by fibrous joint

(c) 9th and 10th pairs of ribs are called floating ribs

(d) Glenoid cavity is depression to which thigh bone articulates

28. Examine the figure of vertebral column (right lateral view) and identify *A*, *B*, *C* and *D*.

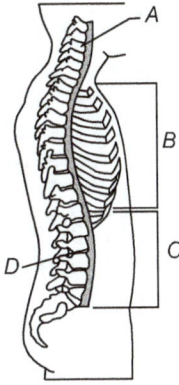

	A	*B*	*C*	*D*
(a)	Lumbar vertebrae	Thoracic vertebrae	Cervical vertebrae	Intervertebral disc
(b)	Cervical vertebrae	Thoracic vertebrae	Lumbar vertebrae	Intervertebral disc
(c)	Thoracic vertebrae	Cervical vertebrae	Intervertebral disc	Lumbar vertebrae
(d)	Cervical vertebrae	Lumbar vertebrae	Thoracic vertebrae	Intervertebral disc

29. The component '*X*' at the extremities of long bones, helps in the elongation of bone.

    What is *X* in the above statement?
    (a) Elastic cartilage
    (b) Sesamoid bone
    (c) Motor end plate
    (d) Epiphyseal plates

30. What is true about acromion process?
    (a) It is the part of pelvic girdle
    (b) It is the small projection of the thigh bone
    (c) It is also linked with coracoid process
    (d) None of the above

31. Out of '*X*' pairs of ribs in human only '*Y*' pairs are true ribs. Select the option that correctly represents values of *X* and *Y* and provides their explanation.

(a) $X = 12, Y = 7$ True ribs are attached dorsally to vertebral column and ventrally to the sternum.

(b) $X = 12, Y = 5$ True ribs are attached dorsally to vertebral column and sternum on the two ends.

(c) $X = 24, Y = 7$ True ribs are dorsally attached to vertebral column, but are free on ventral side.

(d) $X = 24, Y = 12$ True ribs are dorsally attached to vertebral column, but are free on ventral side.

32. The triangular bone scapula is found on
    (a) dorsal part of thorax between 2nd and 7th ribs
    (b) ventral part of thorax between 2nd and 7th ribs
    (c) medial part of thorax between 2nd and 7th ribs
    (d) None of the above

33. Cavity in coxal bone called as acetabulum is formed by the fusion of
    (a) ilium and incus
    (b) ilium and ischium
    (c) incus and ischium
    (d) ilium, ischium and pubis

34. Select the correct function(s) from the options with respect to the diagram given below.

    (a) It provides the surface for muscle attachment
    (b) It helps in the respiratory mechanism
    (c) Both (a) and (b)
    (d) It protects the internal organs in the lumbar region

35. Identify the parts labelled as *A*, *B*, *C* and *D* in the given figure of right pelvic girdle and lower limb bone.

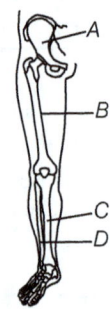

	A	B	C	D
(a)	Coxal bone	Femur	Tibia	Fibula
(b)	Femur	Coxal bone	Tibia	Fibula
(c)	Fibula	Tibia	Coxal bone	Femur
(d)	Femur	Fibula	Tibia	Coxal bone

36. Given below is a list of characters of human skeleton.

    I. Wider, deeper pelvic cavity

    II. More movable coccyx

    III. Rounded obturator foramen

    IV. Narrow sciatic notch

Out of the four, which one shows the characters of female skeleton?

(a) III and IV   (b) II and III

(c) I and II   (d) I and IV

37. A cricket player is fast chasing a ball in the field. Which one of the following groups of bones is directly contributing to this movement?

(a) Malleus, tibia, metatarsals, femur

(b) Pelvis, patella, tarsals, incus

(c) Sternum, femur, tibia, fibula

(d) Tarsals, femur, metatarsals, tibia

38. Select the correct match for the type of the joint with the example in human skeletal system.

	Types of Joint	Examples
(a)	Cartilaginous joint	Between frontal and parietal bones
(b)	Pivot joint	Between 3rd and 4th cervical vertebrae
(c)	Hinge joint	Between humerus and pectoral girdle
(d)	Gliding joint	Between joints of carpals

39. Refer to the following Venn diagram and choose the correct option for *X*.

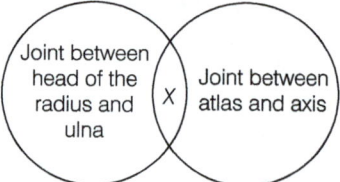

(a) Gliding joint   (b) Eclipsoid joint

(c) Saddle joint   (d) Rotatory joint

40. The diagram given below shows two joints labelled as *X* and *Y*.

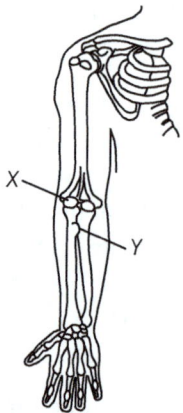

Identify *X* and *Y*.

	X	Y
(a)	Ball and socket	Condyloid
(b)	Hinge	Pivot
(c)	Condyloid	Pivot
(d)	Pivot	Hinge

41 Lack of relaxation between successive stimuli in sustained muscle contraction is known as
(a) fatigue   (b) tetanus
(c) tonus   (d) spasm

MCQs 2 Marks Questions

42. Match the Column I with Column II and choose the correct option from the codes given below.

Column I		Column II
A. Ciliary movement	1.	Phagocytes and macrophages
B. Muscular movement	2.	Movement of sperms towards the ovum
C. Flagellar movement	3.	Respiratory tract
D. Amoeboid movement	4.	Movement of jaw and tongue

Codes
(a) A-2, B-4, C-3, D-1
(b) A-3, B-4, C-2, D-1
(c) A-1, B-2, C-3, D-4
(d) A-4, B-3, C-2, D-1

43. A scientist conducted an experiment to investigate the function of mutated actin protein. He introduced this mutated protein into mice and the changes were noted down.

Apply your knowledge and select the correct set of pair.
I. Abnormal thin filament formation.
II. Normal muscle contraction.
III. Muscles weakness and symptoms of actin- accumulation myopathy.
(a) III and II   (b) I and II
(c) I and III   (d) I, II and III

44. Match the correct bands of myofibril with the respective statements.
I. The dark band of myofibril.
II. The light band of myofibril.

III. At the centre of dark band, comparatively less dark zone is present.

	I	II	III
(a)	I	A	H
(b)	A	I	H
(c)	H	A	I
(d)	I	H	A

45. Study the given table and identify the incorrect set of pair.

	Characters	Red muscle fibre	White muscle fibre
A.	Location	Deeply seated	Relatively superficially
B.	Mitochondria	Few	Many
C.	Sarcoplasmic reticulum	Poorly developed	Well-developed
D.	Glycogen content	Abundant	Low

Codes
(a) C and A   (b) A and D
(c) B and D   (d) B and C

46. Apply your knowledge on the mechanism of muscle contraction and complete the following information given below.

Nerve terminal action potential
↓
A
↓
End plate potential
↓
Muscle fibre action potential
↓
B
↓
Inhibition of tropomyosin-troponin
↓
C
↓
Muscle contraction

Choose the correct option from the table given below.

	A	B	C
(a)	Acetylcholine release	Endoplasmic reticulum calcium release	Motor unit
(b)	Calcium release	Sarcoplasmic acetylcholine release	Actin - myosin interaction
(c)	Acetylcholine release	Sarcoplasmic reticulum calcium release	Actin - myosin interaction
(d)	Acetylcholine release	Sarcoplasmic reticulum calcium release	Actin - myosin inhibition

47. Given below are two statements.

Statement I Isotonic contraction is the type of contraction in which tension remains the same.

Statement II Isometric contraction is the type of contraction in which the length of muscle fibres remains the same.

Choose the correct answer from the options given below.

(a) Both statement I and statement II are correct

(b) Both statement I and statement II are incorrect

(c) Statement I is correct, but statement II is incorrect

(d) Statement I is incorrect, but statement II is correct

48. Select the incorrect statement.

(a) Each half of pectoral girdle consists of a clavicle and scapula

(b) Acromion is a flat, expanded process of ischium containing glenoid cavity

(c) Clavicle is a long slender bone with two curvatures

(d) Force generated by muscles results in locomotion through joints and thus they act as fulcrum

49. Consider the following statements.

I. Human ribs are bicephalic as they possess two articulation surfaces.

II. Floating ribs are not connected to sternum ventrally.

Select the correct option.

(a) I is true, II is false

(b) Both I and II are true

(c) I is false, II is true

(d) Both I and II are false

50. The characteristics and an example of a synovial joint in humans is

	Characteristics	Examples
(a)	Fluid cartilage between two bones, limited movements	Knee joints
(b)	Fluid-filled between two joints provides cushion	Skull bones
(c)	Fluid-filled synovial cavity between two bones	Joint between atlas and axis
(d)	Lymph-filled between two bones, limited movement	Gliding joint between carpals

51. Match the following columns and choose the correct option from the codes given below.

Column I	Column II	Column II
A. Synarthrosis joints	1. Freely movable	(i) Between vertebrae
B. Amphiarthrosis joints	2. Immovable	(ii) Between radio-ulna and carpals
C. Diarthrosis joints	3. Slightly movable	(iii) Between the Ist pair of ribs and the breast bone

Codes

	A	B	C
(a)	2-(iii)	3-(i)	1-(ii)
(b)	2-(i)	3-(ii)	1-(iii)
(c)	3-(iii)	2-(ii)	1-(i)
(d)	1-(ii)	2-(i)	3-(iii)

52. Match the Column I with Column II and choose the correct option from the codes given below.

Column I		Column II
A. Arthritis	1.	Damage to ligaments surrounding the joints
B. Gout	2.	Inflammation of joints
C. Dislocation	3.	Inherited disorder of purine metabolism
D. Myasthenia gravis	4.	Autoimmune neuromuscular disorder

Codes

	A	B	C	D
(a)	1	2	3	4
(b)	2	3	1	4
(c)	1	3	2	4
(d)	4	2	1	3

Direction (Q. Nos. 53 - 55) Given below is the figure showing the signs of a genetic disease X that causes muscle weakness.

53. Identify the disease 'X' from the following options.
(a) Rheumatoid arthritis
(b) Osteoporosis
(c) Muscular dystrophy
(d) Tetany

54. The protein whose production gets affected in the above disease is
(a) actin   (b) myotropin
(c) dystrophin   (d) leucovorin

55. Gene responsible for causing the above disease is found on
(a) Y-chromosome
(b) X-chromosome
(c) autosomal chromosome number-5
(d) autosomal chromosome number-8

56. Which of the following graph represents the pH curve of a muscle cell, which is excessively exercised and then rested?

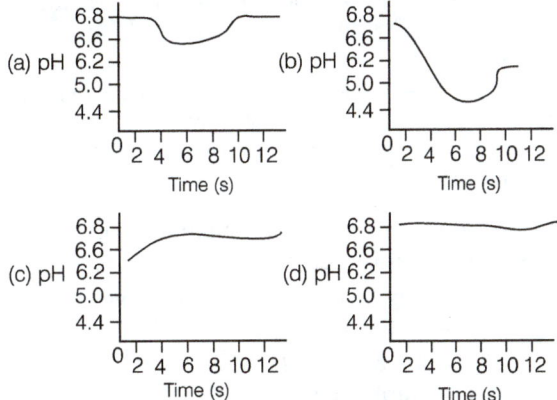

Darken your choice with HB Pencil

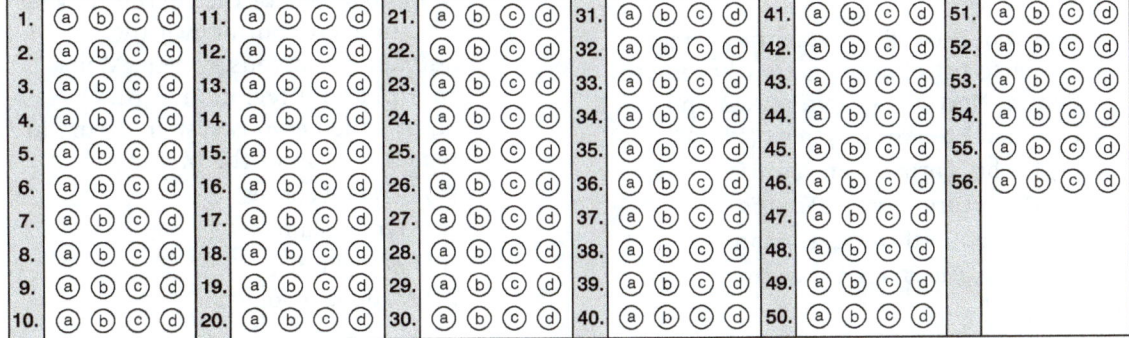

Chapter 13

Control and Coordination

MCQs 1 Mark Questions

1. Complete the flowchart by choosing the correct options.

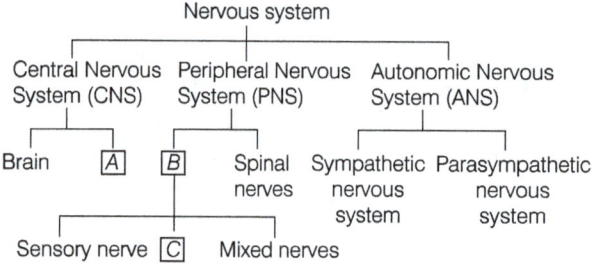

(a) *A* – Motor nerves, *B* – Spinal cord, *C* – Cranial nerves

(b) *A* – Spinal cord, *B* – Cranial nerves, *C* – Motor nerves

(c) *A* – Spinal cord, *B* – Motor nerves, *C* – Cranial nerves

(d) *A* – Cranial nerves, *B* – Spinal cord, *C* – Motor nerves

2. Which of the following is the correct complete list of animals that have both Central Nervous System (CNS) and Peripheral Nervous System (PNS)?

(a) Rabbit, Earthworm, *Planaria*

(b) Earthworm, *Hydra*, *Planaria*

(c) Rabbit, Earthworm, Human

(d) *Hydra*, *Planaria*, Earthworm

3. The nervous system of *X* animal is well-developed and consists of CNS, PNS and SNS. The central nervous system is made up of nerve ring of fused ganglia and ventral nerve cord. Which animal is *X*?

(a) Echinodermata   (b) Mollusca

(c) Platyhelminthes (d) Annelida

4. Vertebrate nervous system are divided into two major divisions: the central nervous system, which include the .... and .... and the .... nervous system, which include all neuron other than those in the brain and spinal cord.

(a) brain, nervous, autonomic

(b) spinal cord, eyes, peripheral

(c) brain, spinal cord, peripheral

(d) ganglia, cerebellum, autonomic

5. Many portions of the central nervous system exert control over the autonomic nervous system. Major control and integration of the autonomic nervous system occurs in which portion of the brain?

(a) Cerebral cortex

(b) Hypothalamus

(c) Cerebellum

(d) Medulla oblongata

6. Overall, ...X... nerves slow down the body and divert energy to digestion and other basic housekeeping tasks, and ...Y... nerves slow down housekeeping tasks and increase overall activity in times of heightened awareness or excitement. Complete the passage by replacing X and Y with correct option.
   (a) X = parasympathetic, Y = sympathetic
   (b) X = sympathetic, Y = parasympathetic
   (c) X = somatic, Y = peripheral
   (d) X = central, Y = autonomic

7. The following diagram shows structure of a neuron. Choose the correct option that labelled the parts from A to D.

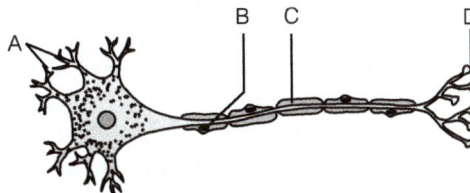

	A	*B*	*C*	*D*
(a)	Axon	Node of ranvier	Cell body	Dendrites
(b)	Dendrites	Schwann cell	Axon	Synaptic knob
(c)	Axon	Schwann cell	Node of ranvier	Synaptic knob
(d)	Axon terminal	Myelin sheath	Cell body	Schwann cell

8. Choose the incorrect match for the type of nerves and their location in the human body.
   (a) Unipolar nerves—Nerves of embryonic stage
   (b) Bipolar nerves—Nerve cell of retina
   (c) Mixed nerves—Nerves in brain
   (d) Multipolar nerves—Nerves cells of cerebral cortex

9. Why does nerve impulse only travel in one direction across a synapse?
   (a) Release of acetylcholine from only one side of synapse to other
   (b) Release of acetylcholine from the other side of the synapse
   (c) Release of acetylcholine from both side of the synapse
   (d) Release of acetylcholine from post-synaptic membrane

10. During synaptic transmission of nerve impulse, X neurotransmitter is released from synaptic vesicles by the action of ions Y. What is X and Y?
    (a) X = Cholinesterase, Y = Ca^{2+}
    (b) X = Acetylcholine, Y = Ca^{2+}
    (c) X = GABA, Y = Na^{+}
    (d) X = Acetylcholine, Y = Na^{+}

11. Few statements about neurotransmitter is given below. Which of the following statements are true?
    I. Neurotransmitter jumps from one junction to another.
    II. Neurotransmitters bind to receptors within the membrane of a post-synaptic neurons.
    III. Neurotransmitters is permanently destroyed after the transmission of nerve impulse.
    (a) I and II
    (b) II and III
    (c) Only I
    (d) Only II

12. During the propagation of a nerve impulse, the action potential results from the movement of
    (a) K^{+} ions from intracellular fluid to extracellular fluid
    (b) Na^{+} ions from extracellular fluid to intracellular fluid

(c) K^+ ions from extracellular fluid to intracellular fluid

(d) Na^+ ions from intracellular fluid to extracellular fluid

13. During the transmission of nerve impulse through a nerve fibre the potential on the inner side of the plasma membrane has which type of electric charge?

   (a) First positive then negative and continue to be negative

   (b) First negative then positive and continue to be positive

   (c) First positive then negative and again back to positive

   (d) First negative then positive and again back to negative

14. In the nerve cells, the reversal of the resting potential occurs due to

   (a) influx of Na^+ (b) influx of K^+

   (c) influx of Ca^{2+} (d) influx of Cl^-

15. Which of the following shows the correct sequence of meninges from inner to outer side?

   (a) Pia mater → Arachnoid mater → Dura mater

   (b) Pia mater → Dura mater → Arachnoid mater

   (c) Dura mater → Arachnoid mater → Pia mater

   (d) Arachnoid mater → Pia mater → Dura mater

16. Choose the correct composition of grey and white matter of the CNS?

   (a) Grey matter = cell bodies, white matter = axons + oligodendrocytes

   (b) Grey matter = axons, white matter = cell bodies + oligodendrocytes

   (c) Grey matter = cell bodies + oligodendrocytes, white matter = axons

   (d) Grey matter = axons + oligodendrocytes, white matter = cell bodies

17. The inner parts of cerebral hemispheres and a group of associated deep structures like amygdala, hippocampus, etc. form a complex structure called

   (a) arbor vitae

   (b) limbic lobe/limbic system

   (c) corpora quadrigemina

   (d) reticular system

18. A part of the brain regulates heart rate and involuntary breathing. It is the centre of swallowing, vomiting and gut peristalsis. Which part of the brain it indicates?

   (a) Hypothalamus

   (b) Cerebellum

   (c) Medulla oblongata

   (d) Cerebrum

19. If the most dorsal (topmost) regions of the primary motor areas on both hemispheres gets damaged, the person will loose the control movement of his

   (a) legs   (b) lips

   (c) hands   (d) tongue

20. A patient was suffering from an abnormally low body temperature, loss of apetite and extreme thirst. His brain scan would probably show a tumor in

   (a) pons   (b) cerebellum

   (c) hypothalamus   (d) medulla oblongata

21. The Broca's area and Wernicke's centre are the association areas situated in cerebrum. These are associated with

   (a) memory   (b) breathing

   (c) blind spot   (d) None of these

22. The part X is situated in the hind brain that is responsible for hand-eye coordination. X represents

   (a) thalamus

   (b) cerebellum

   (c) pons Varolii

   (d) medulla oblongata

23. Which of the following region of the brain is incorrectly paired with its function?

  (a) Hypothalamus – Production of releasing hormones and regulation of temperature, hunger and thirst

  (b) Limbic system – Consists of fibre tracts that interconnect different regions of brain; controls movement

  (c) Corpus callosum – Communication between the left and right cerebral cortices

  (d) Cerebrum – Calculation and contemplation

24. Which of the following structure or region is incorrectly paired with its function?

  (a) Hypothalamus   Production of releasing hormones and regulation of temperature, hunger and thirst

  (b) Limbic system   Consists of fibre tracts that interconnect different regions of brain; controls movement

  (c) Medulla oblongata   Controls respiration and cardiovascular reflexes

  (d) Corpus callosum   Band of fibres connecting left and right cerebral hemispheres

25. Few statements about hormones are given below.

  I. Hormones may be proteinaceous, or amine or steroids.

  II. Hormones are diffusible through cell membranes.

  III. Hormones have high molecular weights.

  Which of the following statement(s) is/are not true?

  (a) I and II   (b) Only III

  (c) Only II   (d) II and III

26. Complete the flowchart by choosing the correct option for A, B and C.

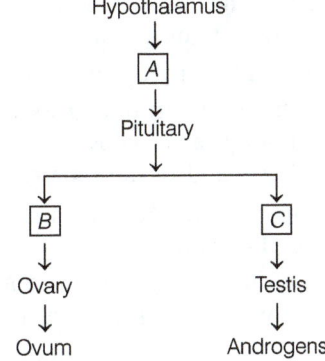

  (a) A-GnRh, B-FSH, C-LH

  (b) A-PRL, B-ICSH, C-GnRH

  (c) A-GH, B-LH, C-FSH

  (d) A-ICSH, B-ISH, C-GnRH

27. Choose the correct option for the parts A-D.

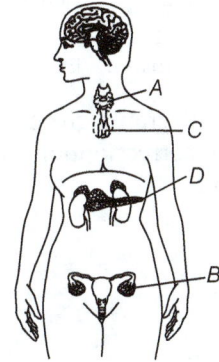

  (a) A-Thymus, B-Gonads, C-Parathyroid, D-Pancreas

  (b) A-Parathyroid, B-Thymus, C-Gonads, D-Adrenals

  (c) A-Parathyroid, B-Gonads, C-Thymus, D-Pancreas

  (d) A-Thymus, B-Parathyroid, C-Adrenal, D-Pancreas

28. A common secretion of the salivary and Brunner's glands that plays a role in growth, repair and regeneration is

  (a) neurotensin   (b) somatostatin

  (c) prostaglandin   (d) adrenalin

29. Few statements about a specific hormone is given below.

    I. It stimulates growth in liver, muscles, cartilages, bones, and other tissue.

    II. It is secreted by the pituitary gland.

    III. It secrete insulin like growth factor from body cells, helps in protein synthesis and tissue repair.

The above features are of which of the following hormone?

(a) Somatotropin   (b) Thyrotropin

(c) Corticotropin   (d) Prolactin

30. Choose the correct option that gives correct information that matches the disease.

Disease	Hormone	Quantity	Gland
(a) Dwarfism	GH	Excess	Pituitary
(b) Acromegaly	GH	Excess	Pituitary
(c) Diabetes insipidus	ADH	Deficiency	Thyroid
(d) Cretinism	Thyroxine	Excess	Parathyroid

31. Study the diagrams given below and choose the correct option for the labelled parts *A* to *D*.

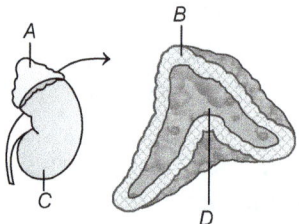

(a) *A*-Kidney, *B*-Adrenal medulla, *C*-Adrenal cortex, *D*-Adrenal gland

(b) *A*-Adrenal gland, *B*-Kidney, *C*-Adrenal cortex, *D*-Adrenal medulla

(c) *A*-Adrenal gland, *B*-Adrenal cortex, *C*-Kidney, *D*-Adrenal medulla

(d) *A*-Adrenal cortex, *B*-Adrenal gland, *C*-Kidney, *D*-Adrenal medulla

32. It has been found in a case study that increased levels of hormones from the .... in the blood of students preparing for final exams. These hormones are produced in response to stress.

(a) pineal gland

(b) adrenal gland

(c) thyroid gland

(d) parathyroid gland

33. A person is frightened by a loud noise that led to an increase in the blood sugar level. Which hormone is responsible for this?

(a) Insulin   (b) Adrenaline

(c) Secretin   (d) Gastrin

34. In an accident, the adrenal cortex of a person was injured. The secretion of which one of the following would likely remain unaffected?

(a) Cortisol   (b) Adrenaline

(c) Aldosterone   (d) Androstenedions

35. A hormone *X* causes dilation of blood vessels, increased oxygen consumption and glucogenesis and the deficiency of *Y* lowers blood calcium level.

Identify *X* and *Y*.

(a) *X*-Adrenaline, *Y*-Parathormone

(b) *X*-Glucagon, *Y*-Adrenaline

(c) *X*-Parathormone, *Y*-Glucagon

(d) *X*-Adrenalin, *Y*-Gastrin

36. Reabsorption of water from urine is increased by the hormone ...., while reabsorption of Na^+ from urine is enhanced by ....

Choose the correct option and complete the paragraph.

(a) antidiuretic, vasopressin

(b) vasopressin, aldosterone

(c) aldosterone, insulin

(d) thyroxine, glucagon

37. 'X' is a butterfly-shaped organ. It produces a hormone which causes a disease called cretinism, which might be due to
(a) absence of insulin
(b) excess adrenaline
(c) excess growth hormone
(d) hyposecretion of thyroid in pregnancy

38. The hormone which regulates basal metabolism in our body secreted from
(a) thymus   (b) thyroid gland
(c) pancreas   (d) adrenal gland

39. Which one of the following endocrine glands stores its secretion in the extracellular space before discharging it into the blood?
(a) Testis   (b) Thyroid
(c) Adrenal   (d) Pancreas

40. If a part of pituitary affected excretory system is removed, it causes atrophy of
(a) adrenal cortex
(b) renal medulla
(c) adrenal medulla
(d) renal pyramids

41. A pregnant woman delivers a baby boy who suffers from stunted growth, mental retardation, low intelligence quotient and abnormal skin. What might be the possible reasons?
(a) Cancer of the thyroid gland
(b) Over secretion of pars distalis
(c) Deficiency of iodine in diet
(d) Low secretion of growth hormone

42. Secretion of PTH is regulated by the circulating levels of
(a) Na^+ ions   (b) I^- ions
(c) Ca^{2+} ions   (d) Fe^{2+} ions

43. A person was suffering from swollen neck, with difficulty in swallowing, cough and hoarseness. Which substance was deficient in his diet?
(a) Iodine   (b) Vitamin-C
(c) Magnesium   (d) Calcium

44. Choose the correct option for the hormone matching with its source and function.
(a) Atrial natriuretic factor—cardiac muscles of the ventricular wall, increases the blood pressure
(b) Melatonin—pineal gland, regulates the normal rhythm of sleepwake cycle
(c) Progesterone—corpus luteum, stimulation of growth and activities of female secondary sex organs
(d) Oxytocin-posterior pituitary, growth and maintenance of mammary glands

45. The intermediate lobe of the pituitary gland produces a hormone which causes a dramatic darkening of the skin of many fishes, amphibians and reptiles. Name this hormone?
(a) Follicle stimulating hormone (FSH)
(b) Melanocyte stimulating hormone (MSH)
(c) Adrenocorticotropic hormone (ACTH)
(d) Luteinizing hormone (LH)

46. A person is having problem with calcium and phosphorus metabolism in his body. Which one of the following glands may not be functioning properly?
(a) Parotid   (b) Pancreas
(c) Parathyroid   (d) Adrenal cortex

47. Swati had a tumour in her endocrine gland which led to weekend bones and unusually high levels of blood calcium. Which of the following was affected?
(a) Pancreas
(b) Parathyroid glands
(c) Adrenal glands
(d) Anterior pituitary

48. A gland which is responsible for the maturation of T-lymphocytes and gradually atrophies at the age of 14-16 due to the activities of sex gland is
(a) thyroid   (b) thymus
(c) pineal   (d) Pancreas

49. Which of the following gland secretes a hormone which is responsible for the conversion of excess glucose to glycogen in liver to maintain the concentration of glucose in blood?

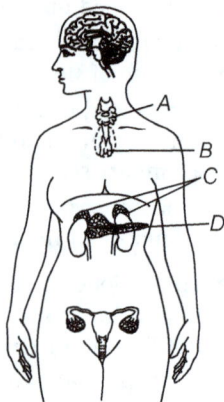

(a) D – Insulin

(b) A – Parathyroid

(c) C – Glucagon

(d) B – Adrenaline

50. Sita's father always complains of constant thirst and excessive passing of urine. After a health checkup it was found that blood glucose and insulin level is normal but he has low blood pressure. What is the disorder and which hormone is responsible for this?

(a) Acromegaly, GnRH

(b) Osteoporosis, oxytocin

(c) Diabetes insipidus, vasopressin

(d) Hyperthyroidism, T_3

51. X hormone is needed to stimulate the increased level of blood glucose during fasting or sustained exercise when glucose is in demand for metabolism. What is X?

(a) Insulin   (b) Glucagon

(c) Somatostatin   (d) Adrenaline

52. A hormone X is released after meal, which controls the level of glucose in the blood. Another hormone Y is released in response to drop in blood sugar during prolonged fasting, exercise. What is X and Y?

(a) X – gastrin, Y – secretin

(b) X – secretin, Y – gastrin

(c) X – insulin, Y – leptin

(d) X – insulin, Y – glucagon

53. The hormone needed to stimulate the increased levels of blood glucose during fasting or sustained exercise when glucose is in demand for metabolism is

(a) insulin   (b) prolactin

(c) glucagon   (d) somatostain

54. A hormone X is often used in over the counter diagnostic test to determine when ovulation has occurred. Name this hormone?

(a) Oestrogen   (b) FSH

(c) LH   (d) Progesterone

55. Which of the following pair of hormones are the examples of those that can easily pass through the cell membrane of the target cell and bind to a receptor inside it?

(a) Insulin, Glucagon

(b) Somatostatin, Oxytocin

(c) Cortisol, Ttestosterone

(d) Thyroxin, Insulin

56. The hormones that initiate ejection of milk, stimulates milk production and growth of ovarian follicles. These are respectively known as

(a) Oxytocin, PRL and FSH

(b) LH, PRL and FSH

(c) PRH, Oxytocin and FSH

(d) Oxytocin, FSH and PRH

57. Which of the following given features are appropriate for androgens?

  (a) Regulates development and maturation of accessory sex organs

  (b) Stimulate muscular growth and influence libido

  (c) Stimulate the formation of spermatozoa

  (d) All of the above

58. The steroid hormones, oestrogen and progesterone are secreted by which part/structure of ovary?

  (a) Ova and Leydig cells, respectively

  (b) Ovarian follicle and corpus luteum, respectively

  (c) Corpus luteum and corpus albicans, respectively

  (d) Graafian follicle and ova, respectively

59. Choose the correct option for the group of hormones that belongs to fat soluble, with sterol group and derived from cholesterol.

  (a) Thyroxine, glucagon, aldosterone

  (b) Epinephrine, insulin, oxytocin

  (c) Oxytocin, testosterone, FSH

  (d) Aldosterone, testosterone, progesterone

60. Hormones of which of the following endocrine glands lacks peptides, amines and sulphur?

  (a) Testes

  (b) Thyroid and adrenal glands

  (c) Anterior pituitary

  (d) Posterior pituitary and pancreas

61. What will happen if receptor molecules are removed from target organs?

  (a) The target organ will not respond to the hormone

  (b) The target organ will continue to respond to the hormone without any difference

  (c) The target organ will continue to respond to the hormone but in the opposite way

  (d) The target organ will continue to respond to the hormone but will require higher concentration

MCQs 2 Marks Questions

62. The diagram given below shows synaptic transmission. Choose the correct option for labelled parts from *A* to *D*.

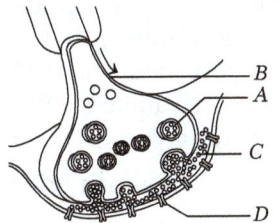

	A	*B*	*C*	*D*
(a)	Synaptic cleft	Post-synaptic membrane	Receptor molecule	Synaptic vesicles
(b)	Synaptic vesicles	Pre-synaptic membrane	Synaptic cleft	Post-synaptic membrane
(c)	Receptor molecule	Post-synaptic cleft	Synaptic vesicles	Synaptic cleft
(d)	Synaptic vesicles	Pre-synaptic membrane	Synaptic cleft	Receptor molecule

63. Which of the following diagram will show an excited nerve fibre or an increased action potential?

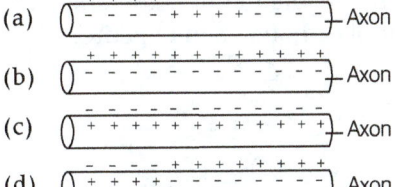

64. The following graph shows an action potential.

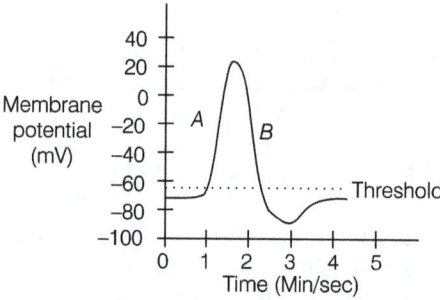

What does *A* and *B* indicate?
(a) *A* – Depolarisation, *B* – Refractory period
(b) *A* – Repolarisation, *B* – Refractory period
(c) *A* – Depolarisation, *B* – Repolarisation
(d) *A* – Refractory period, *B* – Repolarisation

65. The diagram of human brain is shown below.

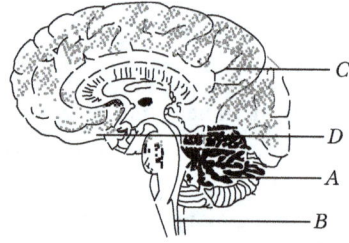

Which part of the brain is concerned with coordination of muscular movements?
(a) *C*   (b) *A*
(c) *D*   (d) *B*

66. The diagram shows sagittal section of the human brain. Which part is responsible for the regulation of body temperature, controls emotions and apetite?

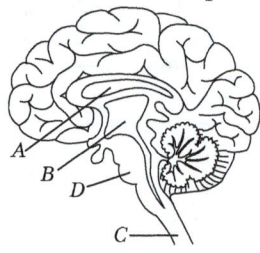

(a) *B*   (b) *C*
(c) *D*   (d) *A*

67. Assertion (A) Spinal cord has a column of both grey and white matter.
Reason (R) Grey matter form the central spinal canal.
(a) Both A and R are true and R is the correct explanation of A
(b) Both A and R are true, but R is not the correct explanation of A
(c) A is true, but R is false
(d) A is false, but R is true

68. The diagram of a human brain is shown below. What is the function of the labelled parts *A* to *D*.

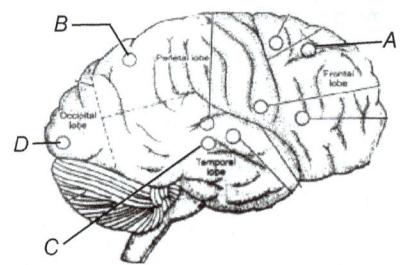

(a) *A* – Sensation of light, *B* – Vision, *C* – Sense of smell, *D* – Understanding speech
(b) *A* – Planning, *B* – Language, *C* – Understanding speech, *D* – Vision
(c) *A* – Sense of smell, *B* – Sensation of light, *C* – Language, *D* – Sense of taste
(d) *A* – Sense of smell, *B* – Sense of taste, *C* – Hearing, *D* – Sensation of light

69. Match the following areas in human cerebral cortex with their function.

Area		Function
A.	Somesthetic area	1. Motor speech
B.	Broca's area	2. Sense of taste
C.	Motor area	3. Sensation of pain, touch
D.	Gustatory area	4. Voluntary movements of muscle

Codes

	A	B	C	D			A	B	C	D
(a)	3	1	4	2		(b)	2	3	1	4
(c)	2	1	4	3		(d)	2	4	3	1

70. The following figure shows cross-section of a spinal cord. Choose the correct option and label the parts *A* to *D*.

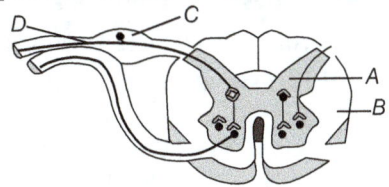

	A	*B*	*C*	*D*
(a)	White matter	Grey matter	Spinal nerve	Dorsal root
(b)	Grey matter	White matter	Central root	Dorsal root
(c)	Grey matter	White matter	Dorsal root	Spinal nerve
(d)	White matter	Grey matter	Central root	Spinal nerve

71. The following table shows the effects of sympathetic and parasympathetic nervous system. Which one option is correctly combined?

	Features	Sympathetic nervous system	Para sympathetic nervous system
(a)	Pupil of the eye	Constricts	Dilates
(b)	Digestion	Inhibits	Stimulates
(c)	Salivation	Stimulates	Inhibits
(d)	Sweat production	Inhibits	Stimulates

72. A boy met with an accident where his anterior pituitary was severely damaged but the boy survived. What is likely to happen?
    (a) The boy will not grow much in height
    (b) High levels of thyroxine will be released
    (c) Spermatogenesis will be stimulated
    (d) The growth of mammary glands will be stimulated

73. **Assertion** (A) Glucocorticoid have anti-inflammatory effects.

    Reason (R) They are secreted by zona glomerulosa of adrenal cortex.
    (a) Both A and R are true and R is the correct explanation of A
    (b) Both A and R are true, but R is not the correct explanation of A
    (c) A is true, but R is false
    (d) A is false, but R is true

74. Complete the following table by choosing the correct option.

Glands	Secretion	Effect on body
Anterior pituitary	*A*	Over secretion leads to gigantism
B	Oestrogen	Maintenance of secondary sexual characters
Posterior pituitary	*C*	Increase loss of water through urine

    (a) *A* – Calcitonin, *B* – Placenta, *C* – Vasopressin
    (b) *A* – Growth hormone, *B* – Ovary, *C* – Vasopressin
    (c) *A* – Vasopressin, *B* – Placenta, *C* – Growth hormone
    (d) *A* – Insulin, *B* – Ovary, *C* – Calcitonin

75. A person entering an empty room suddenly finds a snake right in front on opening the door. Which one of the following is likely to happen in his neurohormonal control system?
    (a) Sympathetic nervous system is activated releasing epinephrine and nor-epinephrine from adrenal medulla
    (b) Neurotransmitters diffuse rapidly across the cleft and transmit a nerve impulse
    (c) Hypothalamus activates the parasympathetic division of brain
    (d) Sympathetic nervous system is activated releasing epinephrine and nor-epinephrine from adrenal cortex

76. The given table enlists various hormones and their chemical nature. Select the option, which complete the table.

Hormones	Chemical composition
(i)	Peptide
Testosterone	(ii)
Thyroxine	(iii)
(iv)	Amino-Acid derivatives

	(i)	(ii)	(iii)	(iv)
(a)	Cortisol	Steroid	Polypeptide	Estradiol
(b)	Oxytocin	Protein	Iodothyronine	Epinephrine
(c)	Cortisol	Protein	Amine	Estradiol
(d)	Oxytocin	Steroid	Iodothyronine	Epinephrine

77. Choose the correct match in relation to glands and disease associate with them.

Disease		Glands
A. Myxedema	1.	Pituitary
B. Addison's disease	2.	Parathyroid
C. Tetany	3.	Thyroid
D. Diabetes insipidus	4.	Adrenal cortex

Codes

	A	B	C	D			A	B	C	D
(a)	3	4	2	1		(b)	2	3	4	1
(c)	4	1	2	3		(d)	4	2	1	3

78. Which of the following pair of hormone is correctly matched with the corresponding information?
(a) Somatostatin—Delta-cells (source)
(b) Insulin—Diabetes mellitus (disease)
(c) Glucagon—Beta cells (source)
(d) Corpus luteum—Relaxin (secretion)

79. Match the following hormones listed with their functions.

	Hormones		Functions
A.	Prolactin	1.	Stimulates ovulation
B.	Progesterone	2.	Lactation after child birth
C.	Oxytocin	3.	Uterine contraction during labour
D.	Luteinizing hormones	4.	Implantation and maintenance of pregnancy

Codes

	A	B	C	D
(a)	2	4	3	1
(b)	4	3	1	2
(c)	4	1	3	2
(d)	3	4	1	2

80. Complete the following table by choosing the correct answer for X and Y.

Hormone	Source	Function
X	Beta cells of Islets of Langerhans	Increases loss of water through urine
Vasopressin	Posterior pituitary	Increase loss of water through urine
Norepinephrine	Y	Normalises the heart beat
Prolactin	posterior pituitary	Regulates growth of mammary glands.

(a) X-Estrogen, Y-Thyroid
(b) X-Insulin, Y-Adrenal medulla
(c) X-Insulin, Y-Placenta
(d) X-Calcitonin, Y-Renal medulla

81. The diagram shows mechanism of steroid hormone action. Label the parts D to I.

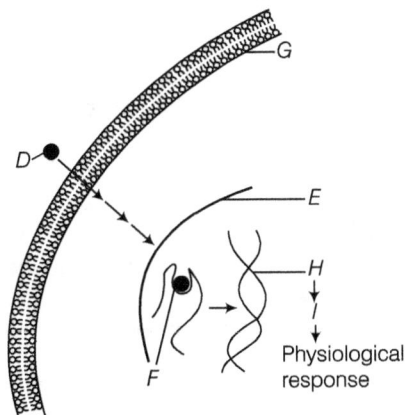

(a) D – Non-steroid hormone, E – Nucleus, F – Genome, G – Hormone-enzyme complex, H – Protein, I – mRNA

(b) D – Steroid hormone, E – Nucleus, F – Hormone-receptor complex, G – Uterine cell membrane, H – mRNA, I – protein

(c) D – Non-steroid hormone, E – Genome, F – mRNA, G – Nucleus, H – Hormone-enzyme complex, I – Protein

(d) D – Steroid hormone, E – Hormone-receptor complex, F – Genome, G – Nucleus, H – mRNA, I – Protein l

Darken your choice with HB Pencil

1.	ⓐ ⓑ ⓒ ⓓ	16.	ⓐ ⓑ ⓒ ⓓ	31.	ⓐ ⓑ ⓒ ⓓ	46.	ⓐ ⓑ ⓒ ⓓ	61.	ⓐ ⓑ ⓒ ⓓ	76.	ⓐ ⓑ ⓒ ⓓ
2.	ⓐ ⓑ ⓒ ⓓ	17.	ⓐ ⓑ ⓒ ⓓ	32.	ⓐ ⓑ ⓒ ⓓ	47.	ⓐ ⓑ ⓒ ⓓ	62.	ⓐ ⓑ ⓒ ⓓ	77.	ⓐ ⓑ ⓒ ⓓ
3.	ⓐ ⓑ ⓒ ⓓ	18.	ⓐ ⓑ ⓒ ⓓ	33.	ⓐ ⓑ ⓒ ⓓ	48.	ⓐ ⓑ ⓒ ⓓ	63.	ⓐ ⓑ ⓒ ⓓ	78.	ⓐ ⓑ ⓒ ⓓ
4.	ⓐ ⓑ ⓒ ⓓ	19.	ⓐ ⓑ ⓒ ⓓ	34.	ⓐ ⓑ ⓒ ⓓ	49.	ⓐ ⓑ ⓒ ⓓ	64.	ⓐ ⓑ ⓒ ⓓ	79.	ⓐ ⓑ ⓒ ⓓ
5.	ⓐ ⓑ ⓒ ⓓ	20.	ⓐ ⓑ ⓒ ⓓ	35.	ⓐ ⓑ ⓒ ⓓ	50.	ⓐ ⓑ ⓒ ⓓ	65.	ⓐ ⓑ ⓒ ⓓ	80.	ⓐ ⓑ ⓒ ⓓ
6.	ⓐ ⓑ ⓒ ⓓ	21.	ⓐ ⓑ ⓒ ⓓ	36.	ⓐ ⓑ ⓒ ⓓ	51.	ⓐ ⓑ ⓒ ⓓ	66.	ⓐ ⓑ ⓒ ⓓ	81.	ⓐ ⓑ ⓒ ⓓ
7.	ⓐ ⓑ ⓒ ⓓ	22.	ⓐ ⓑ ⓒ ⓓ	37.	ⓐ ⓑ ⓒ ⓓ	52.	ⓐ ⓑ ⓒ ⓓ	67.	ⓐ ⓑ ⓒ ⓓ	
8.	ⓐ ⓑ ⓒ ⓓ	23.	ⓐ ⓑ ⓒ ⓓ	38.	ⓐ ⓑ ⓒ ⓓ	53.	ⓐ ⓑ ⓒ ⓓ	68.	ⓐ ⓑ ⓒ ⓓ	
9.	ⓐ ⓑ ⓒ ⓓ	24.	ⓐ ⓑ ⓒ ⓓ	39.	ⓐ ⓑ ⓒ ⓓ	54.	ⓐ ⓑ ⓒ ⓓ	69.	ⓐ ⓑ ⓒ ⓓ	
10.	ⓐ ⓑ ⓒ ⓓ	25.	ⓐ ⓑ ⓒ ⓓ	40.	ⓐ ⓑ ⓒ ⓓ	55.	ⓐ ⓑ ⓒ ⓓ	70.	ⓐ ⓑ ⓒ ⓓ	
11.	ⓐ ⓑ ⓒ ⓓ	26.	ⓐ ⓑ ⓒ ⓓ	41.	ⓐ ⓑ ⓒ ⓓ	56.	ⓐ ⓑ ⓒ ⓓ	71.	ⓐ ⓑ ⓒ ⓓ	
12.	ⓐ ⓑ ⓒ ⓓ	27.	ⓐ ⓑ ⓒ ⓓ	42.	ⓐ ⓑ ⓒ ⓓ	57.	ⓐ ⓑ ⓒ ⓓ	72.	ⓐ ⓑ ⓒ ⓓ	
13.	ⓐ ⓑ ⓒ ⓓ	28.	ⓐ ⓑ ⓒ ⓓ	43.	ⓐ ⓑ ⓒ ⓓ	58.	ⓐ ⓑ ⓒ ⓓ	73.	ⓐ ⓑ ⓒ ⓓ	
14.	ⓐ ⓑ ⓒ ⓓ	29.	ⓐ ⓑ ⓒ ⓓ	44.	ⓐ ⓑ ⓒ ⓓ	59.	ⓐ ⓑ ⓒ ⓓ	74.	ⓐ ⓑ ⓒ ⓓ	
15.	ⓐ ⓑ ⓒ ⓓ	30.	ⓐ ⓑ ⓒ ⓓ	45.	ⓐ ⓑ ⓒ ⓓ	60.	ⓐ ⓑ ⓒ ⓓ	75.	ⓐ ⓑ ⓒ ⓓ	

Practice Set 01

Time : 60 Mins.   Max. Marks : 60

> ### General Instructions
> 1. This question paper contains 50 questions.
> 2. All questions are compulsory. There is no negative marking.
> 3. This question paper is divided into two parts; In first part, there are 40 MCQs of 1 mark each while in second part, there are 10 MCQs of 2 marks each.
> 4. Use HB pencil / Blue ball point pen to mark your choice of answer by darkening the circles on the OMR Sheet.

MCQs 1 Mark Questions

1. Students attending biology class came to know that if a part of the pith from the stem is taken as explant and and cultured on nutrient media, an undifferentiated mass of cell called callus, grows. Which of the following processes is responsible for it?
   (a) Growth
   (b) Differentiation
   (c) Dedifferentiation
   (d) Redifferentiation

2. Select the correct events that occur during inspiration.
   I. Contraction of diaphragm.
   II. Contraction of external inter-costal muscles.
   III. Pulmonary volume decreases.
   IV. Intra pulmonary pressure increases.
   (a) III and IV   (b) I, II and IV
   (c) Only IV   (d) I and II

3. The oxygenation activity of RuBisCO enzyme in photorespiration leads to the formation of
   (a) 1 molecule of 3-C compound and 1 molecule

   (b) 1 molecule of 6-C compound of 2-C compound
   (c) 1 molecule of 4-C compound and 1 molecule of 2-C compound
   (d) 2 molecules of 3-C compound

4. In light reaction, plastoquinone facilitates the transfer of electrons from
   (a) Cyt-$b_6 f$ complex to PS-I
   (b) PS-I to NADP$^+$
   (c) PS-I to ATP synthase
   (d) PS-II to Cyt-$b_6 f$ complex

5. The QRS complex in a standard ECG represents
   (a) depolarisation of auricles
   (b) depolarisation of ventricles
   (c) repolarisation of ventricles
   (d) repolarisation of auricles

6. Presence of which of the following conditions in urine are indicative of diabetes mellitus?
   (a) Uremia and renal calculi
   (b) Ketonuria and glycosuria
   (c) Renal calculi and hyperglycaemia
   (d) Uremia and ketonuria

7. Ray florets have
   (a) superior ovary
   (b) hypogynous ovary
   (c) half inferior ovary
   (d) inferior ovary

8. The process of growth is maximum during
   (a) lag phase   (b) senescence
   (c) dormancy   (d) log phase

9. Parallel venation is the characteristic of monocots. Which of the following is an exception to this
   (a) *Smilax*   (b) *Colocasia*
   (c) *Alocasia*   (d) All of these

10. Bilaterally symmetrical and acoelomate animals are exemplified by
    (a) Platyhelminthes
    (b) Aschelminthes
    (c) Annelida
    (d) Ctenophora

11. Which of the following statements about inclusion bodies is incorrect?
    (a) These are involved in ingestion of food particles
    (b) They lie free in the cytoplasm
    (c) These represent reserve material in cytoplasm
    (d) They are not bound by any membrane

12. Which is the important site of formation of glycoproteins and glycolipids in eukaryotic cells?
    (a) Peroxisomes
    (b) Golgi bodies
    (c) Polysomes
    (d) Endoplasmic reticulum

13. The number of substrate level phosphorylation in one turn of citric acid cycle is
    (a) one
    (b) two
    (c) three
    (d) zero

14. If fimbriae is removed from the bacterial cell, which of the following is expected to happen?
    (a) Bacteria would fail to swim
    (b) Bacteria would fail to adhere to host tissue
    (c) Transportation of molecules across membrane would stop
    (d) Shape of bacteria would alter

15 Which of the following pairs is of unicellular algae?
    (a) *Gelidium* and *Gracilaria*
    (b) *Anabaena* and *Volvox*
    (c) *Chlorella* and *Spirulina*
    (d) *Laminaria* and *Sargassum*

16. Floridean starch has structure similar to
    (a) amylopectin and glycogen
    (b) mannitol and algin
    (c) laminarin and cellulose
    (d) starch and cellulose

17. Identify the correct statement with regard to G_1-phase (Gap 1) of interphase.
    (a) Reorganisation of all cell components, take place
    (b) Cell is metabolically active, grows but does not replicate its DNA
    (c) Nuclear division takes place
    (d) DNA synthesis or replication takes place

18. In a frog, if a hole is punched in the floor of its buccal cavity, the frog does not die. This is because
   (a) buccal respiration does not stop
   (b) pulmonary respiration takes place
   (c) frog can store O_2 for future
   (d) respiration other than lungs continues

19. Select the correctly matched pair.
   (a) Hinge joint   −Between vertebrae
   (b) Gliding joint   −Between carpals
   (c) Cartilagenous joint −Skull bones
   (d) Fibrous joint   −Between phalanges

20. Feeling the tremors of an earthquake, a scared resident of 7th floor start climbing down the stairs rapidly. Which of the following hormones initiated this action?
   (a) Gastrin   (b) Adrenaline
   (c) Glucagon   (d) Thyroxine

21. Name the plant growth regulator which upon spraying on sugarcane crop, increases the length of stem, thus increasing the yield of sugarcane crop.
   (a) Gibberellin   (b) Ethylene
   (c) Abscisic acid   (d) Cytokinin

22. An X-ray of the lower abdomen shows a shadow in the region of ureter suspected to be a ureteric calculus. What would be the possible clinical symptom?
   (a) Anuria and hematuria
   (b) Acute renal failure
   (c) Chronic renal failure
   (d) Motor aphasia

23. Dissolution of the synaptonemal complex occurs during
   (a) zygotene   (b) diplotene
   (c) leptotene   (d) pachytene

24. At what phase of meiosis there are two cells, each with separated sister chromatids which have shifted to opposite spindle poles?
   (a) Anaphase-II
   (b) Anaphase-I
   (c) Telophase-II
   (d) Telophase-I

25. Which of the following would help in prevention of diuresis?
   (a) Reabsorption of Na^+ and water from renal tubules due to aldosterone
   (b) Atrial natriuretic factor causes vasoconstriction
   (c) Decrease in the secretion of renin by JG cells
   (d) More water reabsorption due to undersecretion of ADH

26. Strobili or cones are found in
   (a) *Pteris*   (b) *Marchantia*
   (c) *Equisetum*   (d) *Salvinia*

27. Identify the substances having glycosidic bond and peptide bond, respectively in their structure.
   (a) Glycerol, trypsin
   (b) Cellulose, lecithin
   (c) Inulin, insulin
   (d) Chitin, cholesterol

28. Which one of the following is the most abundant protein in the animals?
   (a) Collagen
   (b) Lectin
   (c) Insulin
   (d) Haemoglobin

29. The ovary is half inferior in
   (a) mustard   (b) sunflower
   (c) plum   (d) brinjal

30. Select the correct statement.
   (a) Glucagon is associated with hypoglycemia
   (b) Insulin acts on pancreatic cells and adipocytes
   (c) Insulin is associated with hyperglycemia
   (d) Glucocorticoids stimulate gluconeogenesis

31. If volume of CO_2 liberated during respiration is more than the volume of O_2 used, then respiratory substrate will be
   (a) carbohydrate   (b) fats
   (c) protein   (d) organic acid

32. Some dividing cells exit the cell cycle and enter vegetative inactive stage. This is called quiescent stage (G_0). This process occurs at the end of
   (a) G_1-phase
   (b) S-phase
   (c) $G_{not} = G_0$-phase
   (d) M-phase

33. Choose the incorrect vertebrate character.
   (a) Ventral muscular heart
   (b) Kidneys for excretion and osmoregulation
   (c) Paired appendages which may be fins or limbs
   (d) None of the above

34. Members of Phycomycetes are found in
   I. aquatic habitats.
   II. on decaying wood.
   III. moist and damp places.
   IV. as obligate parasites on plants.
   Choose the correct answer from the following options.
   (a) I and IV   (b) Only III
   (c) Only II   (d) All of these

35. Select the correctly written scientific name of mango which was first described by Carolus Linnaeus.
   (a) *Mangifera indica* Car. Linn.
   (b) *Mangifera indica* Linn.
   (c) *Mangifera indica*
   (d) *Mangifera Indica*

36. If you are asked to classify the various algae into distinct groups, which of the following characters you should choose?
   (a) Types of pigments present in the cell
   (b) Nature of stored food materials in the cell
   (c) Structural organisation of thallus
   (d) Chemical composition of the cell wall

37. The function of adhering junction is to
   (a) prevent leakage of substances across tissues
   (b) connect the cytoplasm of adjacent cells
   (c) diffuse small ions across tissues
   (d) cement the neighbouring cells together

38. Adipose tissue performs which of the following functions?
   (a) Producing fat   (b) Dissolving fat
   (c) Storing fat   (d) All of these

39. Choose the correct option for the given floral aestivation.

   (a) Valvate, found in *Calotropis*
   (b) Twisted, found in lady finger
   (c) Imbricate, found in China rose
   (d) Vexillary, found in pea

40. Free-central placentation is found in
(a) *Dianthus*   (b) *Argemone*
(c) *Brassica*   (d) *Citrus*

MCQs 2 Marks Questions

Direction (Q. Nos. 41-44) Each of these questions contains two statements : Assertion (A) and Reason (R). Each of these questions also has four alternative choices, any one of which is the correct answer. You have to select one of the codes (a), (b), (c) and (d) given below.

(a) Both A and R are true and R is the correct explanation of A
(b) Both A and R are true, but R is not the correct explanation of A
(c) A is true, but R is false
(d) A is false, but R is true

41. Assertion (A) Platyhelminthes are hermaphrodites.

Reason (R) Fertilisation is internal in Platyhelminthes.

42. Assertion (A) Archaebacteria are able to survive in harsh habitats.

Reason (R) Presence of peptidoglycan in cell wall help Archaebacteria to survive in extreme conditions.

43. Assertion (A) The floral formula of family-Solanaceae starts with the $\oplus$.

Reason (R) The flowers of family-Solanaceae are zygomorphic.

44. Assertion (A) The arrangement of axonemal microtubules in cilia or flagella is called 9 + 2 array.

Reason (R) The axoneme usually has nine pairs or doublets of radially arranged peripheral microtubules and a pair of centrally located microtubules.

Direction (Q. Nos. 45-47) Read the following and answer the questions that follow.

Observe the given diagram and answer the following questions.

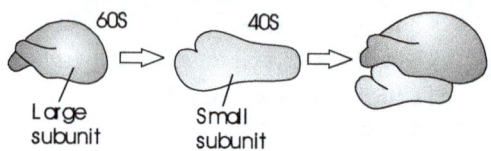

45. Which cell organelle is shown in the above diagram?
(a) Mesosome
(b) Golgi bodies
(c) Ribosome
(d) None of the above

46. 70S ribosomes occur in
(a) bacteria
(b) mitochondria
(c) chloroplasts
(d) All of the above

47. Which of the following ribosomes are engaged in protein synthesis in animal cell?
(a) Ribosomes which occur on nuclear membrane and ER
(b) Ribosomes of only cytosol
(c) Ribosomes of only nucleolus and cytosol
(d) Ribosomes of only mitochondria and cytosol

48. Which of the following statements are true for the phylum–Chordata?
I. In Urochordata notochord extends from head to tail and it is present throughout their life.
II. In Vertebrata, notochord is present during the embryonic period only.

III. Central nervous system is dorsal and hollow.

IV. Chordata is divided into 3 subphyla, Hemichordata, Tunicata and Cephalochordata.

(a) III and I   (b) I and II

(c) II and III   (d) IV and III

49. Identify the wrong statement with reference to transport of oxygen.

(a) Partial pressure of CO_2 can interfere with O_2 binding with haemoglobin

(b) Higher H^+ concentration in alveoli favours the formation of oxyhaemoglobin

(c) Low pCO_2 in alveoli favours the formation of oxyhaemoglobin

(d) Binding of oxygen with haemoglobin is mainly related to partial pressure of O_2

50. The transverse section of a plant shows following anatomical features.

I. Large number of scattered vascular bundles surrounded by bundle sheath.

II. Large conspicuous parenchymatous ground tissue.

III. Vascular bundles conjoint and closed.

IV. Phloem parenchyma absent.

Identify the category of plant and its part.

(a) Monocotyledonous root

(b) Dicotyledonous stem

(c) Dicotyledonous root

(d) Monocotyledonous stem

Darken your choice with HB Pencil

1.	ⓐ ⓑ ⓒ ⓓ	11.	ⓐ ⓑ ⓒ ⓓ	21.	ⓐ ⓑ ⓒ ⓓ	31.	ⓐ ⓑ ⓒ ⓓ	41.	ⓐ ⓑ ⓒ ⓓ
2.	ⓐ ⓑ ⓒ ⓓ	12.	ⓐ ⓑ ⓒ ⓓ	22.	ⓐ ⓑ ⓒ ⓓ	32.	ⓐ ⓑ ⓒ ⓓ	42.	ⓐ ⓑ ⓒ ⓓ
3.	ⓐ ⓑ ⓒ ⓓ	13.	ⓐ ⓑ ⓒ ⓓ	23.	ⓐ ⓑ ⓒ ⓓ	33.	ⓐ ⓑ ⓒ ⓓ	43.	ⓐ ⓑ ⓒ ⓓ
4.	ⓐ ⓑ ⓒ ⓓ	14.	ⓐ ⓑ ⓒ ⓓ	24.	ⓐ ⓑ ⓒ ⓓ	34.	ⓐ ⓑ ⓒ ⓓ	44.	ⓐ ⓑ ⓒ ⓓ
5.	ⓐ ⓑ ⓒ ⓓ	15.	ⓐ ⓑ ⓒ ⓓ	25.	ⓐ ⓑ ⓒ ⓓ	35.	ⓐ ⓑ ⓒ ⓓ	45.	ⓐ ⓑ ⓒ ⓓ
6.	ⓐ ⓑ ⓒ ⓓ	16.	ⓐ ⓑ ⓒ ⓓ	26.	ⓐ ⓑ ⓒ ⓓ	36.	ⓐ ⓑ ⓒ ⓓ	46.	ⓐ ⓑ ⓒ ⓓ
7.	ⓐ ⓑ ⓒ ⓓ	17.	ⓐ ⓑ ⓒ ⓓ	27.	ⓐ ⓑ ⓒ ⓓ	37.	ⓐ ⓑ ⓒ ⓓ	47.	ⓐ ⓑ ⓒ ⓓ
8.	ⓐ ⓑ ⓒ ⓓ	18.	ⓐ ⓑ ⓒ ⓓ	28.	ⓐ ⓑ ⓒ ⓓ	38.	ⓐ ⓑ ⓒ ⓓ	48.	ⓐ ⓑ ⓒ ⓓ
9.	ⓐ ⓑ ⓒ ⓓ	19.	ⓐ ⓑ ⓒ ⓓ	29.	ⓐ ⓑ ⓒ ⓓ	39.	ⓐ ⓑ ⓒ ⓓ	49.	ⓐ ⓑ ⓒ ⓓ
10.	ⓐ ⓑ ⓒ ⓓ	20.	ⓐ ⓑ ⓒ ⓓ	30.	ⓐ ⓑ ⓒ ⓓ	40.	ⓐ ⓑ ⓒ ⓓ	50.	ⓐ ⓑ ⓒ ⓓ

Practice Set 02

Time : 60 Mins.   Max. Marks : 60

General Instructions
1. This question paper contains 50 questions.
2. All questions are compulsory. There is no negative marking.
3. This question paper is divided into two parts; In first part, there are 40 MCQs of 1 mark each while in second part, there are 10 MCQs of 2 marks each.
4. Use HB pencil / Blue ball point pen to mark your choice of answer by darkening the circles on the OMR Sheet.

MCQs 1 Mark Questions

1. Which of the following stages of meiosis involves division of centromere ?
   (a) Metaphase-I   (b) Metaphase-II
   (c) Anaphase-II   (d) Telophase-II

2. Genera like *Selaginella* and *Salvinia* produces two kinds of spores. Such plants are known as
   (a) homosorus
   (b) heterosorus
   (c) homosporous
   (d) heterosporous

3. Plants follow different pathways in response to environment or phases of life to form different kinds of structures. This ability is called
   (a) elasticity   (b) flexibility
   (c) plasticity   (d) maturity

4. Which of the following are not secondary metabolites in plants?
   (a) Morphine, codeine
   (b) Amino acids, glucose
   (c) Vinblastine, curcumin
   (d) Rubber, gums

5. When the centromere is situated in the middle of two equal arms of chromosomes, the chromosome is referred as
   (a) metacentric
   (b) telocentric
   (c) sub-metacentric
   (d) acrocentric

6. Natural cytokinins are synthesised in regions where rapid cell division takes place. Such regions are
   (a) root apices
   (b) developing shoot buds
   (c) young fruits
   (d) All of the above

7. Diadelphous stamens are found in
   (a) China rose
   (b) *Citrus*
   (c) Pea
   (d) China rose and *Citrus*

8. Which of the following algae contains mannitol as reserve food material ?
   (a) *Ectocarpus*   (b) *Gracilaria*
   (c) *Volvox*   (d) *Ulothrix*

9. The plant hormone used to destroy weeds in a field is
   - (a) IAA
   - (b) NAA
   - (c) 2,4-D
   - (c) IBA

10. Which of the following algae produces carrageen?
    - (a) Green algae
    - (b) Brown algae
    - (c) Red algae
    - (d) Blue-green algae

11. In some members of which of the following pairs of families, pollen grains retain their viability for months after release?
    - (a) Poaceae; Rosaceae
    - (b) Poaceae: Leguminosae
    - (c) Poaceae: Solanaceae
    - (d) Rosaceae : Leguminosae

12. Which of the following statement is incorrect?
    - (a) Both ATP and NADPH + H$^+$ are synthesised during non-cyclic photophosphorylation
    - (b) Stroma lamellae have PS-I only and lack NADP reductase
    - (c) Grana lamellae have both PS-I and PS-II
    - (d) Cyclic photophosphorylation involves both PS-I and PS-II

13. Which of the following statement is correct?
    - (a) Fusion of two cells is called karyogamy
    - (b) Fusion of protoplasm between two motile or non-motile gametes is called plasmogamy
    - (c) Organisms that depend on living plants are called saprophytes
    - (d) Some of the organisms can fix atmospheric nitrogen in specialised cells called sheath cells

14. Which one of the following belongs to the family-Muscidae ?
    - (a) Firefly
    - (b) Grasshopper
    - (c) Cockroach
    - (d) Housefly

15. A person breathing normally at rest, takes in and expels approximately half a litre of air during each respiratory cycle. This is called
    - (a) IRV
    - (b) TV
    - (c) ERV
    - (d) VC

16. Which enzyme is responsible for the conversion of inactive fibrinogens to fibrins?
    - (a) Thrombin
    - (b) Renin
    - (c) Epinephrine
    - (d) Thrombokinase

17. The partial pressures (in mm Hg) of oxygen (O_2) and carbon dioxide (CO_2) at alveoli (the site of diffusion) are
    - (a) $pO_2 = 104$ and $pCO_2 = 40$
    - (b) $pO_2 = 40$ and $pCO_2 = 45$
    - (c) $pO_2 = 95$ and $pCO_2 = 40$
    - (d) $pO_2 = 159$ and $pCO_2 = 0.3$

18. Chronic auto immune disorder affecting neuro muscular junction leading to fatigue, weakening and paralysis of skeletal muscle is called as
    - (a) arthritis
    - (b) muscular dystrophy
    - (c) myasthenia gravis
    - (d) gout

19. Erythropoietin hormone which stimulates RBC formation is produced by
    - (a) alpha cells of pancreas
    - (b) the cells of rostral adenohypophysis
    - (c) the cells of bone marrow
    - (d) juxtaglomerular cells of the kidney

20. In frog, mesorchium is a thin fold of membrane extending between
    - (a) two testes
    - (b) liner and kidneys
    - (c) two kidneys
    - (d) kidneys and testes

21. Which one of the following organisms bears hollow and pneumatic long bones?

(a) *Neophron*   (b) *Hemidactylus*

(c) *Macropus*   (d) *Ornithorhynchus*

22. The centriole undergoes duplication during

(a) S-phase   (b) prophase

(c) metaphase   (d) G_2-phase

23. Photosynthesis is carried out by green plants, algae and some bacteria. The source of oxygen evolved during photosynthesis is

(a) H_2O (b) $C_6H_{12}O_6$

(c) CO_2 (d) $n(CH_2O)$

24. Select the favourable conditions required for the formation of oxyhaemoglobin at the alveoli.

(a) High pO_2, low pCO_2, less H^+, lower temperature

(b) Low pO_2, high pCO_2, more H^+, higher temperature

(c) High pO_2, high pCO_2, less H^+, higher temperature

(d) Low pO_2, low pCO_2, more H^+, higher temperature

25. Identify the incorrect pair.

(a) Alkaloids - Codeine

(b) Toxin   - Abrin

(c) Lectins   - Concanavalin-A

(d) Drugs   - Ricin

26. A person is having problem with calcium and phosphorus metabolism in his body. Which gland might not be functioning properly?

(a) Parotid   (b) Pancreas

(c) Adrenal   (d) Parathyroid

27. The organelles that are included in the endomembrane system are

(a) endoplasmic reticulum, mitochondria, ribosomes and lysosomes

(b) endoplasmic reticulum, Golgi complex, lysosomes and vacuoles

(c) Golgi complex, mitochondria, ribosomes and lysosomes

(d) Golgi complex, endoplasmic reticulum, mitochondria and lysosomes

28. Which stage of meiotic prophase shows terminalisation of chiasmata as its distinctive feature?

(a) Leptotene   (b) Zygotene

(c) Diakinesis   (d) Pachytene

29. Which of these is not an important component of initiation of parturition in humans?

(a) Increase in oestrogen and progesterone ratio

(b) Synthesis of prostaglandins

(c) Release of oxytocin

(d) Release of prolactin

30. Identify the types of cell junctions that help to stop the leakage of the substances across a tissue and facilitation of communication with neighbouring cells *via* rapid transfer of ions and molecules.

(a) Gap junctions and adhering junctions, respectively

(b) Tight junctions and gap junctions, respectively

(c) Adhering junction and tight junctions, respectively

(d) Adhering junctions and gap junctions, respectively

31. During muscular contraction, which of the following events occur?

    I. 'H' zone disappears

    II. 'A' band widens

    III. 'I' band reduces in width

    IV. Myosine hydrolyses ATP, releasing the ADP and Pi

    V. Z-lines attached to actins are pulled inwards.

    Choose the correct answer from the options given below.

    (a) I, III, IV and V
    (b) I, II, III and IV
    (c) II, III, IV and V
    (d) II, IV, V and I

32. Which category possesses the least similar characteristic to one another?

    (a) Class
    (b) Order
    (c) Family
    (d) Division

33. The members of phylum–Arthropoda have balancing organ named as

    (a) radula
    (b) statocysts
    (c) choanocyte
    (d) comb plates

34. Which of the following statement is correct?

    (a) Lichens do not grow in polluted areas
    (b) Algal component of lichen is mycobiont
    (c) Fungal component of lichen is phycobiont
    (d) Lichens are not good pollution indicator

35. In which of the following organisms the cell wall is composed of two thin overlapping shells, which fit together like a soap-case?

    (a) Diatoms
    (b) Golden algae
    (c) Slime moulds
    (d) *Gonyaulax*

36. Which one of the following sets of animals belongs to a single taxonomic group?

    (a) Cuttlefish, jellyfish, silverfish, dogfish, starfish
    (b) Bat, pigeon, butterfly
    (c) Monkey, chimpanzee, man
    (d) Silkworm, tapeworm, earthworm

37. Amit observed difficulties in his body activities post his accident.

    On conducting tests, it was found out that his vagus nerve got injured. Which of the following activities will not be affected?

    (a) Tongue movement
    (b) Gastrointestinal movement
    (c) Breathing
    (d) Cardiac movement

38. Each phospholipid molecule in a cell membrane consists of

    (a) one polar head and two non-polar tails
    (b) one polar head and one polar tail
    (c) one non-polar head and one polar tail
    (d) one non-polar head and one non-polar tail

39. The pyrimidine base, which confers additional stability to DNA over RNA is

    (a) adenine
    (b) guanine
    (c) cytosine
    (d) thymine

40. Secondary metabolites such as nicotine, strychnine and caffeine are produced by plants for their

    (a) growth response
    (b) defence action
    (c) effect on reproduction
    (d) nutritive value

MCQs 2 Marks Questions

Direction (Q. Nos. 41-44) Each of these questions contains two statements : Assertion (A) and Reason (R). Each of these questions also has four alternative choices, any one of which is the correct answer. You have to select one of the codes (a), (b), (c) and (d) given below.

  (a) Both A and R are true and R is the correct explanation of A

  (b) Both A and R are true, but R is not the correct explanation of A

  (c) A is true, but R is false

  (d) A is false, but R is true

41. **Assertion** (A) Inorganic catalysts work efficiently at high temperature.
Reason (R) Enzymes get damaged at high temperature.

42. **Assertion** (A) Mitochondria is called 'power house' of the cell.
Reason (R) Mitochondria produce cellular energy in the form of ATP.

43. **Assertion** (A) Cyanobacteria are photosynthetic autotrophs.
Reason (R) They have chlorophyll-*a* and *b* similar to green plants.

44. **Assertion** (A) Chemosynthetic autotrophic bacteria oxidise various inorganic substances.
Reason (R) Energy released during oxidation is used in ATP production.

Direction (Q. Nos. 45-47) Read the following and answer the questions that follow.
Observe the given diagram and answer the following questions.

The following graph shows a person's breathing rate before, during and after a period of vigorous exercise.

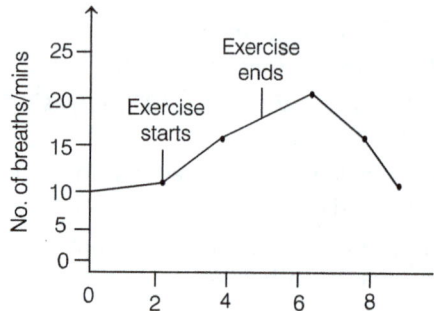

45. What happens to breathing rate is observed?

  (a) Increase in breathing rate during exercise

  (b) Decrease in breathing rate is observed

  (c) Breathing rate remains same all throughout

  (d) None of the above

46. Which of the following hormones is/are known to stimulate breathing?

  (a) Progesterone

  (b) Adrenalin

  (c) Progesterone and thyroxine

  (d) Thyroxine and dopamine

47. Blood analysis of a person who exercises daily versus the person who does not exercise were compared. It was found that the latter had a high quantity of carboxyhaemoglobin content.

This implies that the patient had been inhaling polluted air containing high content of

  (a) CO_2 (b) Chloroform

  (c) CS_2 (d) CO

48. Read the following statements.

   I. Metagenesis is observed in helminths

   II. Echinoderms are triploblastic and coelomate animals.

  III. Round worms have organ-system level of body organisation.

  IV. Comb plates present in ctenophores help in digestion.

   V. Water vascular system is characteristic of echinoderms.

Choose the correct answer from the options given below.

(a) III, IV and V are correct

(b) I, II and III are correct

(c) I, IV and V are correct

(d) II, III and V are correct

49. Following are the statements with reference to lipids.

   I. Lipids having only single bonds are called unsaturated fatty acids.

  II. Lecithin is a phospholipid.

  III. Trihydroxy propane is glycerol.

IV. Palmitic acid has 20 carbon atoms including carboxyl carbon.

V. Arachidonic acid has 16 carbon atoms.

Choose the correct answer from the options given below.

(a) I and III

(b) III and IV

(c) II and III

(d) II and V

50. Given below are same events of a living muscle.

   I. Ca^{2+} released by sarcoplasmic reticulum.

  II. Actin complexes with myosin

  III. ATPase is activated

  IV. Troponin binds Ca^{2+}

For which state the above events are associated with?

(a) Muscle at the beginning of contraction

(b) Relaxed state

(c) Muscle in tetanus

(d) Muscle at the end of contraction.

Darken your choice with HB Pencil

1.	ⓐ ⓑ ⓒ ⓓ	11.	ⓐ ⓑ ⓒ ⓓ	21.	ⓐ ⓑ ⓒ ⓓ	31.	ⓐ ⓑ ⓒ ⓓ	41.	ⓐ ⓑ ⓒ ⓓ
2.	ⓐ ⓑ ⓒ ⓓ	12.	ⓐ ⓑ ⓒ ⓓ	22.	ⓐ ⓑ ⓒ ⓓ	32.	ⓐ ⓑ ⓒ ⓓ	42.	ⓐ ⓑ ⓒ ⓓ
3.	ⓐ ⓑ ⓒ ⓓ	13.	ⓐ ⓑ ⓒ ⓓ	23.	ⓐ ⓑ ⓒ ⓓ	33.	ⓐ ⓑ ⓒ ⓓ	43.	ⓐ ⓑ ⓒ ⓓ
4.	ⓐ ⓑ ⓒ ⓓ	14.	ⓐ ⓑ ⓒ ⓓ	24.	ⓐ ⓑ ⓒ ⓓ	34.	ⓐ ⓑ ⓒ ⓓ	44.	ⓐ ⓑ ⓒ ⓓ
5.	ⓐ ⓑ ⓒ ⓓ	15.	ⓐ ⓑ ⓒ ⓓ	25.	ⓐ ⓑ ⓒ ⓓ	35.	ⓐ ⓑ ⓒ ⓓ	45.	ⓐ ⓑ ⓒ ⓓ
6.	ⓐ ⓑ ⓒ ⓓ	16.	ⓐ ⓑ ⓒ ⓓ	26.	ⓐ ⓑ ⓒ ⓓ	36.	ⓐ ⓑ ⓒ ⓓ	46.	ⓐ ⓑ ⓒ ⓓ
7.	ⓐ ⓑ ⓒ ⓓ	17.	ⓐ ⓑ ⓒ ⓓ	27.	ⓐ ⓑ ⓒ ⓓ	37.	ⓐ ⓑ ⓒ ⓓ	47.	ⓐ ⓑ ⓒ ⓓ
8.	ⓐ ⓑ ⓒ ⓓ	18.	ⓐ ⓑ ⓒ ⓓ	28.	ⓐ ⓑ ⓒ ⓓ	38.	ⓐ ⓑ ⓒ ⓓ	48.	ⓐ ⓑ ⓒ ⓓ
9.	ⓐ ⓑ ⓒ ⓓ	19.	ⓐ ⓑ ⓒ ⓓ	29.	ⓐ ⓑ ⓒ ⓓ	39.	ⓐ ⓑ ⓒ ⓓ	49.	ⓐ ⓑ ⓒ ⓓ
10.	ⓐ ⓑ ⓒ ⓓ	20.	ⓐ ⓑ ⓒ ⓓ	30.	ⓐ ⓑ ⓒ ⓓ	40.	ⓐ ⓑ ⓒ ⓓ	50.	ⓐ ⓑ ⓒ ⓓ

Hints and Explanations

Chapter 1 Biological Classification, Plant and Animal Kingdom

1. (a) 2. (a) 3. (a) 4. (c) 5. (d)
6. (c) 7. (a)
8. (b) Kingdom Monera holds maximum nutritional diversity. Photoautotrophic, chemoautotrophic, and heterotrophic modes of nutrition are all possible. Saprophytic, parasitic, or symbiotic organisms are the examples of heterotrophs.

   Plantae organisms contain most autotrophic forms, whereas Fungi and Animalia contain only heterotrophic form of nutrition.
9. (b) Based on shapes, Bacteria are grouped under four categories that includes: the spherical Coccus, the rod-shaped Bacillus, the comma-shaped Vibrium and the spiral *Spirillum*.
10. (c) Halophiles, thermoacidophiles, and methanogens belongs to domain Archaebacteria of kingdom Monera.
11. (c) 12. (d) 13. (b) 14. (c) 15. (b)
16. (b) The organism in the image is *Paramecium* which is placed under ciliated protozoans.
17. (d) 18. (c)
19. (a) Holozoic nutrition is defined as the process of ingesting organic food with the help of the mouth, followed by digestion, absorption, assimilation, and egestion, after which the food is excreted.
20. (a) 21. (a) 22. (b) 23. (c) 24. (d)
25. (b) 26. (c) 27. (c) 28. (d)
29. (c) The members of Rhodophyceae are commonly called red algae because of the predominance of the red pigment, r-phycoerythrin in their body. Chlorophyll-*b* is major pigment of Chlorophyceae and chlorophyll-*c* and fucoxanthin are major pigments of Phaeophyceae.

30. (a) 31. (c) 32. (d) 33. (a) 34. (c)
35. (b) 36. (c) 37. (c) 38. (b) 39. (d)
40. (a) 41. (c) 42. (b) 43. (a) 44. (b)
45. (d) 46. (d) 47. (a) 48. (a) 49. (d)
50. (d) 51. (c) 52. (d) 53. (b) 54. (a)
55. (b) 56. (a) 57. (c) 58. (d) 59. (d)
60. (c)
61. (c) The digestive tract of birds has additional chambers, the crop and gizzard.
62. (a)
63. (b) Viviparity is defined as the process of development of the embryo inside the body of the mother.
64. (d)
65. (b) The bacterial cell is Gram-positive due to the presence of single-layered and thick cell wall.
66. (a) In a Gram-negative bacterium, the cells will lose the crystal violet stain, when the silde is rinsed. As a result, the cells remain discoloured.
67. (a) The basis of Gram-staining is the lipid content of bacterial cell wall.
    Gram-negative bacteria have high lipid content due to which the lipids dissolve in organic solvents.
68. (c)
69. (b) Both A and R are true, but R is not the correct explanation of A.
    Basidiomycetes are the most advanced fungi as they have fully developed cellular composition in their hyphae. They also sexually reproduce *via* specialised spores known as basidiospores that are present in club-shaped end cells called basidia.
70. (d) 71. (a) 72. (c) 73. (d) 74. (b)

Chapter 2 Morphology of Flowering Plants

1. (d)
2. (a) Majority of the plants have roots growing towards the water content, thus exhibiting positive hydrotropism.
3. (d)   4. (b)
5. (c) Y that represents zone of cell elongation is situated just behind meristematic zone. Cells of this zone become elongated and develop a large central vacuole filled with cell sap.

   These cells have lost the power of division.
6. (c)   7. (a)   8. (a)
9. (b) Mosses are flowerless plants which do not have true roots. Instead, they have thin root like outgrowths called rhizoids to help anchor them.
10. (c) Stem is the ascending part of the axis that bears branches, leaves, flowers, fruits and trichomes along with nodes and internodes.
11. (c)   12. (c)   13. (b)   14. (b)   15. (a)
16. (d)   17. (d)   18. (a)   19. (c)   20. (d)
21. (c)   22. (a)   23. (d)
24. (b) The incorrect match given in option (b). It can be corrected as

   In free central placentation, ovules are borne on the central axis. e.g. Primrose.

   Marigold is an example of basal placentation.
25. (d)
26. (b)   27. (b)   28. (b)   29. (c)   30. (d)
31. (c)   32. (c)   33. (a)   34. (b)   35. (d)
36. (c)   37. (a)   38. (a)   39. (d)   40. (d)
41. (c)   42. (a)   43. (c)   44. (a)
45. (b) Perennial (A) plants complete their life cycle in more than two years. An ephemeral (B) plant is one marked by short life cycles.

   Annual (C) plants complete their life cycle in one year.
   Biennials (D) complete their life cycle in two years.
46. (d) Aquatic plants like

   Pistia, Lemna and *Eicchornia* do not possess root caps. Instead, they have root pockets for buoyancy.
47. (a) I and III are the main function of the stem.

It is the ascending part of the main plant axis and bears branches, leaves, flowers and fruits, etc. Also, it adds new cells and tissues every year to keep continuing the functioning of the plant for longer time period.

48. (a)   49. (a)   50. (a)
51. (c) Plants having hypogynous flowers include mustard, brinjal china rose, rupin, gram, chilli, *Petunia*, tomato, *Withania*, Potato, onion, *Aloe* and tulip.

   Such flowers contain superior ovary.
52. (b) Option (b) represents the correct match in valvate aestivation, petals lie close to each other but do not overlap. It is seen in mustard or *Brassica*.
53. (a)   54. (a)   55. (a)
56. (b) Cashewnut is a nut formed from unilocular, multicarpellary ovary. Pericarp is hard and stony.
57. (b)   58. (a)
59. (c) Various external and internal factors influence seed germination internal factors, include seed viability, dormancy, enzymes, maturity of embryo.

   External factors are water, light, O_2, temperature, etc.
60. (b)

Chapter 3 Anatomy of Flowering Plants

1. (c)   2. (c)
3. (d) In dicot root 2-6 vascular bundles are present.
4. (d) Velamen cells provide support, prevent water loss and assist the plant in absorbing water from the atmosphere.
5. (c) Cortex, endodermis and pericycle.
6. (d)   7. (d)   8. (c)   9. (d)   10. (a)
11. (c)   12. (b)   13. (c)   14. (b)   15. (a)
16. (d)
17. (c) In barley stem, vascular bundles are closed and scattered.
18. (c)   19. (d)   20. (a)   21. (d)   22. (c)
23. (a)   24. (c)
25. (b) In monocot mesophyll is not differentiated into palisade and spongy parenchyma.
26. (a)   27. (d)   28. (b)   29. (d)   30. (d)

31. (b)   **32.** (d)   **33.** (c)   **34.** (b)   **35.** (c)

36. (c)   **37.** (d)

38. (a) When xylem is surrounded by phloem on all sides, such vascular bundles are called amphicribal or hadrocentric.

39. (d)   **40.** (c)

41. (a) Statement given in option (a) is incorrect and can be corrected as

Epidermis is usually single layered which is made up of elongated, compactly arranged cells and form a continuous layer.

42. (a) Statement given in option (a) is incorrect and can be corrected as

Epidermal cells are parenchymatous with a small amount of cytoplasm lining the cell wall and a large vacuole.

43. (a) It is usually occur in uniseriate epidermis.

44. (a) Both A and R are correct and R is the correct explantion of A. It can be explained as In the endodermal cells, lingo-suberised thickening are present on the radial and tangenital cell walls. These are called Casparian strip. Due to this, endodermis acts as biological check post and prevent wall to wall movement of substances between cortex and pericycle.

45. (d) The part labelled as *E* is to be identified as pericycle, these are thick -walled parenchymatous cells which plays a key role in the initiation of lateral roots and vascular cambium during the secondary growth of the plants cells.

46. (b) Both A and R are correct, but R is not the correct explanation of A. It can be explained as

Phloem parenchyma is made up of elongated, tapering cylindrical cells. Which have dense cytoplasm and nucleus. The cell wall is composed of cellulose and has pits through which plasmodesmata connections exist between the cells. The phloem parenchyma stores food materials and other substances, like resins, latex and mucilage. it is absent in most of the monocot as they store their food in other vacuoles.

47. (a) In the monocotyledons, the vascular bundles have no cambium present in them. Hence, since they do not form secondary tissues they are referred to as closed.

48. (c)   **49.** (a)

50. (b) Option (b) is correct, i.e. labelled 2 and 3 are mesophyll cells. These cells contain chloroplast which perform the function of photosynthesis. Mesophyll is a tissue of the leaf between the adaxial and abaxial epidermis. It is differentiated into the palisade parenchyma (composed of tall, compactly placed cells) and the spongy parenchyma (comprising oval or round, loosely arranged cells with intercellular spaces).

51. (a)   **52.** (c)   **53.** (d)   **54.** (c)   **55.** (b)

56. (c)

Chapter 4 Structural Organisation in Animals

1. (b)   **2.** (c)   **3.** (d)   **4.** (c)

5. (a) Frogs change their colour to defend and protect themselves from predators. This process is termed as camouflage and the protective coloration with the help of which it hides in its surroundings is referred as mimicry.

6. (c)   **7.** (d)

8. (b) The body of the frog is divided into 2 parts that includes a head and a trunk. Neck and tail are not present.

9. (a)   **10.** (d)

11. (a) The incorrect match given in option (a). It can be corrected as
The forelimbs and hindlimbs are used for leaping, swimming and burrowing. Feet have webbed digits that help in swimming. Each forelimb of frog has four digits while each hindlimb of frog has five digits.

12. (c) Male frogs can be distinguished by the presence of sound producing vocal sacs and a copulatory pad present on the first digit of the forelimbs which are absent in female frogs.

13. (d) Frogs are carnivores. Frogs feed on insects such as flies, mosquitoes, worms, etc.

14. (a)   **15.** (b)   **16.** (c)

17. (a) Food ingested by the frog is churned with the help of bile, pancreatic juices and hydrochloric acid present in the stomach to produce an acidic mixture known as chyme. This is passed to the duodenum which is the first part of small intestine.

18. (d)   **19.** (a)   **20.** (b)   **21.** (d)   **22.** (d)

23. (a) The heart of the frog has three chambers that includes two auricles and one ventricle. The heart is enclosed by pericardium. Oxygenated blood leaves the heart *via* conus arteriosus.

24. (b) In frogs, RBC's are nucleated and contain red coloured pigment known as haemoglobin.

25. (c) Statement given in option (c) is correct with respect to the anatomy of frog. Other statement are incorrect and can be corrected as
In female frogs, the oviduct and ureters are separate, whereas in male frogs, the urinary and genital ducts fuse to form urinogenital ducts. The urinary bladder is thin-walled and is situated ventral to the rectum. Frogs are ureotelic.

26. (b)   **27.** (b)

28. (c) The medulla oblongata is a part of the hindbrain of frogs. The foramen magnum lies between the medulla oblongata and the spinal cord.

29. (c) The senses for vision (eyes) and hearing (tympanum and internal ears) are well-developed and the rest (organs of touch called sensory papillae, taste buds for taste and nasal epithelium for smell) are cellular aggregations.

30. (d) The mesorchium attaches yellowish, ovoid testes to the upper part of each kidney in male frogs. The mesorchium is a double fold of the peritoneum that joins both the structures.

31. (c) A female frog typically lays around 2500 to 3000 ova at a time. Fertilisation is external in frogs and takes place in water. The development consists of a larval stage called tadpole.

32. (c)   **33.** (a)   **34.** (b)   **35.** (d)

36. (c)   **37.** (a)   **38.** (d)   **39.** (a)   **40.** (b)

41. (b) VA-3, B-4, C-2, D-1. These can be explained as
Vasa efferentia are 10-12 in number that arise from testes.
The ovaries are situated near kidneys and there is no functional connection with kidneys.
Male reproductive organs consist of a pair of yellowish ovoid testes (Figure 7.21), which are found adhered to the upper part of kidneys by a double fold of peritoneum called mesorchium.
The cloaca is a small, median chamber that is used to pass faecal matter, urine and sperms to the exterior

42. (d)

Chapter 5 Cell : The Basic Unit of Life

1. (a)   **2.** (c)   **3.** (a)   **4.** (a)   **5.** (c)
6. (d)   **7.** (d)   **8.** (b)   **9.** (b)   **10.** (a)
11. (a)   **12.** (b)   **13.** (a)   **14.** (a)   **15.** (b)
16. (c)   **17.** (c)   **18.** (b)   **19.** (c)   **20.** (d)
21. (c)   **22.** (c)   **23.** (c)   **24.** (b)   **25.** (a)
26. (d)   **27.** (b)   **28.** (c)   **29.** (d)   **30.** (d)
31. (c)   **32.** (d)   **33.** (b)   **34.** (b)   **35.** (b)
36. (b)   **37.** (c)   **38.** (b)   **39.** (c)   **40.** (c)
41. (b)   **42.** (b)   **43.** (b)   **44.** (b)   **45.** (d)
46. (a)   **47.** (c)   **48.** (c)   **49.** (b)   **50.** (b)
51. (c)   **52.** (d)   **53.** (d)   **54.** (b)   **55.** (c)
56. (a)   **57.** (a)   **58.** (d)   **59.** (b)   **60.** (b)
61. (a)   **62.** (b)   **63.** (b)   **64.** (c)   **65.** (a)
66. (c)   **67.** (c)   **68.** (c)   **69.** (b)   **70.** (b)
71. (a)   **72.** (d)   **73.** (b)   **74.** (b)   **75.** (c)
76. (b)   **77.** (d)   **78.** (d)   **79.** (b)   **80.** (c)
81. (d)   **82.** (a)   **83.** (a)   **84.** (c)   **85.** (b)
86. (c)   **87.** (c)   **88.** (c)   **89.** (c)   **90.** (b)

91. (c) A is true, but R is false.
Eukaryotic cells have membrane-bound cell organelles which performs specific functions.
This feature offers several advantages to eukaryotic cells like, cells can concentrate and isolate enzymes and reactants in smaller volume, increasing the efficiency of chemical reactions, potentially harmful proteins remain bound within membranes, etc.

Eukaryotic organisms are plants and animals. Bacteria, blue-green algae and mycoplasma are prokaryotes. They do not have membrane bound organelles.

92. (b) Statements I and III are correct. Statement II is incorrect regarding nucleus and can be corrected as

Nucleus is present in eukaryotes as a double membrane bound, dense body. In prokaryotes, a true nucleus is absent. They instead possess an incipient or false nuclei.

93. (c)   **94.** (a)   **95.** (b)   **96.** (b)   **97.** (d)

98. (b)   **99.** (a) **100.** (d) **101.** (a) **102.** (a)

103. (a) **104.** (c)

105. (a) Lipase works at pH between 4.5 to 7.5. It gets denatured at high pH. Whereas pepsin require very acidic pH its optimal pH is around 2.

106. (d) **107.** (d) **108.** (b) **109.** (a) **110.** (b)

Chapter 6 Photosynthesis in Higher Plants

1. (d)   **2.** (c)   **3.** (c)   **4.** (d)   **5.** (c)

6. (b)   **7.** (b)   **8.** (c)   **9.** (c)   **10.** (d)

11. (b)   **12.** (b)   **13.** (c)   **14.** (b)   **15.** (a)

16. (d)   **17.** (b)   **18.** (c)   **19.** (a)   **20.** (b)

21. (d)   **22.** (a)   **23.** (c)   **24.** (c)   **25.** (d)

26. (c)   **27.** (a)   **28.** (b)   **29.** (d)   **30.** (d)

31. (b)   **32.** (b)   **33.** (c)   **34.** (c)   **35.** (d)

36. (a)   **37.** (a)   **38.** (c)   **39.** (b)   **40.** (c)

41. (c)   **42.** (a)   **43.** (b)   **44.** (b)   **45.** (c)

46. (a)   **47.** (a)   **48.** (b)   **49.** (a)   **50.** (a)

51. (a)   **52.** (a)   **53.** (b)   **54.** (a)   **55.** (d)

56. (b)   **57.** (c)   **58.** (c)   **59.** (a)   **60.** (a)

61. (a)   **62.** (b)   **63.** (a)   **64.** (b)   **65.** (c)

66. (c)   **67.** (b)   **68.** (c)   **69.** (d)

70. (d) Statement I is incorrect, but statement II is correct. The incorrect statement I can be corrected as
Cyanobacteria store food in the form of starch but synthesise simple sugars as the byproduct of photosynthesis.

71. (c)

72. (c) Statement I is correct, but statement II is incorrect and can be corrected as

Action spectrum is the curve that depicts the relative rate of photosynthesis at different wavelengths of light.

73. (c) Statements I is correct, but statement II is incorrect and it can be corrected as
$NADPH^+ + H^+$ and ATP produced in light reaction constitute assimilatory power.

74. (b)

75. (b) Soft drink contains CO_2 gas and hence, helps in accelerating the rate of photosynthesis in submerged hydrophytes when added into the water. This can be easily demonstrated using Wilmot's bubbler.

76. (a)   **77.** (b)   **78.** (d)   **79.** (d)   **80.** (c)

81. (a)   **82.** (d)   **83.** (b)   **84.** (c)   **85.** (a)

Chapter 7 Respiration in Plants

1. (a)   **2.** (b)   **3.** (b)   **4.** (a)   **5.** (b)

6. (d)   **7.** (c)   **8.** (c)   **9.** (d)   **10.** (c)

11. (c)   **12.** (a)   **13.** (b)   **14.** (b)   **15.** (a)

16. (c)   **17.** (b)   **18.** (c)   **19.** (a)   **20.** (b)

21. (d)   **22.** (d)   **23.** (b)   **24.** (b)   **25.** (c)

26. (d)   **27.** (a)   **28.** (b)   **29.** (c)   **30.** (c)

31. (c)   **32.** (c)   **33.** (c)   **34.** (b)   **35.** (a)

36. (b)   **37.** (d)   **38.** (c)   **39.** (b)   **40.** (d)

41. (c)   **42.** (a)   **43.** (b)   **44.** (c)   **45.** (b)

46. (c)   **47.** (b)   **48.** (b)   **49.** (b)   **50.** (c)

51. (a)   **52.** (c)   **53.** (b)   **54.** (a)   **55.** (d)

56. (c)   **57.** (a)   **58.** (d)   **59.** (b)   **60.** (d)

61. (b)   **62.** (a)   **63.** (c)   **64.** (b)   **65.** (c)

66. (b)   **67.** (c)   **68.** (b)   **69.** (d)

70. (c) A is true, but R is false. R can be corrected as

The terminal phosphate of ATP yields about 7300 calories per mole. The standard free energy of hydrolysis of ATP to ADP and phosphate is -7.30 Kcal at pH 7.0 and temperature of 37°C in the presence of excess magnesium.

71. (a)

72. (c) Option (c) is correct as potassium hydroxide is used in the experiment to show absorption of CO_2 from the plants released during respiration. When KOH absorbs CO_2, it creates a vacuum in the bent glass tube which moves in the conical flask to pull the water in the bent tube further up.

73. (c) **74.** (c) **75.** (b) **76.** (d) **77.** (c)

78. (c) **79.** (b) **80.** (b) **81.** (d) **82.** (c)

83. (c)

84. (c) Statement I is correct, but statement II is incorrect and this can be corrected as

During electron transfer, electron donor gets oxidised while electron-acceptor gets reduced.

85. (b) **86.** (c) **87.** (d)

Chapter 8 Plant Growth and Development

1. (d) **2.** (c) **3.** (b) **4.** (c) **5.** (d)

6. (c) **7.** (b) **8.** (b) **9.** (c) **10.** (c)

11. (b) **12.** (c) **13.** (c) **14.** (b)

15. (a) The incorrectly matched pair given in option (a). It can be corrected as

2, 4, 5-T (2, 4, 5-trichlorophenoxyacetic acid) is used as a herbicide. It is chemically synthesised auxin.

16. (a) **17.** (d) **18.** (c) **19.** (b) **20.** (c)

21. (d) **22.** (c) **23.** (b) **24.** (b) **25.** (b)

26. (c)

27. (d) Statement given in option (d) is false. It can be corrected as.
In dwarf plants, the gibberellin is not expected to be present in higher amount. This is because high level of gibberellin induces tallness in stem, which is not a characteristic associated with dwarf (short heighted) plants.

28. (a) Different concentration of IAA have differing effects on root growth. These effects may vary from one species to another. However, at any concentration IAA promotes growth in shoot areas of plant. Very high concentration of auxin inhibits plant shoot growth while only a small amount of IAA can stimulate growth in the roots.
Thus, graph (a) correctly represents the best response of IAA on shoot and root development.

29. (c) Cytokinins are plant hormone which promote cytokinesis or cell dividsion. It also helps in opening of stomata, delaying ageing in leaves, etc.

30. (c) ABA (Abscisic acid) induces stomatal closure. This is done by an ATP dependent proton pump present in plasma membrane of guard cells. Increased ABA will not allow the stomata to open completely thereby reducing the evaporative cooling of the plant which inturn will raise the internal temperature of plant.

31. (c) **32.** (a)

Chapter 09 Breathing and Exchange of Gases

1. (c) **2.** (b) **3.** (b) **4.** (a) **5.** (b)

6. (c) **7.** (a)

8. (a) When a person inhales, the diaphragm muscles contract and pull it down. The external intercoastal muscles also contract and pull the ribcage upwards and outwards.

9. (d) **10.** (c) **11.** (c) **12.** (c) **13.** (c)

14. (c) **15.** (a) **16.** (a) **17.** (c) **18.** (d)

19. (b) **20.** (c) **21.** (c) **22.** (b) **23.** (a)

24. (a) Partial pressure of O_2 and CO_2 in atmospheric air and alveolar air is 159mm Hg and 0.3 mm Hg, respectively.
Thus, option (a) is correct

25. (c) **26.** (c) **27.** (b) **28.** (c) **29.** (c)

30. (a) **31.** (a) **32.** (d) **33.** (c) **34.** (a)

35. (c) **36.** (d) **37.** (d) **38.** (c) **39.** (b)

40. (d) **41.** (b) **42.** (c) **43.** (c) **44.** (c)

45. (c) **46.** (a) **47.** (d) **48.** (a) **49.** (b)

50. (c) **51.** (c) **52.** (c)

53. (d) At point C on the graph, the diaphragm gets lowered. When we breathe in or inhale, the diaphragm contracts and moves downward. This increases the space in chest cavity and lungs to expand, i.e. inspiration.

54. (c) The correct option is (c).
Composition of inhaled air
$A - CO_2 = 0.04\%$
$B - $ Nitrogen $= 78\%$
$C - $ Oxygen $= 20.95$ %
Composition of exhaled air
$A - CO_2 - 4.4\%$
$B - $ Nitrogen - 78%
$C - $ Oxygen - 16.4 %

55. (c)

56. (c) Statement I is correct, but statement II is incorrect and it can be corrected as

Type II alveolar cells, also known as granular pneumocytes and great alveolar cells are cuboidal in shape, having approximately 1/40 of mean alveolar surface area of type I cell.

57. (b)   **58.** (b)

59. (d) TLC = VC + RV

TLC = (TV + IRV + ERV) + RV

5800 mL = (500 + 2850 + 1000)mL + RV

5800 mL - 4350 mL = RV

RV = 1450 mL

60. (d)   **61.** (a)

62. (b) B due to difference in concentration, i.e. diffusion gradient occurs and CO_2 moves out of lungs. Muscle action during exhalation also helps in excretion of CO_2

63. (b)   **64.** (c)

Chapter 10 Body Fluids and Circulation

1. (b)	**2.** (a)	**3.** (d)	**4.** (c)	**5.** (d)
6. (c)	**7.** (c)	**8.** (b)	**9.** (a)	**10.** (d)
11. (a)	**12.** (b)	**13.** (c)	**14.** (b)	**15.** (b)
16. (d)	**17.** (a)	**18.** (a)	**19.** (a)	**20.** (d)
21. (c)	**22.** (a)	**23.** (d)	**24.** (a)	**25.** (c)
26. (d)	**27.** (c)	**28.** (d)	**29.** (b)	**30.** (d)
31. (d)	**32.** (a)	**33.** (b)	**34.** (c)	**35.** (b)
36. (b)	**37.** (b)	**38.** (a)	**39.** (d)	**40.** (d)
41. (c)	**42.** (a)	**43.** (c)	**44.** (c)	**45.** (c)
46. (a)	**47.** (b)	**48.** (a)	**49.** (c)	**50.** (a)
51. (c)	**52.** (c)	**53.** (b)	**54.** (c)	**55.** (a)
56. (a)	**57.** (b)	**58.** (b)	**59.** (a)	**60.** (b)
61. (c)	**62.** (b)	**63.** (a)	**64.** (c)	**65.** (b)
66. (d)				

67. (b) X represents RBC's or erythrocytes. These are biconcave, enucleated, haemoglobin containing blood cells. The haemoglobin in RBCs bind to oxygen and helps to transport it throughout the body. These range from 52 Lacs/mm^3 in males and 47 Lacs/mm^3 in females. Hence, option (b) is correct.

Rest functions like coagulation, antibody production and development of hypersensitivity are performed by platelets, lymphocytes and mast cells, respectively.

68. (c)	**69.** (a)	**70.** (b)	**71.** (a)	
72. (d)	**73.** (a)	**74.** (d)	**75.** (a)	**76.** (d)
77. (d)	**78.** (a)	**79.** (a)	**80.** (c)	**81.** (c)

Chapter 11 Excretory Products and Their Elimination

1. (a)	**2.** (b)	**3.** (b)	**4.** (c)	**5.** (a)
6. (a)	**7.** (a)	**8.** (b)	**9.** (a)	**10.** (d)
11. (b)	**12.** (b)	**13.** (b)	**14.** (c)	**15.** (b)
16. (c)	**17.** (d)	**18.** (b)	**19.** (a)	**20.** (a)
21. (d)	**22.** (c)	**23.** (c)	**24.** (c)	**25.** (b)
26. (c)	**27.** (d)	**28.** (a)	**29.** (d)	**30.** (d)
31. (a)	**32.** (a)	**33.** (d)	**34.** (ac)	**35.** (b)
36. (b)	**37.** (c)	**38.** (b)	**39.** (a)	**40.** (c)
41. (d)	**42.** (b)	**43.** (a)	**44.** (a)	**45.** (a)
46. (c)	**47.** (d)	**48.** (a)	**49.** (b)	**50.** (d)
51. (c)	**52.** (b)	**53.** (a)	**54.** (a)	**55.** (d)
56. (d)	**57.** (b)	**58.** (a)	**59.** (b)	**60.** (c)
61. (b)	**62.** (c)	**63.** (a)	**64.** (a)	**65.** (d)

66. (d) Urea is produced by domination in liver cells or hepatocytes. It is transported to kidneys by renal artery where it is filtered from blood and temporarily stored in bladder as a constituent of urine before being expelled from the body.

67. (a)   **68.** (a)

69. (d) GHP = 60 mm Hg, BCOP = 30 mm Hg, CHP = 20 mm Hg

Glomerular Filtration Pressure = GHP − (BCOP + CHP)

= 60 − (30 + 20) = 10 mm Hg

70. (d)	**71.** (d)	**72.** (b)	**73.** (d)	**74.** (a)
75. (a)	**76.** (b)	**77.** (b)	**78.** (a)	

79. (b) Both A and R are true, but R is not the correct explanation of A. R can be corrected as

ADH or vasopressin is effective in reabsorption of water by changing permeability of DCT, collecting tubules and collecting ducts. It triggers the release of aldosterone which further increases the concentration of Na$^+$ in the blood. The increased salt concentration in the blood increases the blood osmotic potential which further increases the reabsorption of water into the collecting tubule and thus, the urine released is the concentrated one. In the absence of vasopressin, the water reabsorption is considerably reduced.

80. (b) Both A and R are true, but R is not the correct explanation of A.

    During micturition, urine is prevented from backflow due to the presence of urethral sphincters.

    The urethral sphincters located at the junction of ureter and urinary bladder to prevent the backflow of urine when the bladder pressure is high.

81. (c)

Chapter 12 Locomotion and Movement

1.	(c)	**2.**	(c)	**3.**	(b)	**4.**	(c)	**5.**	(a)
6.	(d)	**7.**	(b)	**8.**	(c)	**9.**	(b)	**10.**	(b)
11.	(c)	**12.**	(d)	**13.**	(a)	**14.**	(a)	**15.**	(a)
16.	(c)	**17.**	(b)	**18.**	(c)	**19.**	(c)	**20.**	(d)
21.	(d)	**22.**	(b)	**23.**	(a)	**24.**	(c)	**25.**	(d)
26.	(d)	**27.**	(b)	**28.**	(b)	**29.**	(d)	**30.**	(c)
31.	(a)	**32.**	(a)	**33.**	(d)	**34.**	(c)	**35.**	(a)
36.	(c)	**37.**	(d)	**38.**	(d)	**39.**	(d)	**40.**	(b)
41.	(b)	**42.**	(b)	**43.**	(c)	**44.**	(b)	**45.**	(d)
46.	(c)	**47.**	(a)	**48.**	(b)	**49.**	(b)	**50.**	(c)
51.	(a)	**52.**	(b)						

53. (c) 'X' is muscular dystrophy, a group of genetic disease that cause progressive weakness and loss of muscle mass. In this disease, abnormal genes (mutations) lead to muscle degeneration. Most of the forms are apparent at birth or develop during childhood.

54. (c) Muscular dystrophy is caused by mutation of the Duchenne muscular dystrophy gene on the X-chromosome. The gene regulates the

production of a protein called dystrophin that is found in association with the inner side of the membrane of skeletal and cardiac muscle.

55. (b)　56. (a)

Chapter 13 Control and Coordination

1.	(b)	**2.**	(c)	**3.**	(d)	**4.**	(c)	**5.**	(b)
6.	(a)	**7.**	(b)	**8.**	(c)	**9.**	(a)	**10.**	(b)
11.	(a)	**12.**	(b)	**13.**	(d)	**14.**	(a)	**15.**	(a)
16.	(a)	**17.**	(b)	**18.**	(c)	**19.**	(c)	**20.**	(c)
21.	(d)	**22.**	(b)	**23.**	(b)	**24.**	(b)	**25.**	(b)
26.	(a)	**27.**	(c)	**28.**	(b)	**29.**	(a)	**30.**	(b)
31.	(c)	**32.**	(b)	**33.**	(b)	**34.**	(b)	**35.**	(a)
36.	(b)	**37.**	(d)	**38.**	(b)	**39.**	(b)	**40.**	(a)
41.	(c)	**42.**	(c)	**43.**	(a)	**44.**	(b)	**45.**	(b)
46.	(c)	**47.**	(b)	**48.**	(b)	**49.**	(a)	**50.**	(c)
51.	(b)	**52.**	(d)	**53.**	(c)	**54.**	(c)	**55.**	(c)
56.	(a)	**57.**	(d)	**58.**	(b)	**59.**	(d)	**60.**	(a)
61.	(a)	**62.**	(d)						

63. (a) Option (a) is correct.

    An excited neuron is the one in which action potential is generated. In figure (a) we can see difference in the permeability of Na$^+$ ion inside and outside the membrane which is due to depolorisation caused by a stimulus.

64. (c)

65. (b) Label 'A' is cerebellum, which coordinates voluntary movements and helps to maintain posture, balance and equilibrium.

66. (a) B–Hypothalamus is responsible for regulation of body temperature, controls emotions and apetite.

67. (b)　68. (b)　69. (a)　70. (c)　71. (b)

72. (a)

73. (c) A is true, but R is false. R can be corrected as

    Glucocorticoids are secreted by the zona fasciculata of the adrenal cortex region.

74. (b)　75. (a)　76. (d)　77. (a)　78. (a)

79. (a)　80. (b)　81. (b)

Practice Set 01

1.	(c)	2.	(d)	3.	(a)	4.	(d)	5.	(b)	6.	(b)	7.	(d)	8.	(d)	9.	(d)	10.	(a)
11.	(a)	12.	(b)	13.	(a)	14.	(b)	15.	(c)	16.	(a)	17.	(b)	18.	(b)	19.	(b)	20.	(b)
21.	(a)	22.	(a)	23.	(b)	24.	(a)	25.	(a)	26.	(c)	27.	(c)	28.	(a)	29	(c)	30.	(d)
31.	(d)	32.	(d)	33.	(d)	34.	(d)	35.	(b)	36.	(a)	37.	(d)	38.	(c)	39.	(b)	40.	(a)
41.	(b)	42.	(c)	43.	(c)	44.	(a)	45.	(c)	46.	(d)	47.	(a)	48.	(c)	49.	(b)	50.	(d)

Practice Set 02

1.	(c)	2.	(d)	3.	(c)	4.	(b)	5.	(a)	6.	(d)	7.	(c)	8.	(a)	9.	(c)	10.	(c)
11.	(d)	12.	(d)	13.	(b)	14.	(d)	15.	(b)	16.	(a)	17.	(a)	18.	(c)	19.	(d)	20.	(d)
21.	(a)	22.	(a)	23.	(b)	24.	(a)	25.	(d)	26.	(d)	27.	(b)	28.	(c)	29	(d)	30.	(b)
31.	(a)	32.	(d)	33.	(b)	34.	(a)	35.	(a)	36.	(c)	37.	(a)	38.	(a)	39.	(d)	40.	(b)
41.	(b)	42.	(a)	43.	(c)	44.	(b)	45.	(a)	46.	(c)	47.	(d)	48.	(d)	49.	(c)	50.	(a)

www.ingramcontent.com/pod-product-compliance
Lightning Source LLC
Chambersburg PA
CBHW062149060526
44654CB00050B/1590